Because I Am Compassionate

Because I Am Compassionate

Humanitarianism in the Book of the Covenant and Cuneiform Law

DAVID NONNENMACHER JR.

☙PICKWICK *Publications* · Eugene, Oregon

BECAUSE I AM COMPASSIONATE
Humanitarianism in the Book of the Covenant and Cuneiform Law

Copyright © 2025 David Nonnenmacher Jr. All rights reserved. Except for brief quotations in critical publications or reviews, no part of this book may be reproduced in any manner without prior written permission from the publisher. Write: Permissions, Wipf and Stock Publishers, 199 W. 8th Ave., Suite 3, Eugene, OR 97401.

Pickwick Publications
An Imprint of Wipf and Stock Publishers
199 W. 8th Ave., Suite 3
Eugene, OR 97401

www.wipfandstock.com

PAPERBACK ISBN: 979-8-3852-5127-8
HARDCOVER ISBN: 979-8-3852-5128-5
EBOOK ISBN: 979-8-3852-5129-2

Cataloguing-in-Publication data:

Names: Nonnenmacher, David, Jr., author.

Title: Because I am compassionate : humanitarianism in the Book of the Covenant and cuneiform law / David Nonnenmacher Jr.

Description: Eugene, OR: Pickwick Publications, 2025. | Includes bibliographical references and index.

Identifiers: ISBN 979-8-3852-5127-8 (paperback). | ISBN 979-8-3852-5128-5 (hardcover). | ISBN 979-8-3852-5129-2 (ebook).

Subjects: LCSH: Book of the Covenant. | Law, Assyro-Babylonian. | Jewish law.

Classification: BS410 N36 2025 (print). | BS410 (epub).

VERSION NUMBER 09/23/25

Unless otherwise noted, Scripture translations are the author's.

Scripture quotations marked (NASB) are taken from the (NASB®) New American Standard Bible®, Copyright © 1960, 1971, 1977, 1995, 2020 by The Lockman Foundation. Used by permission. All rights reserved. www.lockman.org.

Scripture quotations marked NKJV is taken from the New King James Version®. Copyright © 1982 by Thomas Nelson. Used by permission. All rights reserved.

Scripture quotations marked (NIV) are taken from the Holy Bible, New International Version®, NIV®. Copyright © 1973, 1978, 1984, 2011 by Biblica, Inc.™ Used by permission of Zondervan. All rights reserved worldwide. www.zondervan.com

Scripture quotations marked (JPS) are reprinted from *Tanakh: The New JPS Translation According to the Traditional Hebrew Text*. Copyright © 1985, 1999 by The Jewish Publication Society with the permission of the publisher.

Figure "Three Pillars of Israel's Worldview" is taken from Daisy Yulin Tsai, *Human Rights in Deuteronomy*, © 2014 by De Gruyter. Used by Permission. All rights reserved.

For Sarah,
whose love and support made this project possible,
and for our children,

Phoebe and Corban,
who were on my mind throughout the writing process

וְהָיוּ הַדְּבָרִים הָאֵלֶּה אֲשֶׁר אָנֹכִי מְצַוְּךָ הַיּוֹם עַל־לְבָבֶךָ וְשִׁנַּנְתָּם לְבָנֶיךָ
Deut 6:6–7a

Contents

List of Illustrations and Tables | x
Acknowledgments | xi
Abbreviations | xii

1 Introduction and Project Significance | 1
2 Compassion as a Starting Place for Humanitarian Values | 29
3 The Deliverance from Slavery as a Basis for the Book of the Covenant | 81
4 The Book of the Covenant's "Scale of Values" in Light of Its ANE Contemporaries | 119
5 The Book of the What? Humanitarian Values and the "Big Picture" | 167
6 Conclusion and Final Contemplations | 193

Bibliography | 203
Subject Index | 221
Scripture and Ancient Sources Index | 231

Illustrations and Tables

ILLUSTRATIONS

The Structure of the Book of the Covenant | 90
The Literary Framing of Exod 21:12—23:9 | 98
The Three Pillars of Israel's Worldview | 107
Depiction Atop Hammurabi's Stela | 171

TABLES

ANE Law Collections | 20
Literary Expressions in Selected Laws | 46
Compassion in Exod 3 vs. Exod 22 | 115
People vs. Property in ANE Legal Collections | 149

Acknowledgments

CREDIT FOR THE COMPLETION of this dissertation is hardly my own. The journey leading up to this point has been fraught with family and friends who unwaveringly supported me through prayer, advice, encouragement, funding, watching and loving my children, critical feedback, welcome distraction, and the giving of their time to listen to my ups and downs. It is not an exaggeration to say that these people are simply too numerous to recall in their entirety. Some of my long-time supporters include my parents, grandparents, in-laws (and "out-laws"), pastor(s), various university and seminary professors, academic colleagues, church family at-large, and especially my wife, Sarah, whom I met very early on in my program and has not yet known me apart from my identity as a PhD student.

I am particularly thankful for my first and second readers, Drs. Richard Averbeck and Lawson Younger, whose teaching, wisdom, patience, encouragement, and specialized skill in biblical interpretation were very formative for me as I worked toward the completion of my program requirements. They have forever impacted the way in which I read the Bible and their recent retirements truly feel like the end of an era. I am also thankful for Andrew "Gil" and Maggie Gilbert who poured untold hours into proofreading and engaging with the entirety of this work. Finally, I am grateful for and continually humbled by the sound advice I received upon my acceptance at Trinity to "treat my desk as an altar." The wisdom of this counsel became increasingly apparent with each passing day and ultimately brought me to a place where the process of writing became a means of worship.

Abbreviations

ANE	Ancient Near East
BC	Book of the Covenant
HL	Hittite Laws
LE	Laws of Eshnunna
LH	Laws of Hammurabi
LL	Laws of Lipit-Ishtar
LU	Laws of Ur-Namma
MAL	Middle Assyrian Laws
MT	Masoretic Text
NBL	Neo-Babylonian Laws
NT	New Testament
OT	Old Testament

1

Introduction and Project Significance

Then he took the Book of the Covenant and read it aloud to the people. They responded, "We will do everything the LORD has said, and we will be obedient."[1]

—EXOD 24:7

Law without (what I call) religion degenerates into a mechanical legalism. Religion without (what I call) law loses its social effectiveness.

—HAROLD J. BERMAN, *THE INTERACTION OF LAW AND RELIGION*

OVER THE COURSE OF the last century, studies regarding the Book of the Covenant (BC) have seen a remarkable comeback.[2] This is undoubtedly a result of the discovery of the Laws of Hammurabi in 1901 along with subsequently discovered legal collections in the years following, all of

---

1. Unless otherwise stated, any translations of the Hebrew text are my own.

2. The BC is generally understood as including Exod 21–23. Where some have opted to label this selection of text the "Covenant Code," the name "Book of the Covenant" will be used here as seen in Exod 24:7. Additionally, this study will refrain from using "code" as a descriptor for any other biblical or cuneiform legal texts, preferring instead to use terms such as "law collection." This is to avoid the assumption that each law collection exists purely as legislation without any literary context or textual history.

which contain shocking similarities with the BC's structure and content. The unearthing of these cuneiform law collections provided no small grounds for new conversation. Indeed, "no area of biblical studies has benefited more from the recovery of ancient Near Eastern [ANE] literature than law."[3] So impactful were these discoveries that a new approach for examining biblical law, now known as the comparative method, rapidly grew in popularity.[4] To date, the insights provided by this method can hardly be overstated, as more is now known than ever before about the context in which the Old Testament (OT) is set. While this new window into the past revealed how the BC in many ways reflected its cultural and historical setting, it also set it apart as a work that revolutionized how law collections were to be read, understood, and practiced.

Taking the time to read and meditate on a literary work provides substantial insight into the character and values of the author. While most texts are inviting to such a process, the BC goes a step further by employing a rhetoric that yearns for the reader's attention and offers motivation toward introspection and action. Additionally, it is the first (and only) law collection to begin with the topic of slavery—a subject that other ANE law collections unpack only after matters of personal property.[5] This change in order would not have been missed by its ancient audience. As Averbeck notes, "For the debt-slave laws to be at the beginning of this very important section of laws is conspicuous both historically and theologically."[6] Moreover, the BC challenged the existing perception and treatment of women, provided exemptions from punishment on the basis of criminal intent, and promoted harmony and accountability in one's relationships with others regardless of social class or standing. Such concepts fall within the purview of God's most important requirements: to fear the LORD, walk in his ways, love him, serve him, and obey him (Deut 10:12–13). The prophet Micah, in direct reference to the way in which the BC should be read and applied, simplified these requirements even further: to do justice, love mercy, and walk humbly with God (Mic 6:8).[7]

---

3. Patrick, *Old Testament Law*, 28. For an overview of the impact cuneiform law has had on the study of biblical law, see C. B. Hays, *Hidden Riches*, 121–45.

4. Also known as the "contextual method."

5. There is much debate as to whether or not the ordering of the laws in the BC contains significant relevance. For a viewpoint suggesting that the ordering of the laws in the BC could be arbitrary, see Greengus, *Laws in the Bible*, 9.

6. Averbeck, "Law," 133.

7. For a very helpful study on the relationship between God's character and the structure of the BC, see Hess, "Structure of the Covenant Code." In his research, Hess

When read in light of the surrounding covenant narrative, these seemingly small changes to the ancient legal formula, amongst others to be highlighted later on in this project, display a remarkably humanitarian agenda. Gane adds,

> The narrative framework of biblical law preempts conflict between social justice and human vested interests by presenting the legislation as promulgated by the covenant deity, Yhwh, through Moses. [Yhwh] demonstrated his power, beneficent character, and concern for the freedom and well-being of all Israelites by delivering them from slavery in Egypt. Having provided a powerful example, he required them to treat each other with similar justice and kindness.[8]

With this observation in mind, it is unsurprising that the BC has found a foothold in both theological and anthropological circles, though collaboration between these two fields leaves more to be desired. In other words, "biblical scholars have not given commensurate attention to the relationship between [the biblical laws'] theological significance and humanitarian concerns."[9] The BC's insistence on integrating moral and religious values along with its inclusion within a covenant narrative serves as further evidence that it; and, by extension, its author places the rights and well-being of people far above other matters.

REVIEW OF LITERATURE

One would be hard-pressed to find a scholar who argues against the importance of context. Rather, the struggle is generally found in what part of a text's context receives more attention. Should matters of geography and chronology, amongst other such elements, provide the authoritative basis for textual comparison, or should a text's narrative/literary setting claim the brighter spotlight? This is, of course, a false dichotomy. Greengus notes, "We cannot escape recognition of the fact that the Covenant Code, as we have received it in the MT [Masoretic Text], is itself embedded in a larger framework that is not a law code."[10] In turn, Patrick states,

---

uses Mic 6:8 to summarize the values of God as they are reflected in the BC.

8. Gane, "Social Justice," 29. Reading OT law within the context of its covenant narrative is not only recommended, but it is, as Averbeck notes, "realistic" (see Averbeck, "Law," 114–15, for a quick overview of the relationship between law and genre analysis).

9. Tsai, *Human Rights in Deuteronomy*, 2.

10. Greengus, "Some Issues Relating to the Comparability of Law," 73–74.

"There is no one method of comparative study. The ancient Near Eastern texts are useful in understanding Hebrew words, idiomatic expressions, and technical terminology and in identifying types of law."[11] Careful consideration of the BC's surrounding narrative alongside extant ANE legal collections is therefore warranted.

The BC in Its Literary Context

Examination of Scripture as a literary work dates back to the time of the church fathers, but it wasn't until the twentieth century that it became a more formalized practice.[12] Unfortunately, there has been little work done with specific regard to the Book of the Covenant on this matter, especially when it is considered alongside its ANE legal counterparts. In 1965, Shalom Paul completed his dissertation titled "The Book of the Covenant: Its Literary Setting and Extra-Biblical Background." Later published in 1970 under a new title, he argued that "law is an index of a civilization which reflects the underlying value concepts inherent within that civilization . . . law then must be seen as an integral part of the entire structural complex of the society under study."[13] The focal point of his research centered around how the Mesopotamian "prologue-corpus-epilogue" framework in legal compilations may provide insight into the literary context of the BC. He ultimately concluded that cuneiform law and the BC were compatible for fruitful comparison with the assumption that literary context is appropriately considered alongside the more popular and numerous diachronic measures. His work exemplified both of these approaches being in harmony.[14]

While there was some modest progress concerning the study of biblical law's literary elements following Paul's publication, the BC itself would not gain the center spotlight again until the late 1980s. It was at this time that Chirichigno attempted to fill this gap. He points out that "little has been written about biblical narratives which are connected with legal material. This is true particularly for the narrative account of

---

11. Patrick, *Old Testament Law*, 28.

12. For a survey on how the Bible has been treated as a literary work over the centuries, see Ryken, "The Bible as Literature," 51–60.

13. Paul, *Studies in the Book of the Covenant*, 1; published from Paul, "The Book of the Covenant."

14. Paul, *Studies in the Book of the Covenant*, 99–105.

the theophany of God at Mt. Sinai in Exod 19–24."[15] By examining resumptive repetition, his work highlighted the importance of perspective, noting that the Exod 19–24 narrative could be read in two ways: first, from the perspective of Yhwh, which emphasizes the formulation of the covenant and the nature of holiness; and, second, from the perspective of the people, particularly in Exod 20:18–21 and 24:1–8 where the former serves as a preface and introduction to the BC and the latter acts as a bookend for the ratification of the covenant.[16]

A few years later, in 1994, Sprinkle endeavored to bring clarity to the literary approach as he masterfully applied it to the study of the BC. His approach is as follows:

> The 'literary approach' to be adopted here ... looks at the text in a synchronic rather than a diachronic way ... [it] centers on a 'close reading' of the text itself, with an eye to inner coherence, rather than its historical development or production ... A critic adopting this approach, when faced with an incongruity in the text, attempts to find authorial purpose where source critics tend to find scribal misadventure, seams between sources, disorder, contradiction, or corruption.[17]

Moreover, he proposed a way to revise the literary methods used up to this point by drawing upon the strengths of pre-existing approaches and other methods while also being wary of their shortcomings. In summary, his revision can be seen as two-fold. (1) It draws upon some of the techniques of the comparative method to aid in literary analysis, and (2) it de-emphasizes methods that divide rather than unite the text.[18] Sprinkle's work is helpful in that it winsomely promotes the literary unity of Exod 19–24, though the scope of his publication stops short of seeing the Sinai narrative in light of the entire Exodus account—a scope that would not be fully embraced until about two decades later.

---

15. Chirichigno, "The Narrative Structure of Exod 19–24," 457–79.

16. Chirichigno, "The Narrative Structure of Exod 19–24," 479. For a helpful and concise overview of resumptive repetition in the BC, see Dozeman, *God on the Mountain*, 145–75. See esp. 147–50 for an explanation on its unifying and dividing natures.

17. Sprinkle, *'The Book of the Covenant,'* 12–14. For a brief history of this school of thought, see Sprinkle, "Literary Approaches to the Old Testament," 299–310.

18. Sprinkle, *'The Book of the Covenant,'* 14–15. Sprinkle mentions the works of D. Daube, A. Philips, B. S. Jackson, and R. Westbrook. Where he differs from them is that he opts to view the text in a more rhetorical fashion, seeing it as literature rather than law.

Averbeck's treatment of the BC begins with an observation of the broader boundaries of biblical law (Exod 19–Deut 26) and slowly moves inward toward the Sinai event in order to more fully understand its literary setting.[19] Along the way, he affirms the strong ties between the law and the Exodus narrative in which it is placed: "According to the text as it stands, there would be no Law without the Exodus."[20] This statement is further bulwarked by a conversation on the debt slavery and manumission regulations found within all three major sections of law in the Torah.[21] According to Averbeck, these laws in particular not only connect the entire law to the Exodus narrative in which the Israelites were themselves slaves in Egypt, but it also addresses the historical background and rationale of the law as a whole.[22] Simply put, the narrative and the law do not make sense independently—each depends on the other.

The BC in Its ANE Context

While the BC has received little in the way of literary analysis over the years (see above), the same cannot be said of the attention it has been given via the comparative approach. Not long after the discovery of the Laws of Hammurabi (LH), C.H.W. Johns surmised that "the interest of the subject will, doubtless, lead to a considerable literature, which every student of Old Testament and of ancient history will make himself acquainted with."[23] Johns's statement here could not have been more on point, especially when considering the numerous other legal collections that would later be unearthed. What follows is therefore a concise overview of how the BC has been viewed in light of its ANE backdrop.

Chilperic Edwards was quick to offer up his take concerning the relationship between the BC and the LH. He posited that "if there be any relationship between the Hebrew and the Babylonian legislations, there is only one possible conclusion, and that is that the Hebrew was borrowed

---

19. Averbeck, "The Egyptian Sojourn," 143–75.

20. Averbeck, "The Egyptian Sojourn," 166.

21. I.e., the BC, the Holiness Collection (Lev 17–26), and the Deuteronomic Laws (Deut 12–26).

22. Averbeck, "The Egyptian Sojourn," 174–75. See also his works "The Exodus, Debt Slavery, and the Composition of the Pentateuch," 26–48; along with "Slavery in the World of the Bible," 423–30.

23. Johns, "The Code of Hammurabi," 257–58.

from the earlier Babylonian."[24] Edwards helpfully identified parallels between the LH and the BC in his work, but his question of source would continue to be a point of interest behind such examination.[25] In the decades following, form criticism was increasingly used in the analysis of ancient jurisprudence, ultimately leading to Albrecht Alt's work in the mid-1930s. It would be an understatement to say that Alt's contributions changed the flow of the conversation. His terms "casuistic law" and "apodictic law" are still widely used today, despite being relatively dated. Alt rejected the notion put forth by Edwards, opting instead for the viewpoint that the BC was formed through already-existing traditions within Israelite culture, largely due to the unique presence of apodictic laws.[26] This opinion did not go unchallenged. In 1955, George Mendenhall suggested that Alt's comparative scope was too narrow in that he did not consider treaty texts in his work.[27] Ten years later, Erhard Gerstenberger broadened the scope even further to include wisdom literature.[28] Both Mendenhall and Gerstenberger provided worthy examples of extra-biblical apodictic structure, thus raising the bar for future comparative efforts.

Taking up the mantle in 1980 was Hans Boecker who insisted on the importance of considering cultural and theological factors. He states that the BC "has its basis in Israel's relationship with God as constituted by God's election," qualifying this as a "decisive and essential feature of OT law."[29] Informing some of Boecker's conclusions was the work of Volker Wagner. While both scholars affirmed the BC as being "put together deliberately and systematically,"[30] Boecker ultimately agreed with Alt in that it originated with the Israelites while Wagner's analysis of the motive clause led him to the belief that the BC lends itself to a more "pre-Israelite, nomadic setting."[31]

---

24. Edwards, *The Hammurabi Code*, 115. Edwards's insistence that biblical literature by and large owes itself to earlier Mesopotamian writings was typical of this time in biblical scholarship. For more on this, see Delitzsch, *Babel and Bible*.

25. For another early resource on this topic, see Cook, *The Laws of Moses and the Code of Ḥammurabi*.

26. Alt, *Essays on Old Testament History and Religion*, 86.

27. Mendenhall, *Law and Covenant in Israel*, 7.

28. Gerstenberger, "Covenant and Commandment," 49.

29. Boecker, *Law and the Administration of Justice*, 136.

30. Boecker, *Law and the Administration of Justice*, 138–39.

31. Wagner, *Rechtssätze*, 65–66. See also Wagner, "Zur Existenz des sogannanten 'Heiligkeitsgesetzes,'" 307–16. Clausal analysis of ancient legal collections was becoming quite popular during this time. For a helpful overview and masterful study of the use of the motive clause, see Sonsino, *Motive Clauses in Hebrew Law*.

The question of tradition quickly rose to the forefront of the conversation. In his publications surrounding 1990, Raymond Westbrook suggests that the BC as a coherent text may indeed be of Israelite origin, but that the very framework of Israelite tradition is rooted in pre-existing cuneiform scribal schools.[32] In 2009, Bruce Wells, in conjunction with Westbrook, re-affirms this viewpoint, stating, "[There is a] common legal tradition that was prevalent throughout the ancient Near East. It is already in place when written records first appear in the Early Bronze Age and continues unabated into the Hellenistic period. Biblical Israel does not escape the influence of this tradition . . . its inherent system [does] not differ from the pattern."[33] While other scholars such as Bernard M. Levinson were supporting the notion of Israelite adaptation of a larger Mesopotamian legal tradition during this time, Westbrook largely paved the way in formalizing such a thought.[34]

Reminiscent of Edwards's conclusion one hundred years prior, David P. Wright decided to focus less on an underlying ancient legal tradition and more on the specific relationship between the BC and the LH. He bluntly states that "the CC depends rather directly on LH," further adding that "[their] similarities cannot be explained satisfactorily by coincidence, independent genesis, oral tradition, or dependence upon unknown cuneiform or Northwest Semitic text."[35] This assertion once again stirred the pot, drawing criticism from a number of scholars. Perhaps the most noticeable amongst them was Wells, who attempted to deconstruct D. P. Wright's assumptions regarding the nature of textual similarities.[36] Despite such feedback, D. P. Wright pushed forward in his endeavors, eventually publishing a comprehensive work on the matter in 2009.[37] Though many still

---

32. Westbrook, *Studies in Biblical and Cuneiform Law*, 1–4; Westbrook, "What Is the Covenant Code?"

33. Westbrook and Wells, *Everyday Law in Biblical Israel*, 23.

34. See Levinson, "Is the Covenant Code an Exilic Composition?," 288–97. For an earlier take on this understanding, see also Wagner, "Zur Systematik in dev Codex Ex:21:2—22:16," 176–82, where Wagner discusses a type of *Schultradition* that permeated ANE scribal networks.

35. D. P. Wright, "The Laws of Hammurabi," 11–87. Throughout his works, Wright opts for the title "Covenant Code" (CC) rather than BC. Moving forward, these titles will be considered as interchangeable for the purposes of interacting with other scholars.

36. Wells, "The Covenant Code and Near Eastern Legal Traditions," 85–118. See also Collins, "Divine Actions in the Hebrew Bible," 221–39.

37. D. P. Wright, *Inventing God's Law*. See 16–24 for a history of scholarship on this topic.

hold disagreements with D. P. Wright's conclusions, his work nonetheless contains significant contributions and represents impressive scholarship.

In 2021, Milstein offered up a new perspective, suggesting that Israel never actually made use of cuneiform law collections in their legal formulations, nor did they endeavor to mimic the ANE style or genre. Rather, they "put the conventions that are associated with the genre toward radically new ends."[38] The crux of her work is found in the notion that while biblical law was not *dependent* on the LH (or any other legal collection), it drew heavy inspiration from ancient legal-pedagogical texts such as the "Laws about Rented Oxen" and the "Sumerian Laws Exercise Tablet."[39] "With respect to Exod 21:18—22:16," she concludes, "the limited scope of the unit, combined with its ambiguities and errors, suggest origins in a scribal exercise, not a law collection per se." Milstein's work largely represents a new avenue for discussion relating to the comparability of biblical law with its ANE contemporaries.

The BC in Its Humanitarian Context[40]

The field of ethics was not exempt from the impact of the discovery of cuneiform law collections. As interest in the ANE context of the OT grew more prevalent (see above), the interaction between the study of human rights, biblical law, and ethics in general stepped further into the spotlight, especially over the last five decades.[41] Whatever one's take on the origin and development of human rights may be, it is difficult to ignore the OT's significant contributions. Ishay, for example, points out that "unlike Hammurabi's Code, ancient Jewish laws did not differentiate between the rights of patricians (or free individuals) and those of commoners. Jewish

---

38. Milstein, *Making a Case*, 4.

39. Milstein, *Making a Case*, 4. The titles for these legal-pedagogical texts were coined by Roth in her foundational publication *Law Collections from Mesopotamia and Asia Minor*.

40. William S. Morrow is amongst the first to label the BC as having a "humanitarian context," suggesting that the author(s) had certain values and strategies in mind which emanated from their unique setting and identity. For a more detailed explanation, see Morrow, *An Introduction to Biblical Law*, 98–105.

41. See, for example, Walton and Walton, *The Lost World of the Torah*; Goldingay, *Old Testament Ethics*; Green and Lapsley, *The Old Testament and Ethics*; Witte and Alexander, *Christianity and Law*; Rogerson, *Theory and Practice in Old Testament Ethics*; Weinfeld, *Social Justice in Ancient Israel*; Otto, *Theologische Ethik des Alten Testaments*; Greenburg, "Biblical Attitudes toward Power," 101–12; and Harrelson, *The Ten Commandments and Human Rights*.

laws even went a step further, explicitly placing the rights of Jews and Gentiles on equal footing."[42] Otto further asserts that "biblical law was a decisive cradle for an explicit ethics," and, unlike ANE law, "had the function of minimizing conflicts and regularizing conduct."[43] This break from the ancient norm would have first been seen in the BC as it represents the earliest body of biblical law.[44]

One of the first observations highlighting the humanitarian context of the BC was made by Albright in the 1960s. He explains,

> One of the most remarkable features of Mosaic legislation ... is its humanity to man. It is the most humanitarian of all known bodies of laws before recent times. The laws about slavery, which envisage the liberation of Hebrew slaves after seven years, are a good example. But there are also laws protecting the poor: interest was prohibited (always high in the ancient East), and again there was a moratorium on payments after a term of years. Furthermore, it was not permitted to take a man's clothing in payment for a debt ... Not only do we find numerous special provisions for the humane treatment of human beings, but even the well-being of animals received attention.[45]

Roughly 20 years later, Kaiser offered up a more concise synopsis of the BC's priorities with respect to its ANE counterparts, claiming that "in [the BC], human values are constantly elevated over material ones."[46] While these observations by Albright and Kaiser find themselves near the outset of this conversation, it could be argued that initial interest was brought about by grammatical studies, namely through continued clausal analysis of the BC's case laws. By the 1970s, most of the BC's casuistic laws were counted as remedial in nature in that they simply aim to set some form of compensation or penalty when personal or community interests have

---

42. Ishay, *The History of Human Rights*, 19–20. See pp. 17–61 for a more thorough overview of the OT and early ethical contributions.

43. Otto, "Ethics," 276.

44. While the chronological order of the biblical law collections is the topic of an ongoing conversation, it is widely agreed upon that the BC is the oldest. For a more detailed conversation on this matter, see Alexander, "Book of the Covenant," 94–101. For an opposing view, see Doorly, *The Laws of Yahweh*, 7–8. See also Van Seters, *A Law Book for the Diaspora*, 8–18, 82–95. Here, Van Seters argues that humanitarian ethics are first seen implicitly in the Deuteronomic laws and later stated explicitly in the BC.

45. Albright, *Yahweh and the Gods of Canaan*, 181.

46. Kaiser, *Toward Old Testament Ethics*, 96.

been harmed.⁴⁷ Patrick points out, however, that certain casuistic laws show more interest in establishing primary rights and duties than in demarcating particular penalties for violations.⁴⁸ In 1975, Gilmer published a study identifying such laws as having an "if-you" structure, meaning that many of them begin with the phrase "If you . . ." and are followed up by a type of moral responsibility (e.g., Exod 21:2; 22:24 [ET 25], 25–26 [26–27]; 23:4, 5).⁴⁹ These "if-you laws," Gilmer notes, "insist upon ethical and religious values of a markedly humanitarian outlook and are designed to evoke sympathy for those in dire circumstances."⁵⁰

In 1993, using the grammatical and ethical foundations set up in the decades prior, Marshall endeavored to produce the first purely anthropological study on the BC. His method involved a thorough examination of Israelite social and political norms as well as a reconstruction of their culture based on the implicit values found within the BC.⁵¹ While Marshall's publication focuses more heavily on understanding Israel's hierarchy of authority than its ethical underpinnings, he often draws upon the BC's humanitarian context, especially when there is a question of motivation. He notes, for example, that the Sabbath ordinance in Exod 23:12 "may demonstrate a humanitarian purpose" in that it "regulates the work week and provides the necessary rest to laborers."⁵² Moreover, he continually points out the BC's heavy emphasis on the protection of individual rights regardless of role or social standing.⁵³

Like Marshall, Rodd (2001) sees the Sabbath requirement as exemplifying humanitarian values in its concern for the poor, but he especially notes the significance of the collateral cloak law in this regard: "The explanation that the poor man's garment taken in pledge must be given

---

47. Morrow, *An Introduction to Biblical Law*, 100.

48. Patrick, "Casuistic Law Governing Primary Rights and Duties," 180–84.

49. Gilmer, *The If-You Form in Israelite Law*, 46–51. Gilmer notes that "if-you laws" are often accompanied by a motive clause, thus increasing the ethical dimensions of the law in question. For more information on the role of motive clauses, see Gemser, "The Importance of the Motive Clause in Old Testament Law," 50–66; Uitti, "The Motive Clause in Old Testament Law"; and Sonsino, *Motive Clauses in Hebrew Law*.

50. Gilmer, *The If-You Form in Israelite Law*, 47.

51. Marshall, *Israel and the Book of the Covenant*. See pages 29–59 for a detailed explanation of Marshall's methodology.

52. Marshall, *Israel and the Book of the Covenant*, 159. For more on this, see Van Houten, *The Alien in Israelite Law*, 56; and Childs, *The Book of Exodus*, 482.

53. Marshall, *Israel and the Book of the Covenant*, 113–30.

back at night (Exod 22:25–26 [English 26–27])[54] reaches beyond merely declaring the reason for the requirement and stresses the humanitarian purpose behind the law, an emphasis which is backed up by a second motive clause expressing God's support for the poor man."[55] From here, he lists other laws in the BC that share the same purpose. These include the prohibition of taking bribes to ensure justice for the poor (23:7–8); the command to care for the widow and the orphan (22:21–23); and, most importantly, the ordinance to have sympathy with the resident aliens within their own society (22:20; 23:9).[56] Rodd concludes that laws such as the above offer a window into the Israelites' communal identity inspired by their time as slaves in the land of Egypt.[57]

The theme of protection as a primary motivation in the BC was further expounded upon by Van Wijk-Bos in 2005. She states, "If there is an ethos that inspires the entire Book of the Covenant, it is that the God of ancient Israel, to whom the people owe exclusive loyalty, requires of the people who live within the divine-human covenant relationship to protect those who are most vulnerable in the society and to refrain from pushing them further to the margins and exploiting their weakness."[58] She supports this conclusion by illustrating eight different categories of protection found within the BC. These include the protection of slaves (21:1–11); against violent persons, both intended and unintended (21:12–27); against violence of animals (21:28–36); against violence toward property and restitution (21:37—22:14); of the weak and vulnerable (22:15–26); of the relationship to God (22:27–30); of the weak (23:1–9); and of the weakest (including animals) through Sabbath rest (23:10–13).[59] She further argues that these directives are only lived out as intended when practiced within the context of the worship regulations intentionally placed at the beginning and end of the BC (20:21–25 and

---

54. This volume will henceforth favor the Hebrew text's verse numeration with respect to Exodus chapter 22; the English text's numeration will occasionally follow in brackets for clarity.

55. Rodd, *Glimpses of a Strange Land*, 115.

56. Rodd, *Glimpses of a Strange Land*, 115.

57. Rodd, *Glimpses of a Strange Land*, 148–49. See also Gamoran, "The Biblical Law against Loans on Interest," 127–34. Using the BC's condemnation of interest as an example, Gamoran explains that laws such as these are brought about Israel's "unique historical experience. It was unique in the economic, the political, the religious, and the psychological sense."

58. Van Wijk-Bos, *Making Wise the Simple*, 191.

59. Van Wijk-Bos, *Making Wise the Simple*, 181–83.

23:14–19, respectively). This way, covenant readers are empowered to "live the common life of the community in such a way that it fosters the well-being of the community."[60]

It was around the turn of the millennium that commentators began to more thoroughly explore the underlying values found within the BC. Hiers, for example, points out that members of the community seem to have been entitled to bodily integrity, that is, to be free from being harmed by others. This includes freedom from actions by others that resulted in loss of or damage to property.[61] He goes on to state that "implicitly, each member of the community had a duty of care . . . the dignity, worth, or value of each member of society was taken as given, even, though with significant qualifications, in the case of slaves."[62] Dozeman goes a step further by suggesting that these understood values emanate from God's character, namely from his compassionate nature that humans are meant to mirror. His primary rationale for this stems from Exod 22:26 [27] where God declares in the first-person, "because I am compassionate."[63] He goes on to opine that this divine quality of compassion is "a spontaneous gift that can exist only in the relationship between God and humans or between humans who mirror the character of God. It is not a possession or a commodity."[64] Otto later offered up a succinct summary of these notions in his 2015 Oxford Encyclopedia entry:

> In the Book of the Covenant, the ethical sentences appealed directly to the addressees and did not threaten legal consequences; note, for example, the humanitarian appeals to solidarity with the poor and needy in the manumission of slaves and especially in the protection of the sojourner and poor. These latter sentences present an ethos of solidarity with the poor that is legitimized by YHWH's compassion for them: "for I am compassionate." YHWH is thus a model for the ethos of the addressees of the Book of the Covenant Code.[65]

More recently, in 2017, Morrow laid out a case for the preexisting presence of a "humanitarian context" behind the BC using the slave laws as his point of reference. He argues that the rest of the laws in the BC

60. Van Wijk-Bos, *Making Wise the Simple*, 181.
61. Hiers, *Justice and Compassion in Biblical Law*, 22.
62. Hiers, *Justice and Compassion in Biblical Law*, 22.
63. Dozeman, *Exodus*, 546.
64. Dozeman, *Exodus*, 546.
65. Otto, "Ethics," 276.

set up a precedent for how the Israelites were to view and treat others regardless of social class or standing, therefore establishing the backdrop for the humane treatment of slaves. "The writers of the Covenant Code integrated laws about slaves into patterns of instructions that connect fair treatment of socially disadvantaged persons with the worship of Yhwh."[66] There are four of these patterns to observe: (1) as with Exod 21:2, the Sabbath laws in 23:10–12 contain the 6/7 motif; (2) Exod 21:2 begins with the "if-you" formula (see above); (3) Exod 22:24–26 [25–27] aims to prevent indebtedness; (4) the esteem of freedom is reinforced by Exodus memory and expectations for the participation of free males in Israel's pilgrim festivals.[67] It is the BC's humanitarian context, Morrow concludes, that sets it apart from its ANE counterparts, most evidently in the way it highlights the interest of slaves. In 2019, Otto expounded on this context, stating that a "decisive difference between cuneiform and biblical law in the Covenant Code was the absolute esteem for the value of a human life."[68] He illustrates this point in two ways: first, no material compensation for a human life could be adequate; second, the punishment of vicarious retaliation is excluded (that is, the punishment of related, yet innocent parties). He goes on to assert that "these differences indicate that to speak of the law of the Covenant Code as 'common law' of ancient Near Eastern law underestimates the characteristics of biblical law in comparison with cuneiform law."[69]

PROJECT OVERVIEW & THESIS

This study will seek to demonstrate that the Book of the Covenant contains a unique, inherent, and innovative humanitarian outlook which is founded upon the compassionate character of Yhwh, the proclaimed only true God, as modeled by his actions in the exodus narrative.[70] This

---

66. Morrow, *An Introduction to Biblical Law*, 98–99.

67. Morrow, *An Introduction to Biblical Law*, 99. For more on the first pattern, see Otto, *Theologische Ethik*, 83. For more on the third, see Shevka, "Biblical Laws of Loans," 269. For more on the fourth, see Houtman, *Exodus*, 112; Daube, "The Exodus Pattern in the Bible," 116; and Dozeman, *Exodus*, 527–28.

68. Otto, "Offenses against Human Beings," 38.

69. Otto, "Offenses against Human Beings," 38. For an invaluable conversation on such comparisons, see J. Berman, *Inconsistency in the Torah*, 107–15.

70. C. J. H. Wright affirms this position, stating that "the practical outcome of [following biblical law . . .] is humanitarian. But the origin and motive are theological, and this is what is ethically most significant about it. It is here that we see . . . that a

compassion, proclaimed in Exod 22:26 [27] (חַנּוּן), not only establishes the basis for the BC's set of humanitarian values, but it also provides the worthy motivation required of its covenant readers in order to appropriately live according to its directives.[71] The preceding survey illustrates that a comprehensive understanding of the BC's humanitarian concerns is still developing and that other topics such as literary or historical dependence on extant ANE legal collections usually receive the majority of the spotlight. While the examination of such issues is invaluable, ranking them too highly risks losing the ability to see through a legal collection's legislative framework and observe the underlying values it is trying to impress upon the reader.[72] In other words, "we must go beyond the individual rules; for it is not possible to comprehend the law of any culture without an awareness of its key concepts, its value judgments."[73]

There is no doubt that the BC shares several principles with cuneiform law. As a culture immersed in the ancient world, it should not come as a surprise to find out that the law of the Israelites mirrors familiar qualities found elsewhere. Similarities should therefore be embraced. Amongst the foremost differences, however, is the character and identity of the lawgiver. Indeed, OT law represents the only ANE legislation to claim divine authorship—a subject that has not gone unnoticed by scholars from a variety of methodological practices.[74] This claim alone provides ample ground for the BC's unique humanitarian foundation. This humanitarianism is both intrinsic and pervasive, simultaneously coming from and contributing to the biblical narrative in which it is embedded. This is, of course, not to imply that other legal collections in the ancient world are without humanitarian laws—that would be reductionistic and

---

wholehearted covenant commitment to God requires that his people reflect his character, as revealed in his actions on their behalf." See C. J. H. Wright, *An Eye for an Eye*, 157–58.

71. This is very notably the first declaration of this divine quality in the OT and seems to offer a broad motivation for the reader to not only keep the laws in the BC, but to also adopt its implicit values. See Otto, *Wandel der Rechtsbegründungen*, 10, for an argument asserting that this declaration serves as the "center" of the entire BC.

72. Levinson, "The Right Chorale," 15; 30–31.

73. Greenberg, "Some Postulates of Biblical Criminal Law," 8; see also Gane, *Old Testament Law for Christians*, 17–38; and B. S. Jackson, *Studies in the Semiotics of Biblical Law*, 171–207.

74. Gane, *Old Testament Law for Christians*, 129; Sternberg, *The Poetics of Biblical Narrative*, 58; Levinson, "The Right Chorale," 32–33; Paul, *Studies in the Book of the Covenant*, 100–101; Boecker, *Law and the Administration of Justice*, 136; amongst many others.

unfair. Rather, it is simply to say that "the OT laws manifest the justice of their *divine* lawgiver, just as the ANE collections can demonstrate the justice of the *human* rulers who sponsored them."[75] As such, this study will ultimately claim that the BC's humanitarian foundation emanates from the compassionate character of God as represented within its surrounding narrative context: the exodus. While it could be argued that this is characteristic of all biblical law, the BC in particular has been chosen for such analysis.[76]

RESEARCH METHODOLOGY

This project will operate with the understanding that there is no single, best method to lean on when studying a text. While some approaches will inevitably receive more time in the spotlight than others, the aim will be to consult a plurality. The highlights, in this case, will include practices such as comparative legal study, biblical exegesis, ethics, and literary analysis. There are two principles to be upheld in this process: the first is to remain aware of the strengths, weaknesses, and limitations of each method (including the ways in which they may or may not complement each other);[77] and the second is to be sensitive to what is happening in the text itself, working it "as it stands" before resorting to other measures. In other words, the goal is "to be willing and able to follow the text wherever it takes us, even if we have trouble fitting it into what we have been taught or currently believe based on our current level of understanding."[78] With these principles serving as a foundation, it becomes easier to qualify methods as "helpful tools" while giving the text first priority.

The Torah has been subject to a variety of treatments over the past century that have directly influenced an understanding of its law

---

75. Gane, *Old Testament Law for Christians*, 127. Emphasis added.

76. For a similar study performed on the laws in Deuteronomy (with a special emphasis on the slave laws), see Tsai, *Human Rights in Deuteronomy*. Tsai masterfully observes a variety of methodologies and perspectives with the goal of illustrating Deuteronomy's unique human rights values and their theological origins. Her work represents a massive stride in the integration of comparative law and legal sociology which this project will seek to emulate and build upon, namely by shifting the spotlight to the (whole) BC where such values tend to be more implicit and by incorporating the significance of literary context.

77. Osborne, *The Hermeneutical Spiral*, 365–73.

78. Averbeck, "Pentateuchal Criticism and the Priestly Torah," 156. See also Averbeck, "The Egyptian Sojourn," 165.

collections. As a quick and simplified overview, "meaning" in the early twentieth century was largely seen as belonging to the original authors, thus paving the way for historical-critical methodologies such as source and form criticism. This led to an era in which, as Vanhoozer opines, "the text came to be seen as a means to a historical end, namely, the reconstruction of what really happened... Increasingly, the historical-critical method displaced other methods of reading the Bible and, at least in the university, was thought to be the only rational approach to the text."[79] It was in the second half of the twentieth century, however, that this mentality began to experience a growing pushback, namely the desire to "restore meaning... to the biblical text."[80] This transition ultimately led to two major methodological schools of thought: diachrony (observance through time) and synchrony (observance at a fixed time), respectively. Stated charitably, scholars empathizing more with the latter have had a tendency to either break away from or minimize the former as a response to its uncontested and dominating era, asserting each school as having two completely different objectives.[81] Instead of affirming this dichotomy, it is better to acknowledge that both are different yet work together toward the same goal.[82] In other words, "knowledge *about* the text serves the purpose of interpretation only when it puts us in a better position to know what the text is *about*. The good commentary both reduces our puzzlement and enriches our appreciation of what is going on in a text."[83]

Since the research presented in this essay will largely focus on the underlying values found within the laws as they currently stand (as opposed to offering up solutions as to how they are to be carried out practically), a more synchronic approach—that is, an approach that assumes the unity of the text and takes it in its final form—will be adopted. This will not be done, however, at the absolute exclusion of diachronic measures, especially when the text itself presents a historical-critical issue. As

---

79. Vanhoozer, *Is There a Meaning in This Text?*, 285.

80. Levinson, "The Right Chorale," 14.

81. See, for example, Sternberg, *The Poetics of Biblical Narrative*, 22; and Westbrook, "What is the Covenant Code?," 36, where he states that diachronic measures are outdated and unhelpful.

82. Levinson, "The Right Chorale," 9–24. See esp. 11 where he explains that "At least in its origins... the diachronic method no less than the synchronic was concerned with the question of meaning. Even if the diachronic method as currently practiced is not true to its origins, that method is still essential to the proper understanding of Israelite literary creativity."

83. Vanhoozer, *Is There a Meaning in This Text?*, 286.

Levinson states, "Adequate comprehension of the structure and significance of the biblical text must be informed by both."[84] Because the biblical legal collections are a part of the Torah, they continue to benefit from the broader methodological efforts touched on above,[85] but the ways they have been observed in their own right have continued to evolve. What follows is therefore an overview of some of the more prominent, contemporary methodologies regarding the study of biblical law:

(1) *Law as Literature*: The relationship between law and literature in the Bible is a wide topic that touches on a variety of domains. In general, literary approaches aim to focus on the text in its present form, accepting it as a unified whole rather than delving into stages of development, redaction, and analysis of its proposed fragments.[86] Additionally, reading Scripture in this way means having significant sensitivity to the text's genre and surrounding content.[87] Perhaps the most noteworthy issue to surface in the application of this method to biblical law is how the law collections relate to their surrounding narratives. Do the collections function more like judicial decrees which inform (and are informed by) their narrative context, or are they more akin to commentaries on the narrative traditions of the Bible?[88] Wherever one may fall on this supposed spectrum, several scholars over the last few decades have made it increasingly clear that maintaining some form of cohesion between OT law collections and their surrounding narratives is a vital practice. Fokkelman, for example, states, "The enactments of God are purposefully embedded; they stand in fruitful interaction with the narrative mass . . . and share their themes with it."[89] In turn, Josipovici argues, "The Israelites placed their laws within a narrative context . . . Are we good readers

---

84. Levinson, "The Right Chorale," 15.

85. For a brief history of this larger discussion, see Alexander, *From Paradise to the Promised Land*, 3–5. For a collection of works delving into the specifics of each individual method and their histories, see LeMon and Richards, *Method Matters*.

86. Also known as literary criticism or new criticism, not to be confused with new literary criticism or new pluralism. See Clines and Exum, "The New Literary Criticism," 11–25, along with pages 60–65 for helpful summaries on the latter.

87. Ryken and Longman, *A Complete Literary Guide*, 19.

88. The first question is discussed at length in the third volume of the *Collected Works of David Daube*, while the second is proposed by Carmichael in *Law and Narrative in the Bible*, 16–17.

89. Fokkelman, "Exodus," 62.

when we split up what has been put together this way? Is it not up to us to try to understand what that putting together might imply?"[90]

A narrative reading of biblical law, in contrast with most traditional readings, is interdisciplinary and relatively new, focusing less on enacted policies and awarding more attention to the characters and events relating to the legal collections themselves. In defense of such a reading, Bartor adds that "narrative is a mode of thought, a cognitive tool which allows us to attribute significance to actions and events, and therefore serves as a foremost means for the recognition of the world, humankind, and human reality and as a means of argumentation and persuasion."[91] The "law as literature" approach therefore largely sees each component as being complementary. The history and teachings found within the biblical narrative, for example, are made more continual and imminent through their interaction with law, and the law likewise achieves a more prominent status and is made increasingly more significant through its interaction with the narrative. More artfully stated, this method advocates that "law is an arena in which human stories are presented."[92]

(2) *ANE Comparisons*: At the time of this writing, the comparative method (as it relates to ancient legal studies) recently celebrated its 130th birthday. Since its origin with the discovery of the LH, discussion on this front has been vast and, at times, complicated. The drive to locate a comparable idea or institution in ANE culture for every biblical one has spurred on what many have called "parallelomania."[93] Additionally, comparative studies have all too often been hijacked by presuppositions and agendas. "Whether defending the Bible or defending the ancient Near East," states Walton, "some scholars became enmeshed in using cultural and comparative studies as a means to a polemical end. As is often the case in polemics of any stripe, techniques such as selectivity and special pleading can create distortion."[94] Younger notes that haste has also played a large role in poor comparative analysis: "In a number of instances, scholars have been too quick in attempting to do comparative

90. Josipovici, *The Book of God*, 92.

91. Bartor, "Law and Narrative," 225. For an invaluable work on the role of persuasion in biblical law, see Watts, *Reading Law*, 89–130.

92. Bartor, "Law and Narrative," 224.

93. Morrow, *An Introduction to Biblical Law*, 37. For the original sentiment on "parallelomania," see Sandmel, "Parallelomania," 1–13.

94. Walton, *Introducing the Conceptual World of the Hebrew Bible*, 7. See also Malul, *The Comparative Method*, 68–70, for a deeper discussion on some of the pitfalls of comparative studies.

study without allowing time to fully establish the proper reading and understanding of the newly discovered text."[95]

As such, several methodological principles have been proposed for the sake of paving a fruitful way forward. Four of these, established by Talmon in 1977, continue to hold authority to this day: (1) keep in mind the time and place of authorship; (2) prioritize inner biblical parallels over extra-biblical parallels; (3) seek to understand the corresponding social functions; and (4) read the whole text in question rather than picking isolated parts.[96] Hallo later added to this list in his assertion that scholars must be perceptive to both comparison *and* contrast.[97] Indeed, biblical authors shared a fair amount of conventions with their ancient contemporaries, but they also displayed unique perspectives independent of their setting.

The study of biblical law, as demonstrated earlier on in this chapter, has abundantly benefited from the comparative method. This is especially true of the past several decades with the practice of comparison continuing to improve and more source materials becoming available. Due to the biblical legal collections showing up relatively late to the ancient scene, it stands to reason that reading them with a keen awareness of their ANE predecessors will offer valuable insights. Below is a list of discovered ANE legal collections, all of which contain noteworthy (and sometimes shocking) similarities with biblical ones:

Table 1. ANE Law Collections

Sumerian	Laws of Ur-Namma	(LU) *tablet*	ca. 2100 BC
	Laws of Lipit-Ishtar	(LL) *stela*	ca. 1930 BC
Akkadian	Laws of Eshnunna	(LE) *tablet*	ca. 1770 BC
	Laws of Hammurabi	(LH) *stela*	ca. 1750 BC
	Middle Assyrian Laws	(MAL) *tablet*	ca. 1076 BC
	Neo-Babylonian Laws	(NBL) *tablet*	ca. 700 BC
Hittite	The Hittite Laws	(HL) *tablet*	ca. 1650–180 BC

95. Younger, "The 'Contextual Method,'" xxxvi. For a more recent unpacking of this issue, see Weeks, "Problems with the Comparative Method," 287–306.

96. Talmon, "The 'Comparative Method' in Biblical Interpretation," 320–36. See also Averbeck, "Sumer, the Bible, and Comparative Method," 88–125.

97. Hallo, "Compare and Contrast," 1–30. See also Hallo, "Biblical History," 1–26.

As often as comparative legal studies illuminates the biblical collections, it also brings more questions to the table. How were these texts meant to be used? Do they demand specific adherence to their decrees, or do they function more like guidelines for judicial thought? What role does the lawgiver play in their administration?[98] Due to the sheer breadth of such topics, comparative analysis tends to work best when coupled with other methodologies, making it a worthy and irreplaceable interdisciplinary tool.[99] In echoing the sentiment of C. Hays, "the goal of reading the Bible in its context is simply to gain cultural literacy, a basic prerequisite for any interpreter who aspires to any authority."[100]

(3) *Modern Legal Theory*: At the risk of being reductionistic, modern legal theory (or legal science) generally aims to understand the relationship between law and the distribution of social power. Methods relating to this field of thought remain skeptical of the claims made by certain ANE legal collections, such as the LH, that authority belongs to a single, autonomous individual (namely, the king).[101] Rather, they prefer to analyze social and political institutions, traditions, procedures, potential biases, and ideologies. There are a number of focal points to consider in such a process such as the judicial systems at play and their protected interests without the consideration of morals (institutionalism or legal positivism);[102] the local social structure of the culture in question and its beneficiaries (instrumentalism or legal realism); and the ideologies fueled by gender, race/ethnicity, and socio-economic class as they relate to privilege and control (critical legal theory).[103]

---

98. There are a number of works that aim to address questions like these. See, to name a few, J. Berman, *Inconsistency in the Torah*; Walton, *Ancient Near Eastern Thought and the Old Testament*; Bottéro, *Mesopotamia: Writing, Reasoning, and the Gods*, 156–84; C. Hays, *What's Divine About Divine Law?*; Charpin, *Writing, Law, and Kingship*; and LeFebvre, *Collections, Codes, and Torah*.

99. For a thorough overview on the execution of the comparative method in four stages (choosing, reading, and comparing texts before finally drawing conclusions), see Hersey, "The Marriage at Mount Sinai," 36–39.

100. C. B. Hays, *Hidden Riches*, 3.

101. Morrow, *An Introduction to Biblical Law*, 36.

102. See, for example, Westbrook and Wells, *Everyday Law in Biblical Israel*, 1, where they define this approach as "law understood by jurists. It comprises those rules that regulate relationships between humans who are the members of a society in the conduct of their everyday lives, protecting their economic, social, corporal, and psychological interests."

103. For a very thorough unpacking of all of these methods and their histories beginning with the earlier concept of natural law, see Magdelene, "Legal Science Then and Now," 25–29. See also D. P. Wright, "Methods in Studying Ancient Law," 27–38.

The sample of modern legal theories outlined above are chronologically listed and can be seen as continually "zooming out" in their scopes. Legal positivism limits its perspective to the goals of the jurists while legal realism looks at the broader social situation that those jurists belong to, stating that scribes are ultimately a part of a larger system at play. Most recently, critical legal theory upholds that all cultural systems are prone to universal biases best understood through the lens of sociology. Modern legal theory therefore brings a "hermeneutic of suspicion" to the field of biblical legal studies as it questions the basis of authority and the distribution of power in the ancient world.[104]

Understanding Biblical Humanitarianism

To be clear, what is meant by "humanitarianism" in this research is the general treatment of other people—usually the poor, marginalized, weak, oppressed, and unfortunate—that manifests itself in the form of outward service and is often coupled with the desire to enact and execute justice on their behalf. It bears repeating here that humanitarian concerns were not invented by the Bible. All of the legal collections in the ANE espoused to notions of justice and enforced actions protecting the general well-being of their subjects. Understanding "biblical" humanitarianism, then, requires a deeper look at the values and principles which lie behind the behavioral regulations:

> Law is the order of justice and right to which individuals and groups should conform and which judicial authority should enforce. Rules will necessarily play some role in this order, but there also will be principles and values which form a consistent system, cover all possible situations, and belong to the collective conscience of the community. By this definition, explicit rules—laws—are only the tip of the iceberg of the phenomenon of Law.[105]

In adopting Gane's definitions for clarity, a principle is an objective, absolute, changeless truth that governs human nature and relationships. An example of this includes laws like, "you shall not murder" (Exod 20:13). The definition of a value, however, contains more nuance. From a *human* vantage point, a value is generally understood as a subjective, changeable

---

104. Morrow, *An Introduction to Biblical Law*, 36. See also Knight, *Law, Power, and Justice in Ancient Israel*, 82–86.

105. Patrick, *Old Testament Law*, 4.

perspective which comes about from past experiences and interactions within culture. It places a relatively high degree of importance on a course of action generally regarded as right and supposedly results in a good life. From a *divine* (biblical) perspective, a value is similar to a principle in that it is also objective and changeless; but instead of being expressed in the form of an absolute statement, it places ideas on a scale of relative worth or importance, as contrasted with things that are less valuable or rejected.[106] An example of this includes statements like "it is *better* to preserve life *rather than* harming or taking life." In other words, taking life is not necessarily condemned since there are situations which make allowances for such an act, but it is always a less valuable decision than preserving life when possible (e.g. Exod 22:1–2 [2–3]).

Such concepts were not foreign to the teachers of the law during the time of Christ. Matthew 22 recounts a rabbi asking the question, "Of all the commandments, which is the *most* important?" Jesus famously replies with the dual commands—one from Deut 6:4–5 (total love for God), the other from Lev 19:18 (love for one's neighbor as oneself)—adding that "there is no commandment *greater than* these."[107] "In other words," as C. Wright concludes, "here are the primary values, the overriding priorities, that govern the rest of the detailed legislation."[108] Ordering values in this way provides a framework with which one can measure and qualify other values; it also enables the hearer to learn more about what the lawgiver sees as more important. Divine values and principles are therefore "God's priorities which God shares with human beings in order to guide their lives in accordance with his reliable, good, and beautiful will and character."[109]

Is a study on the underlying values within the BC a reasonable (or even feasible) task? If these values are indeed *shared* with human beings by God, as Gane states, then it not only makes sense to say that such an understanding is achievable, but it is also encouraged.[110] As the first Psalm points out, "Rather, his delight is on the law of the LORD, and on it he

---

106. Gane, *Old Testament Law for Christians*, 22–23. See also B. S. Jackson, *Studies in the Semiotics of Biblical Law*, 171–207.

107. C. J. H. Wright, *Old Testament Ethics*, 305. Emphasis added.

108. C. J. H. Wright, *Old Testament Ethics*, 305.

109. Gane, *Old Testament Law for Christians*, 23.

110. Several scholars maintain the importance of looking for underlying values and principles in OT law. See, for example, Kaiser, "A Principlizing Model"; Sprinkle, *Biblical Law and Its Relevance*; and J. D. Hays, "Applying the Old Testament Law Today," 21–35.

meditates day and night." In choosing a starting point for this process—or this meditation, so to speak—this volume will begin its analysis with Exod 22:26 (27), namely the declaration by God concerning his compassionate character. This starting place has been selected for two reasons. First, the character and identity of the author plays a significant role in interpretation. Old Testament law, after all, is first distinguished from other legal collections by the source and authority that the Bible claims for it: Yhwh, the one and only true God. Second, while there are several other characteristics of God that undoubtedly illuminate a sound reading of his law (his loving-kindness, mercy, tolerance, goodness, holiness, etc.), compassion is the characteristic that the BC specifically mentions and promotes as a point of reflection, interpretation, and motivation.[111]

Chapter 2 will make a case for the BC's inherent humanitarianism through an examination of its grammar and syntax, legal formulations, and the ordering of the laws themselves. Specific laws not seen within cuneiform collections will be selected for review. These include the laws regarding the collateral cloak (22:25–26), the enemy's donkey (23:4–5), and the sabbath laws (23:10–12), all of which contain a noteworthy, first-person involvement from the Lord in their contexts. Several scholars have offered up interpretive models to aid in such a process. With regard to literary expression, Gane suggests working with the following features: positive and negative formulations, the manner of address, apodictic and casuistic formulations, recurring formulas expressing consequences, and motivational elements. "Awareness of such elements," he states, "is useful for interpreting the logic and meanings of different kinds of laws."[112] With regard to genre and form, Averbeck recommends observing the law within the canon, noting the style and grammar of the law, comparing the laws in the biblical text with one another, looking for parallels with ANE literature, and seeking to determine the meaning of words, phrases, clauses, sentences, and paragraphs.[113]

C. J. H. Wright appropriately offers a warning against so-called "look-for-the-principle" approaches, stating that on their own, they can "lead to the eventual discarding of the specific realities of the Old Testament text, the concrete, earthy history of Israel, the good, the bad and the

---

111. Dozeman, *Exodus*, 546; and Otto, "Ethics," 276.

112. Gane, *Old Testament Law for Christians*, 80–81. See the pages to follow for a more specific breakdown of these five features.

113. Averbeck, "Law," 130–31.

ugly. Once you have a principle in your pocket, why keep the wrapping?"[114] Three steps (chapters 3–5) will be implemented following the above analysis in order to avoid this all-too-common pitfall. The first step includes an exploration of the relationship between the BC and its surrounding narrative (its historical claims along with its literary elements), ultimately asserting that one cannot be read at the exclusion of the other. W. Janzen notes the absolute importance of observing the biblical story when undergoing any form of OT interpretation:

> Story is the literary genre that, next to actual cultic practice, was most important in the transmission of theological-ethical instruction in ancient Israel itself ... the Old Testament as a whole, in all its diversity, is in a sense a story. Even its legal collections, including the Ten Commandments, have been incorporated into that story in the final canonical text. They no longer function as self-contained law codes, as they once did, but have become sermons heard by Israel in a particular story context ... In our quest for the Old Testament's message, then, we stay closest to its own voice if we begin our search by listening to stories modeling the God-pleasing life.[115]

Indeed, all of Scripture's genres play a role in holistic character development (2 Tim 3:16). The values and principles within OT law should be understood within the totality of biblical revelation, recognizing that the various genres need each other to effectively convey God's moral instructions.[116] In other words, as Vanhoozer points out, truth and reality are multifaceted like a rich white light that can only be fully understood when observed through a "spectrum" of diverse literary forms.[117] Moreover, to discredit the BC's literary context would be to separate it from the very narrative that the BC itself points out as critical in understanding its contents (see Exod 20:22; 22:20; 23:9, 15).

With the understanding that the BC was not generated in a vacuum, the second step will open up the conversation to include ANE legal collections (see Table 1 for a list of these texts). The amount of laws available for comparison is not to be underestimated. In making such selections, Wells recommends keeping in mind what he calls the "continuum of degrees of closeness" (points of identicalness, correspondences, similarities,

114. C. J. H. Wright, *Old Testament Ethics*, 70.
115. W. Janzen, *Old Testament Ethics*, 2.
116. Gane, *Old Testament Law for Christians*, 182.
117. Vanhoozer, "The Semantics of Biblical Literature," 85.

and resemblances, ranged from closer to farther),[118] while Tsai suggests using a legal categorical system to distinguish laws in three levels of similarities and differences (topics, issues, and situations).[119] Such factors highlight two categories of law for review, especially as they relate to the BC's humanitarian concerns: the slave laws (Exod 21:2–11)[120] and the laws concerning the goring ox (21:28–32).[121] Much can be said about the history of these laws and their possible textual transmissions.[122] While this study will seek to address such matters as needed, the primary focus will be on the "scale of values" present within them. Specifically, this scale includes matters of (1) life and property, (2) persons and punishment, and (3) needs and rights.[123] As Tsai points out, "Laws that share the same subject matter . . . may differ fundamentally in their legislative spirits, ethical values, social-economic motivations, political intentions, or theological rationales."[124]

Lastly, the functions of the legal collections and the big-picture questions they are trying to address will be taken into consideration. This will be done in the effort to see their influence on the humanitarian concerns present within the laws themselves especially as they relate to the scale of values above. Both historiography and theology play important roles in this conversation. With regard to the former, Walton recommends working the following questions: (1) who is the sponsor,[125] (2) what or who is

---

118. Wells, "The Covenant Code and Near Eastern Legal Traditions," 91.

119. Tsai, *Human Rights in Deuteronomy*, 23.

120. For some important works on the topic of slavery in the Bible and ANE, see Averbeck, "The Exodus, Debt Slavery, and the Composition of the Pentateuch"; and Chirichigno, *Debt-Slavery in Israel and the Ancient Near East*.

121. See Finkelstein, *The Ox that Gored*; and Patrick, "Studying Biblical Law as a Humanities," 27–47.

122. Morrow highlights these two sections of law as being amongst the most discussed in this regard. See, for example, D. P. Wright, *Inventing God's Law*, 123–53 and 205–28, respectively.

123. C. J. H. Wright maintains that these three value scales are especially helpful when studying biblical and ANE law as they reveal the author's standing on important subjects like the unique worth of human life (*Old Testament Ethics*, 307–14).

124. Tsai, *Human Rights in Deuteronomy*, 23.

125. Scholars are quick to point out, for example, the inverse dynamic between biblical and ANE law. In the former, the author is taking on the role of messenger, claiming that Yhwh is the originator of the laws, while the authors of the latter claim to be the source of law, albeit with the blessing of the deity they represent.

the text promoting,[126] and (3) who is the intended audience?[127] Concerning the latter, he adds that "the existential position of the authors and their matrix for interpreting reality would be significant in how they chose to write their history."[128] Topics such as these, along with a discussion on the problems and benefits of comparing cuneiform law with biblical law, will establish a framework with which to analyze the background of each side.[129] The overall approach of this study can therefore be described as progressively "zooming out" in scope, beginning with the motivation offered in Exodus 22:26 and ending with a more holistic perspective that informs the treatment of others.

PROBLEM STATEMENT AND PROJECT SIGNIFICANCE

What does it mean to have distinctly *biblical* humanitarian values? Interestingly, just as there are several similarities between the BC and other ANE legal collections, there is a decent amount of overlap between a modern understanding of human rights and what the OT upheld to be true of its human recipients. According to the Universal Declaration of Human Rights, established in 1948 by the U.N. General Assembly, all people are of equal dignity and "endowed with reason and conscience and should act towards one another in a spirit of brotherhood" (UDHR §1), entitling them to life and security (§3), freedom from arbitrary punishment (§9), and the presumption of innocence (§11), amongst other proclamations.[130] Such principles were first seen in biblical law, but are they still dependent on the Bible for their continued relevance and practice?[131]

---

126. The majority of recent scholarship maintains that the purpose of ANE law is largely to legitimize the reign of the king. "These collections appear to be legal treatises that provide models of judicial wisdom. As such, they could be used by kings who sponsored them to demonstrate their judicial wisdom and thereby support the legitimacy of their reigns" (Gane, *Old Testament Law for Christians*, 126; see also Walton, *Ancient Near Eastern Thought and the Old Testament*, 202–3). Biblical law, on the other hand, is offered as a gift to the Israelites (it belongs to the people, not Moses). For more on this, see Garrett, *The Problem of the Old Testament*, 223.

127. Walton, *Introducing the Conceptual World of the Hebrew Bible*, 204.

128. Walton, *Introducing the Conceptual World of the Hebrew Bible*, 204. On this, Wenham states that biblical law cannot be fully understood without a proper understanding of the worldview established in Genesis 1–2. See his work *Story as Torah*.

129. The discussion is still ongoing, for example, as to whether or not the prologue-epilogue-corpus formula found in ANE law can be equitably observed in biblical law.

130. See http://www.un.org/en/universal-declaration-human-rights/.

131. Gane, *Old Testament Law for Christians*, 308–10. See also Otto, "Human Rights," 1–20.

When OT law *is* consulted, it is often misunderstood. It has been wrongfully used, for example, to justify slavery,[132] to depict God as legalistic and overbearing,[133] and even to repel and condemn others in lieu of obeying the laws explicitly promoting kindness and compassion (e.g., Exod 23:4). Given that the direct application of OT laws for modern covenant readers contains considerable nuance, misapprehensions like these are bound to take place, but the ramifications of misinterpreting or misapplying them are nonetheless dire.[134] The way forward, then, should strive to bring concrete clarity to the role of the law in biblical-ethical living.

Outwardly, the humanitarian values of the world can appear similar to biblical humanitarianism, but the latter should not be confused with the former, no matter how alike they appear.[135] "The object of [worldly] humanitarianism is not to identify with the world in its shame and affliction (Jas 1:27), nor to permeate the world with the leaven of the Gospel, but to remold the world in the image of enlightened humanity."[136] The Book of the Covenant highlights two clear points of meditation for its readers to consider: Yhwh's compassionate nature and the deliverance of the Hebrew people out of Egypt. This study will ultimately aim to show that a "compassionate reading" of the BC offers up a unique model regarding the treatment of other people while the inclusion of the exodus narrative enables readers to stay in tune with the bigger picture: deliverance. In other words, "do not labor for the food which perishes, but for the food which endures to eternal life" (John 6:27).

---

132. Noll, "Battle for the Bible," 20–25.

133. Garret, *The Problem of the Old Testament*, 29–30.

134. Modern debates surrounding sexuality and religious pluralism, for example, can be associated with a lack of understanding concerning biblical law (Morrow, *An Introduction to Biblical Law*, 5).

135. Bloesch, *Faith and Its Counterfeits*, 47.

136. Bloesch, *Faith and Its Counterfeits*, 47–48.

2

Compassion as a Starting Place for Humanitarian Values

This is what the Lord Almighty said: "Administer true justice. Display mercy and compassion to one another. Do not oppress widows, orphans, foreigners, or the poor. Do not scheme against one another."

—Zechariah 7:9–10

When kindness is separated from the other elements of love, it involves a certain fundamental indifference to its object.

—C. S. Lewis, *The Problem of Pain*

WHAT IS THE LORD like? The Torah, which contains a variety of genres of literature, very often rewards readers who are in the habit of asking questions like this.[1] Some segments, such as the narratives, provide answers by inviting the reader into their stories and enabling them to reflect on their implications. Law, on the other hand, is far more direct, often telling people what to do or what not to do or how to go about judging a

---

1. For a rich conversation on how the Torah (or the genre of *instruction*) is best read and absorbed, see Van Wijk-Bos, *Making Wise the Simple*, 1–14.

particular situation.² It is thanks to this directness that the answer to the above question is not left up to speculation, as the Book of the Covenant contains the all-too-clear pronouncement, "I am compassionate." While this is certainly not the only characteristic of God at play, the BC specifically invokes his compassion as a way to instruct the reader on how to better serve and treat others.

This chapter will endeavor to lay out a case for the BC's unique and inherent humanitarian outlook by dividing the conversation into two parts. With special reference to his self-revelation in Exod 34:6–7, part one will include an exploration of the compassionate character of God—its connections with mercy and justice—along with a pithy discussion on what it means to emulate this character (*imitatio Dei*).³ In other words, what is God trying to reveal to the reader when he calls himself compassionate, and what does he now expect from the reader following this proclamation? Such discussions, according to Van Wijk-Bos, tap into the Torah's convention of "listening and obeying." She states, "The people are required to "listen" so that they may "learn" and "do." . . . In Exodus 24, where the making of the covenant between God and the crowd in the wilderness at Sinai is described as brokered by their leader, Moses, the people promise to listen, to be attentive, to have an open ear, since the covenant represents the living presence of God."⁴ Part two will move the conversation from "listening and learning," so to speak, to "obeying and doing." This will involve an exegetical analysis of three of the BC's laws including the laws of the collateral cloak (22:25–26 [26–27]), the enemy's donkey (23:4–5), and the Sabbath (23:10–12). These laws were chosen for the following reasons: all three lack direct cuneiform parallels; they contain a heightened variety of literary expressions that may provide insight into the BC's unique humanitarian concerns; and all three contain first-person involvement from the LORD in their contexts, enabling the reader to further connect the practical and behavioral requirements of the written laws with the character and desires of their ultimate author.⁵

---

2. Averbeck, *The Old Testament Law for the Life of the Church*, 82.

3. When it comes to rightful relationship with one's neighbor, Otto argues that God leads by example: "God's dealings with humans can be a model for the way humans should deal with each other; this testimony is the core of an Old Testament ethics." See Otto, "Forschungsgeschichte," 20.

4. Van Wijk-Bos, *Making Wise the Simple*, 12.

5. The relationship between Exod 23:4–5 and its immediate surrounding context (23:1–9, often labeled as the "laws of justice and mercy" or the "judicial laws") has been the subject of debate. For a concise overview of this discussion, see Childs, *The Book of*

PART ONE: A COMPASSIONATE GOD

Sometimes translated as "gracious" or "merciful," Exod 22:26 [22:27] contains the Bible's first instance of the divine declaration: "I am חַנּוּן [compassionate]." Though short, glossing over this statement would mean missing out on what several scholars recognize as integral to a proper reading of the laws in Exodus. Otto, for example, identifies it as the organizational and theological center of the BC.[6] He understands the BC to have a "very clear and simple structure," containing two chiastic frameworks with the ending of Exod 22:26 acting as the dividing line or "center point" between them. The first framework, consisting of Exod 21:2—22:26a, is illustrated as follows:[7]

Chiasm 1: Exod 21:2—22:26a [27a]

A. 21:2-11 (Laws for the protection of the underprivileged)
  B. 21:12-17 (Laws worthy of the death penalty)
    C. 21:18-32 (Laws regarding bodily integrity)
      D. 21:33-34 (Laws of restoration)
    C'. 21:35—22:15 [16] (Laws regarding bodily integrity)
  B'. 22:17-19 [18-20] (Laws worthy of the death penalty)
A'. 22:20-26a [21-27a] (Laws for the protection of the underprivileged)

"This chiastic unit is made complete with *ki ḥănnûn 'anî* [because I am compassionate] in Exod 22:27b," Otto goes on to explain, "which is detached from the surrounding context and encompasses the entire collection of Exod 21:2—22:27 and summarizes it theologically in the motif of the compassionate God."[8] Following this critical mid-point is the second framework which consists of Exod 22:27 [28]—23:12:[9]

Exodus, 480-481.
  6. Otto, *Wandel der Rechtsbegründungen*, 9-11.
  7. Adapted from the illustration in Otto, *Wandel der Rechtsbegründungen*, 10-11.
  8. Otto, *Wandel der Rechtsbegründungen*, 10. Translation my own.
  9. Otto's decision to exclude the remainder of Exod 23 is grounded in his understanding that it was added later on and thus should not be included in the original framework. See Otto, *Wandel der Rechtsbegründungen*, 7-8.

Chiasm 2: Exod 22:27—23:12

A. 22:27–30 [28–31] (Laws of apportionment)
   B. 23:1–3 (Laws to safeguard the justice system)
      C. 23:4–5 (Commandment to care for your enemy)
   B'. 23:6–8 (Laws to safeguard the justice system)
A'. 23:10–12 (Laws of apportionment)

Otto's inspection of God's compassion in the BC eventually transitions away from the avenues of form criticism and moves toward ethical analyses. He points out, for example, that the BC houses an abundance of concern for the poor and needy, even to the extent of promoting solidarity with them (especially in 22:20–26). This solidarity is legitimized by the Lord's compassion for them in Exod 22:26b: "When they cry out to me, I will hear, *because* I am compassionate." Through this reasoning, Otto concludes that God takes on the role of the ideal ethical model for the readers of the BC.[10]

The elevation of compassion as a special point of interest in the BC is affirmed by Durham. He states, "The confession of Yahweh חַנּוּן אָנִי 'I am compassionate,' may be understood as the foundational explanation of all of the commands and 'guiding principles' having to do with the defenseless members of the covenant community."[11] W. Janzen furthers these lines of thought, suggesting that a sound reading of the laws seeks out the character of God above the specific letter: "People cannot precisely define and quantify the myriad of life situations offering opportunity for oppression on one hand, and compassion and generosity on the other. These 'laws' are really appeals to an ethically sensitive conscience modeled on Israel's experience of the character and will of God."[12] With these sentiments in mind, attention will now be given to the qualities and defining features surrounding the biblical concept of compassion.

---

10. Otto, "Ethics," 276.

11. Durham, *Exodus*, 329.

12. W. Janzen, *Exodus*, 309. For more reflections on how the BC helps the reader understand the character and will of God, see Enns, *Exodus*, 465–68.

Understanding Biblical Compassion[13]

While the BC contains the first mention of God's compassionate character, this is certainly not the only time this divine attribute is referenced. God is directly described as being חַנּוּן eleven other times in the OT (Exod 34:6; 2 Chr 30:9; Neh 9:17, 31; Ps 86:15; 103:8; 111:4; 116:5; 145:8; Joel 2:13; and Jonah 4:2). Seven of these instances include the most common credal witness to God seen in the Hebrew Bible, namely the proclamation that he is "compassionate and merciful, slow to anger, and full of steadfast love" (Exod 34:6; Joel 2:13; Jonah 4:2; Ps 86:15; 103:8; 145:8; Neh 9:17).[14] While there are notable dissimilarities between some of these instances (such as a change in word order or the addition of further traits or qualifications), scholars are in general agreement that they point toward a singular formula known by the Hebrew people to describe the nature of their God, Yhwh.[15]

Of particular interest to the understanding of biblical compassion is the first of these creedal witnesses found in Exod 34:6–7. "This passage is one of the most important theological texts in Scripture," Laney explains, "because it is the only place where God actually described Himself, listing His own glorious attributes."[16] The significance of Laney's statement was not missed by the biblical authors. As J. G. Janzen observes, "The opening clauses of the proclamation in Exod 34:6 recur again and again throughout the Old Testament; and they reappear in various ways in the New Testament as well."[17] Conspicuous also is Exod 34's connection with the covenant ratified at Sinai, a placement that cements its association with the order to obey everything which the Lord commands (34:10–11). For these reasons, Janzen concludes that God's self-revelation in Exod 34:6–7

---

13. What follows is a foundational survey concerning the qualities of God's compassion. A more specific analysis of the declaration in Exod 22:26 [27] as it relates to its surrounding context (namely the collateral cloak law in 22:25–26 [26–27]) will be offered in part two of this chapter.

14. Cf. Num 14:18.

15. For more on this, see Propp, *Exodus 19–40*, 610; Childs, *Exodus*, 612; and Hamilton, *Exodus*, 576. For a review of ANE parallels to this creed, see Dozeman, *Exodus*, 735–36.

16. Laney, "God's Self-Revelation in Exodus 34:6–8," 36. There is a minority opinion that suggests Moses is the subject (and therefore the speaker) in this passage rather than God. For an advocate of this viewpoint, see Hyatt, *Exodus*, 322.

17. J. G. Janzen, *At the Scent of Water*, 36.

establishes the "customized default setting" to which the rest of the Bible refers thereafter.[18]

Two factors stand out in Exod 34:6–7 as being invaluable to a holistic understanding of God's compassionate character. The first is the combination of חַנּוּן with רַחוּם in v. 6 (God is both compassionate *and* merciful).[19] The second is the seemingly contradictory statement in v. 7 which emphasizes God's strict sense of justice: "But he will certainly not leave the guilty unpunished." Are these two concepts at odds, or are they complementary? Moberly notes that these verses "strongly emphasize the mercy of God, yet do so in such a way as not to deny or abrogate his wrath and judgment," going on to say that "the point is not that the people experience either wrath or mercy, but that both wrath and mercy are in the character of God."[20] In other words, compassion and justice constitute two sides of the same coin; one cannot be fully recognized or understood without the other.[21]

Compassion and Mercy

The word חַנּוּן is very frequently paired with the adjective רַחוּם "merciful." This combination occurs within every passage listed in this segment's introduction and is first seen in Exod 34, the renewing of the covenant at Sinai.[22] J. G. Janzen captures well the significance of the joining of compassion and mercy within God's self-revelation: "Given the fact that this proclamation of God as merciful and gracious [compassionate] introduces the scene in which that covenant is renewed, it is easy to gain the impression that this proclamation is integral to the Sinai covenant and its logic. If that is so, it is because the logic of the Sinai covenant, with its life-or-death sanctions, has become tempered by the compassionate ethos of the ancestral paradigm."[23] Though often coupled, רַחוּם and חַנּוּן bear different meanings and are not interchangeable in the original text. (This can be confusing considering both of these Hebrew words are translated

---

18. J. G. Janzen, *At the Scent of Water*, 35.

19. For more on the other attributes listed in Exod 34:6–7 (patience, loving-kindness, and eagerness to forgive), see Hamilton, *Exodus*, 646; and Garrett, *A Commentary on Exodus*, 652–53.

20. Moberly, *At the Mountain of God*, 87.

21. Hiers, *Justice and Compassion in Biblical Law*, 4.

22. See also Exod 33:19 where both are used together as verbs rather than adjectives.

23. J. G. Janzen, *At the Scent of Water*, 36.

into English as "compassionate," "merciful," or "gracious" depending on the context and the translation one selects.)[24]

The word רַחוּם speaks toward a "gut-level, emotional reaction of sympathy and tender-hearted mercy" similar to how one may think about a parent's disposition toward his or her children.[25] An expression of this can be found in the 103rd Psalm: "Just as a father has mercy on his children, so the LORD has mercy on those who fear him" (Ps 103:13). Girdlestone adds that it communicates a "deep and tender feeling of compassion, such as is aroused by the sight of weakness or suffering in those that are dear to us or need our help."[26] God's merciful nature is also associated with his unconditional choice (Exod 33:19), faithfulness (Deut 4:31), and desire to forgive (Ps 78:38).[27]

The word חַנּוּן is similar to רַחוּם in that it highlights the tenderness and emotion of its object, but it differs in that it "connotes responding favorably to someone's desire for mercy, help, or forgiveness."[28] In other words, חַנּוּן refers to more than just a kind or sympathetic disposition; it implies a tendency to take action and respond positively to cries for aid in moments of distress.[29] Moreover, this form of compassion usually refers to a stronger, superior, or more privileged party offering to help a weaker one who has no claim for such favorable treatment.[30] Yamauchi, with due consideration of these nuances, offers a more simplified definition of חַנּוּן, stating that it depicts a "heartfelt response by someone who has something to give to one who has a need."[31]

It has become somewhat commonplace to tritely label mercy as "the withholding of deserved punishment" and compassion as "the giving of undeserved favor." While not incorrect in the strictest sense, these descriptions tend to misrepresent these terms as amounting to nothing more than their end results. A proper understanding of חַנּוּן and רַחוּם,

---

24. See Koehler and Baumgartner, *HALOT*, s.v., "חַנּוּן" and "חנן" for a range of interpretations.

25. Garrett, *A Commentary on Exodus*, 652. Cf. Gen 43:30 as well as Mark 6:34; 8:2; and Luke 7:13 for the Greek equivalent, ἐσπλαγχνον.

26. Girdlestone, *Synonyms of the Old Testament*, 108.

27. Laney, "God's Self-Revelation," 43–44. Interestingly, רַחוּם comes from the noun רחם, meaning "womb," further highlighting its emotional underpinnings (Garrett, *A Commentary on Exodus*, 652).

28. Garrett, *A Commentary on Exodus*, 652.

29. Garrett, *A Commentary on Exodus*, 652.

30. Laney, "God's Self-Revelation," 44. See also Alexander, *Exodus*, 645–47.

31. Yamauchi, "חַנּוּן," 302.

however, shows that God's compassion is not simply an abstract notion, but a tangible expression of his personhood. It involves an intimate and emotional response of tender-heartedness (רַחוּם) as well as a desire and willingness to act on behalf of those in need (חַנּוּן). There is consideration of how God *feels* as well as how he chooses to *act* on that feeling. As will be discussed below, his compassionate nature is further defined and understood through contemplation of his robust sense of justice, but the main point of his self-declaration in Exod 34 is that he is full of compassion and mercy. The final stanza in v. 7 is a qualification and not the fundamental lesson (Lam 3:22–23; Jas 2:13; 5:11).[32] "The heart of Israel's faith," Garrett proclaims, "is that God is good and merciful."[33]

Compassion and Justice

At first glance, compassion and justice seem to be at odds with one another; one emphasizes forgiveness (Exod 34:6) while the other emphasizes due punishment (34:7). In reality, the removal of one greatly diminishes the potency of the other. Hiers, for example, points out that justice without compassion devolves into rigidness, imposing certain standards or punishments without care for the well-being of those affected. In turn, compassion without justice can be seen as soft-hearted (if not soft-headed) and sentimental, holding no regard for fairness or equity.[34] Garrett agrees, "The qualification, that Yhwh offers no blanket amnesty, means that he does not indulge sin. The unrepentant person cannot escape punishment under a general amnesty; that person remains unforgiven. Forgiveness, moreover, does not necessarily imply release from all consequences for one's actions, although it does mean that one will not pay the full penalty that God would otherwise impose, and it also means that one will, in the end, experience redemption."[35] Beyond simply being complemented, compassion *needs* justice in order to be appropriately realized. Even God's punishments can be seen as acts of love and mercy because they discipline wrongdoers with the aim of motivating them to repent so that they can be forgiven or, at the very least,

---

32. Garrett, *A Commentary on Exodus*, 653; see also Moberly, *At the Mountain of God*, 87.
33. Garrett, *A Commentary on Exodus*, 655.
34. Hiers, *Justice and Compassion in Biblical Law*, 4.
35. Garrett, *A Commentary on Exodus*, 653.

stop them from causing further harm to others (Jer 30:11; Ps 78:34–35).[36] This relationship is best summarized in Proverbs 3:12: "For the LORD disciplines the one he loves, just as a father disciplines the son in whom he delights" (cf. Heb 12:5–6).

Perhaps the best OT illustration of God's compassion and justice is seen in his constant concern for the poor, needy, and oppressed. C. J. H. Wright notes that "because [biblical justice] is fundamentally relational, it always blends into *compassion* for those who are vulnerable."[37] This dynamic not only applies to God's relationship with the poor, but also to his covenant readers (see Exod 22:20–22; Lev 23:22; Deut 15:7–11). On this, Wright continues: "Compassion is, of course, a matter of the heart and emotions, but it is also a covenantal duty and can therefore be commanded."[38] So important is this commandment that whoever fails to heed it will not be heard by God when they cry out (Prov 21:13), practices a defiled religion (Jas 1:27), and ultimately contains no understanding of God's love (1 John 3:17). "The duty of justice to the afflicted is so central that if it is not fulfilled, God will not even accept the divinely ordained sacrifices and worship. When they fail to carry out justice, people do not have the true God as the object of their worship and devotion (Jer 22:15–16)."[39]

Today, the topic of caring for the poor falls within the purview of "social justice," a particular expression of justice that primarily concerns itself with equal rights, economic and social benefits, and the eradication of poverty.[40] There is much that can be said about the positive and negative contributions surrounding the modern application of social justice; but for the purposes of this study, its differences with biblical "social justice" will be quickly reviewed.[41] Gane offers several identifiers to consider in this regard, pointing out that modern social justice often seeks to overturn or adjust the social order, focuses more on the individual, appeals to or pressures corporate groups and power structures for redress

---

36. Gane, *Old Testament Law for Christians*, 321.

37. C. J. H. Wright, *Old Testament Ethics*, 167. See also Wolterstorff, *Justice: Rights and Wrongs*.

38. C. J. H. Wright, *Old Testament Ethics*, 167.

39. Mott, *A Christian Perspective in Political Thought*, 79.

40. Gane, "Social Justice," 19.

41. While the term "social justice" was coined later on and therefore cannot be found in the Bible, Weinfeld argues that the biblical ideal of doing "justice and righteousness" (*mishpat utsedeqah*) "implies maintaining social justice in the society, so that equality and freedom prevail." See Weinfeld, *Social Justice in Ancient Israel*, 5.

to socio-political injustices, and leans on statutory law codes. Conversely, biblical social justice seeks to preserve the health of the existing social order which contained pre-existing privileges;[42] focuses on kinship by covenant which emphasizes each member's place within their respective families;[43] obligates or seeks to persuade individuals possessing social or material advantages to assist the less fortunate; and provides holistic teaching (Torah), including laws that can only be enforced by God (Exod 20:17; Lev 5:1; 19:18, 34; Num 5:12–13) and exhortations that point beyond minimum legal requirements (Deut 15:7–11).[44]

It is important to understand that the above distinctions between modern and biblical social justice, while indeed helpful in exegetical endeavors, speak very little about the relevant aspects of the law's target society. There are several inadequacies to keep in mind that impact the way in which social justice in biblical law is understood. For example, access to Israelite society is limited to a select body of texts (the Bible and a few other inscriptions)[45] and therefore cannot be exhaustive. Moreover, the texts which *are* available do not systematically construct a philosophy of social justice for direct comparison; this must be inductively derived. Perhaps the most significant challenge, however, is the general disconnect that comes along with living in modern times. It is difficult to imagine what life and thought might have been like in an era without today's social systems and amenities.[46]

How, then, can one come to an understanding of biblical social justice? Unlike today's system, which is based on the morality of social relationships,[47] biblical social justice is more religiously based on the character of Yhwh, his historical deliverance of the Israelites from Egypt, and his covenant with them which formed a divine-human relationship that was unique in the ancient Near East.[48] In other words, God's character, actions, and covenantal requirements determine the grounds for what is just. Birch concurs: "The entire Hebrew canon is concerned with

---

42. Westbrook and Wells, *Everyday Law in Biblical Israel*, 143–44, 160. See also Unterman, *Justice for All*, 41.

43. Block, "Marriage and Family in Ancient Israel," 38–40.

44. Gane, "Social Justice," 19–21.

45. See Donahue, *Seek Justice That You May Live*, 53.

46. Gane, "Social Justice," 28.

47. Houston, *Contending for Justice*, 97.

48. Gane, "Social Justice," 20. See also Walton, *Ancient Israelite Literature in its Cultural Context*, 89.

theological/ethical testament to the character, activity, and will of God on the one hand, and the call to response by God's people on the other hand."[49] True justice (Zech 7:9–10) can therefore never be understood solely in sociological terms as the modern approach presumes.[50] The preferred method is instead theological. God's values of compassion and justice "must be taught, encouraged, and accepted as a major part of the collective worldview, as a 'character of society'; it is not enough to legislate and enforce them."[51]

Responding to God's Character

While the emphasis thus far has been on God and his compassionate nature (declared in Exod 22:26 [27] and expounded upon in 34:6–7), attention must inevitably be given to how his people (Exod 6:7) are called to respond. Deuteronomy highlights this transition well: "For the LORD your God is the God of gods and the Lord of lords, the great God, mighty and awesome, who shows no partiality and accepts no bribes. He executes justice for the orphan and the widow, and he loves foreigners, providing them with food and clothing. *You shall also love foreigners . . .*" (10:17–19a). Ethicists and theologians have long discussed the impetus for obeying such a command, showing particular interest in how God's character shapes the morality of his covenant readers. On what grounds are the ethical norms of the OT binding? Are people to obey out of obligation and duty on one hand, or out of goal-oriented conduct on the other (deontology versus teleology, respectively)?[52] Three models have been proposed that claim to have significant bearing on the foundation of the OT's ethical concerns: obedience to God's revealed will, natural law, and the imitation of God (*imitatio Dei*).[53]

Obedience to God's revealed will represents the more traditional usage of the Old Testament in Christian ethics. In short, this model suggests that moral norms are primarily located in commandments, laws, or explicit moral admonitions such as often seen in the prophets.[54] While

49. Birch, "Moral Agency," 24.
50. Birch, "Moral Agency," 29. See also various articles in Cochran and Calo, *Agape, Justice, and Law*.
51. Gane, "Social Justice," 33.
52. Barton, *Understanding Old Testament Ethics*, 45.
53. Barton, *Understanding Old Testament Ethics*, 29.
54. Birch, "Moral Agency," 30.

perhaps the most easily understood and straightforward, the obedience model contains some notable pitfalls if insisted upon too heavily. Hempel, for example, understood "obedience" to be synonymous with complete submission without any autonomy or right to question.[55] This conclusion, however, assumes that God himself is not also a moral agent. Rather than submitting to "pure divine whim," covenant readers are commanded to adhere to the same ethical guidelines that God holds as the standard for his own character and actions.[56] "Although obedience to God's revealed will and the role of commandment are important in the Hebrew canon," says Birch, "a singular focus here separates moral demand from the person of God. In the Hebrew Bible ethics arise not as a matter of obedience to an external model or code of morality but as a result of entering into the life of God."[57]

Natural law, as the name implies, refers to conformity to a pattern of natural order (a vague phrase which is meant to be suggestive rather than defining).[58] This view claims that the basis of ethics is not found in direct command, but rather in the belief that "creation somehow works according to moral principles, of which God as creator is in some sense the 'source' and guarantor . . . In this approach human ability to detect the moral norms by reason, rather than dependence on the revelation of God, is stressed."[59] This explanation encounters some difficulties, however, in that it is through the revelation of Scripture that knowledge of the natural order is received.[60] Moreover, the natural order is made more explicit via direct commands and regulations (e.g. Deut 22:6–7, 10; 25:4; Lev 19:19). As Averbeck notes, "All these kinds of regulations are patterned on the way God designed the world to begin with, and his determination that his people should live according to his patterns and the distinctions between his created categories."[61] In sum, God indeed established a natural order, but an over-insistence on the philosophies of "natural law" leads to the unfortunate exclusion of divine revelation and obedience to his revealed will.

---

55. Hempel, *Das Ethos des alten Testaments*.
56. Otto, "Forschungsgeschichte," 19.
57. Birch, "Moral Agency," 30.
58. Barton, *Understanding Old Testament Ethics*, 29.
59. Barton, *Understanding Old Testament Ethics*, 29.
60. For more on this paradox, see Barr, *Biblical Faith and Natural Theology*.
61. Averbeck, *The Old Testament Law for the Life of the Church*, 159.

The phrase "imitation of God" may conjure up feelings of reservation for some. On one hand, Gen 3 makes it very clear that imitating God, at least in a certain sense, is abhorrent,[62] but on the other hand, there are explicit commands advocating for such a concept: "You shall be holy, for I the Lord your God am holy" (Lev 19:2). To be clear, what is meant by the "imitation of God" in this study is the task of God's covenant readers to "do as God does: to take God's character as the pattern of their character and God's deeds as the model for theirs."[63] This concept has received increasing traction as of late. For example, Barton states that "the purpose of the Old Testament is not primarily to give information about morality . . . but to provide materials which, when pondered and absorbed into the mind, will suggest the pattern or shape of a way of life lived in the presence of God."[64] In other words, "ethics is not so much a system of obligations as a way of communion with God."[65] C. J. H. Wright adds that "the reality of Yhwh's character implies the authority for an ethic of imitation and reflection of that character in human behaviour. We ought to behave in certain ways because that is what Yhwh is like, and that reality is sufficient authority."[66] More succinctly, Nasuti explains that Israel's identity, in having received his law, is largely "defined by the need to imitate God."[67]

Support for the *imitatio Dei* as a basis for OT ethics is only reinforced by its inclusion of the other models. There is no argument against the fact, for example, that the Torah contains direct commands to be obeyed, but the Torah is much more than an archive of dutiful directives (deontology)—it is *instruction*. It offers teachings and advice on how to "follow the path that will take the hearer or the reader to the goal God has in mind" (teleology).[68] Even within the laws themselves, one encounters a myriad of motive clauses seeking to reach beyond mere behavioral regulation. The intentions and desires of one's heart are targeted as the grounds for proper and meaningful obedience, and it is from there that actions flow (Ps 19:14; 40:8). "This might be one of the many possible senses of being made 'in the image of God,'" states Barton, "that Yahweh

62. See Patrick, *The Rendering of God in the Old Testament*.
63. Barton, *Understanding Old Testament Ethics*, 51.
64. Barton, "Approaches to Ethics in the Old Testament," 130.
65. Barton, "Approaches to Ethics in the Old Testament," 130.
66. C. J. H. Wright, *Old Testament Ethics*, 460.
67. Nasuti, "Identity, Identification, and Imitation," 17.
68. Barton, *Understanding Old Testament Ethics*, 52.

and humanity share a common ethical perception, so that God is not only the commander but also the paradigm of all moral conduct."[69]

Paramount to imitating God is the fervent pursuit of his character. "Be holy because I am holy" (Lev 19:2). In what ways is God holy? "Be merciful, just as your Father is merciful" (Luke 6:36). How does God display his mercy? "We love because he first loved us" (1 John 4:19). What did God do to express his love? Humankind is, of course, not able to mimic God in his fullest capacities, but they, being made in his image, are able to reflect his qualities. "Yahweh asks of men that they shall reflect His own character, so far as it can be reflected within the limitations of human life . . . When the prophets denounced harshness and oppression and called for compassion for the unfortunate they were calling men to reflect the character which was uniquely expressed in God's deliverance of His people."[70]

A question more pertinent to this study, then, would be "what does it mean to be compassionate like God?" (Exod 22:26b). As surveyed in the previous section, to reflect God's compassion—his חנון character—is to not neglect the role of justice (Exod 34:7), to be postured toward tender-hearted mercy in all situations (34:6), and to defend the cause of the poor and needy (Exod 22:26a; Jer 22:16). The BC, which brings explicit attention to God's חנון character, was later summarized by the prophet Micah in similar fashion: "He has shown you, O mortal, what is good. What does the LORD require of you? Seek justice, love mercy, and walk humbly with your God" (Mic 6:8).[71] God therefore not only commands these precepts ("what does the LORD require of you?"), but he also demonstrated them for proper replication ("he has shown you"). The values promoted and displayed through obedience to these commands reflect the values of the commander—what he considers to be worthy and acceptable ("what is good").[72] "Indeed, grace and compassion, justice and generosity, are the prime qualities of the LORD mirrored by 'the one who fears the LORD.'"[73]

---

69. Barton, *Understanding Old Testament Ethics*, 52; cf. Col 3:10. See also Jacob, "Les bases théologiques de l'éthique de l'Ancien Testament," 39–51, for early remarks on this notion.

70. Rowley, *The Unity of the Bible*, 25.

71. According to Hess, Micah 6:8 not only emphasizes the sum teachings of the BC, but it also dictates its structure. See Hess, "Structure of the Covenant Code."

72. Gane, *Old Testament Law for Christians*, 55.

73. C. J. H. Wright, *Old Testament Ethics*, 168.

חַנּוּן Humanitarianism

It was stated in chapter 1 that this volume would begin its analysis of biblical humanitarianism by first meditating on God's compassionate character. The goal of this process, prompted by the BC itself in Exod 22:26b [27b], was to provide a solid basis with which to more accurately understand the motivations behind biblical humanitarian concerns and how these motivations might influence the way in which God's covenant readers treat others. A written work is better understood, after all, when the character of the author is made known. Exod 34:6–7, which J. G. Janzen sees as establishing the "settled character of God," expounds on the initial proclamation of God's compassion in the BC, highlighting the critical inclusion of justice and mercy along with a desire to identify with the poor and needy.[74] This is what it means to be compassionate—to be חַנּוּן. Humanitarian actions fueled by the desire to imitate this divine character must then also be חַנּוּן.

As a reminder, this project understands humanitarianism (in a broad sense) to mean "the general treatment of other people—usually the poor, marginalized, weak, oppressed, and unfortunate—that manifests itself in the form of outward service and is often coupled with the desire to enact and execute justice on their behalf." This working definition is not limited to biblical law and can be seen at play in other ANE legal collections. Even the assertion that humanitarian concerns emanate from compassionate avowals is not unique to Scripture.[75] What is unique, however, is the חַנּוּן compassion found within the character of the BC's author, Yʜᴡʜ. Humanitarian actions motivated by God's compassionate character therefore contain distinctive principles. Fretheim, for example, opines that such actions are set apart in three primary ways: (1) they seek relational growth; (2) they are done with the expectation of repetition as needed; and (3) they are considered acts of worship. They are: "beneficent actions and are freely offered or received and contribute to the well-being of another or to the health of an ongoing relationship . . . it is assumed that these will not be isolated actions, but constitute the ongoing shape of life. These actions are not only pleasing to God but are considered as

---

74. J. G. Janzen, *At the Scent of Water*, 35.

75. Ur-Namma states, for example, "I did not deliver the orphan to the rich. I did not deliver the widow to the mighty." In similar fashion, Hammurabi proclaims, "I have not been careless or negligent toward humankind." See Roth, *Law Collections from Mesopotamia and Asia Minor*, 16 and 133, respectively.

done unto the LORD himself and carry their own reward."[76] Garrett adds that חַנּוּן acts seek to renew human dignity: "The essential point is, just as we seek the restoration of our own human dignity by the grace of God, so also we should see in others—however broken they may be—a dignity that is worthy of merciful treatment from us."[77] With these sentiments in mind, practicing חַנּוּן humanitarianism, as opposed to mere general humanitarianism, means caring for others in a way that pleases God and reflects his revealed character.

Is such a practice possible? Are God's covenant readers truly capable of receiving his חַנּוּן character as their own? In the only instance when the word חַנּוּן is not used to describe God, Psalm 112 says, "Praise the LORD. Blessed are those who fear the LORD and who find great delight in his commands ... Even in darkness, light dawns for the upright, for the compassionate [חַנּוּן], merciful [רַחוּם], and righteous [צַדִּיק] ones (112:1, 4).[78] Additionally, it is often used verbally to describe active kindness or generosity exhibited particularly toward those in need (Deut 28:50; Prov 28:8; Dan 4:27). Such imitation, as Dozeman notes, could never arise out of human strength, rather "it [God's compassion] is a spontaneous gift that can exist only in the relationship between God and humans or between humans who mirror the character of God. It is not a possession or a commodity."[79] A good illustration of this is seen when Job begs for compassion (חָנֻּנִי) from his three friends; but in their representation as those who do not understand God's character, they were unable to deliver (Job 19:21). Similar to these antagonists in Job are the priest and the Levite from the parable of the good Samaritan (Luke 10:25–37). They maintained a persona of holy living but lacked in understanding the "weightier matters of the law" (Matt 23:23). "Knowing God is not a matter of mere inner spirituality," C. J. H. Wright concludes, "but a matter of transformation of values and resulting practical commitment."[80] Covenant readers, having heard about God's חַנּוּן character and having seen it demonstrated, are commanded to "go and do likewise" (Luke 10:37).

---

76. Fretheim, "חנן," 204.

77. Garrett, *A Commentary on Exodus*, 520.

78. Cf. Ps 15:1–2.

79. Dozeman, *Exodus*, 546. For opposition to the notion that humans are capable of being חַנּוּן, see Laney, "God's Self-Revelation," 45.

80. C. J. H. Wright, *Old Testament Ethics*, 267.

PART TWO: EXEGESIS OF SELECT LAWS

Humanitarian ethics in the BC are, for the most part, implicit.[81] This is not to say that they are hidden or somehow lesser than what is more explicitly stated. Rather, they are largely assumed by the BC's original readers as being part of its underlying "fabric." Morrow suggests, for example, that the BC was originally penned with humanitarianism in mind in that it contains early strategies for appealing to the readers' conscience. "Overall," he states, "[the laws'] tactics reflect an ethic of concern for the vulnerable, a major theme in the Torah."[82] Watts adds that persuasion was a key element in relaying implicit concerns, especially with the understanding that law was meant to be read out loud. "The accounts of readings depict these texts as influencing the audience's thoughts and persuading them to alter their behavior. Persuasion was thus a principle reason for reading law aloud in public."[83] Such conclusions could lead to feelings of manipulation or to the belief that the BC houses some covert agenda in favor of the poor, but it is important to acknowledge at the outset that this is not the case—God contains no partiality (Exod 23:3; Deut 10:17; Prov 22:2; Acts 10:34; Col 3:25). Humanitarian concerns remain a central point of emphasis in the BC not because God loves the poor and needy more or that they should receive more than their just claims, but because it is within God's character to take up the cause of those who are weak or more frequently victims of injustice (Jer 22:16).[84] The law then provides opportunities for its readers to participate in that endeavor.

The BC's humanitarian principles can be more explicitly observed through a concentrated awareness of some of its key literary expressions. These include examinations of any positive and negative commands, repeating formulas, manners of address, apodictic and casuistic formulations, and motivational elements.[85] Three laws from the BC have been chosen for such analysis, all of which exemplify several of these literary expressions: the collateral cloak (22:25–26 [26–27]), the enemy's donkey (23:4–5), and the sabbath laws (23:10–12). Additionally, both the collateral cloak and enemy's donkey laws contain "if-you" formulations in their casuistic structures. According to Gilmer, laws containing these

---

81. Otto, "Ethics," 276.
82. Morrow, *An Introduction to Biblical Law*, 98.
83. Watts, *Reading Law*, 32.
84. Mott, *Political Thought*, 79; C. J. H. Wright, *Old Testament Ethics*, 268–69.
85. Gane, *Old Testament Law*, 81. Watts, *Reading Law*, 61–88.

formulations often "insist upon ethical and religious values of a markedly humanitarian outlook and are designed to evoke sympathy for those in dire circumstances."[86] Below is a list of each law's literary features:

Table 2. Literary Expressions in Selected Laws

	Collateral Cloak	Enemy's Donkey	Sabbath Laws
Positive/Negative Commands		X	X
Repeating Formulas	X		X
Notable Manners of Address	X	X	X
Apodictic/Casuistic Structures		X	X
Motivational Elements	X	X	X
"If-You" Clauses	X	X	
Direct First-Person Involvement	X		
Indirect First-Person Involvement		X	X

Notably, all three selected laws are connected with first-person involvement from the Lord,[87] a feature that is frequently seen throughout the BC (21:13; 22:21 [22], 23, 24, 26, 28, 29, 30; 23:7, 13, 15). Such involvement, as this study will go on to illustrate, is extremely significant to understanding the role Yhwh plays—his sharing of judicial authority and his self-portrayal in contrast with the Mesopotamian office of king—in the administration of his laws.[88] Additionally, these instances serve to further reveal his character and points of emphasized concern ("I am compassionate" [22:26]; "I will not let the guilty go unpunished" [23:7]; "be careful to do everything I have said to you" [23:13], etc.). In accordance with the above, attention will now be given to the three aforementioned laws. Analysis will include an observation of each law in its

---

86. Gilmer, *The If-You Form in Israelite Law*, 51.

87. While the Lord's first-person involvement is not directly mentioned within Exod 23:4–5 or 23:10–12, it is mentioned within the same immediate context (the same grouping of laws) and is indirectly connected. See, for example, Exod 23:7 and 23:13, respectively. Such connections, as will be further touched on below, indicate that the topics at hand are nothing short of personal for the BC's author.

88. Watts, *Reading Law*, 97.

immediate context along with comparisons with other similar texts as applicable, a discussion concerning relevant literary and grammatical expressions, and a theological/ethical overview as it relates to humanitarian concerns. The laws in question are detailed as follows:

Exod 22:25–26 [26–27]

אִם־חָבֹל תַּחְבֹּל שַׂלְמַת רֵעֶךָ עַד־בֹּא הַשֶּׁמֶשׁ תְּשִׁיבֶנּוּ לוֹ כִּי הִוא [כְסוּתָה] (כְסוּתוֹ) לְבַדָּהּ הִוא שִׂמְלָתוֹ לְעֹרוֹ בַּמֶּה יִשְׁכָּב וְהָיָה כִּי־יִצְעַק אֵלַי וְשָׁמַעְתִּי כִּי־חַנּוּן אָנִי

(25) If you take your neighbor's cloak in a pledge, be sure to return it to him by sunset, (26) for it is his only covering;[89] it is a garment for his skin. What else will he sleep in? If he cries out to me, I will hear, because I am compassionate.

Exod 23:4–5

כִּי תִפְגַּע שׁוֹר אֹיִבְךָ אוֹ חֲמֹרוֹ תֹּעֶה הָשֵׁב תְּשִׁיבֶנּוּ לוֹ כִּי־תִרְאֶה חֲמוֹר שֹׂנַאֲךָ רֹבֵץ תַּחַת מַשָּׂאוֹ וְחָדַלְתָּ מֵעֲזֹב לוֹ עָזֹב תַּעֲזֹב עִמּוֹ

(4) If you come across your enemy's stray ox or donkey, you must return it to him. (5) If you see the donkey of someone who hates you struggling under its load, then even if you want to refrain from helping,[90] be sure to help him (Exod 23:4–5).

---

89. This translation rules in favor of the ketiv-qere (כְסוּתָה to כְסוּתוֹ) suggested in the Masorah Parva as this would yield correct gender agreement with the cloak owner. It is also worth noting that there has been some debate regarding the adjective "only" (the translation used here reflects the majority opinion). For a brief overview on how this word has been treated in the past, see Propp, *Exodus*, 261.

90. There exists some confusion with the clause וְחָדַלְתָּ מֵעֲזֹב לוֹ since it can be hard to tell if וְחָדַלְתָּ is a part of the protasis ("if/when" clause) or the apodosis ("then" clause). The translation here sides with the former; if it were the latter, the translation would be something like "then stop yourself (from abandoning him)." Cp. Propp, *Exodus*, 276 with Alexander, *Exodus*, 507, respectively.

Exod 23:10–12

וְשֵׁשׁ שָׁנִים תִּזְרַע אֶת־אַרְצֶךָ וְאָסַפְתָּ אֶת־תְּבוּאָתָהּ וְהַשְּׁבִיעִת תִּשְׁמְטֶנָּה
וּנְטַשְׁתָּהּ וְאָכְלוּ אֶבְיֹנֵי עַמֶּךָ וְיִתְרָם תֹּאכַל חַיַּת הַשָּׂדֶה כֵּן־תַּעֲשֶׂה לְכַרְמְךָ
לְזֵיתֶךָ שֵׁשֶׁת יָמִים תַּעֲשֶׂה מַעֲשֶׂיךָ וּבַיּוֹם הַשְּׁבִיעִי תִּשְׁבֹּת לְמַעַן יָנוּחַ שׁוֹרְךָ
וַחֲמֹרֶךָ וְיִנָּפֵשׁ בֶּן־אֲמָתְךָ וְהַגֵּר

(10) Sow your land for six years and gather its produce, (11) but during the seventh year, let it rest and leave it uncultivated so that the poor among you may eat from it and so that the wild animals may consume what they leave. Do the same with your vineyard and your olive trees. (12) Work for six days, but rest on the seventh day so that your ox and your donkey may rest, and so that the son of your maidservant and the foreigner may be refreshed.[91]

The Collateral Cloak in Exod 22:25–26 [26–27]

The law concerning the collateral cloak, God's self-proclamation and its theological implications aside, holds more importance than one may initially realize. The act of taking someone's cloak in a pledge presented new opportunities for those in higher positions to abuse their power over the poor and needy, a tendency that, by this point, should be quickly recognized as contemptible to the LORD. Regardless, the prophet Amos found it necessary to criticize the northern Israelites for doing precisely that, saying "they trample on the heads of the poor like the dust on the ground and they deny justice for the oppressed . . . they lie down next to every altar on garments which were taken in pledge. In the house of their God they drink wine obtained through fines" (Amos 2:7a, 8). This treatment of the poor—of one of "God's people" (Exod 22:24 [25])—bears serious consequences for the offender (22:23 [24]). A proper understanding of the collateral cloak law and the character of the God that authored it would have no doubt been of benefit to the Israelites during Amos's day.

---

91. Interestingly, the Hebrew verb וְיִנָּפֵשׁ "may be refreshed" can also be understood to mean "catch one's breath" (Alexander, *Exodus*, 519). This word choice bears some significance in that it appears again in Exod 31:17 with respect God's rest on the first Sabbath after creation.

The Collateral Cloak in Context

The collateral cloak law is regarded by many as belonging to a series of laws in the BC, namely Exod 22:20–26, that concern themselves with matters of social justice and humanitarian practices. Garrett goes so far as to say that these laws in particular are primarily meant to protect and ensure respect for human dignity. "There are two ways we can abuse human dignity," he says, "the first is by involving ourselves in, and promoting, degrading behavior, and the second is by treating others in a disrespectful manner. Both are affronts to the fact that we are made in God's image."[92] He labels this section of laws as expressing concern for three specific vulnerable groups: foreigners/aliens (21), widows and orphans (22–24), and borrowers (25–27).[93] Sprinkle, in agreement with Garrett, highlights that the treatment of each of these groups is outlined with commands to avoid oppression along with a motivation that gives Israel reasons for obeying the imperatives. He notes that these laws are "precepts demanding humanitarian treatment of disadvantaged classes."[94] Unlike the groupings proposed by other scholars, he also includes v. 28 as a generalizing conclusion which capstones the humanitarian stipulations seen in vv. 21–27. The ethical structure of this passage can therefore be understood as follows:[95]

1. Treatment of the Foreigner in Exod 22:20 [Eng. 22:21]

    - Instruction: Do not mistreat or oppress foreign residents.
    - Rationale: You once shared their experience in Egypt—remember your own vulnerability.

2. Treatment of Widows and Orphans in Exod 22:21–23 [Eng. 22:22–24]

    - Instruction: Do not cause harm or distress to the socially unprotected.
    - Rationale: God hears their cry and will respond accordingly if they are afflicted.

---

92. Garrett, *A Commentary on Exodus*, 515.
93. Garrett, *A Commentary on Exodus*, 517.
94. Sprinkle, 'The Book of the Covenant,' 167.
95. Adapted from the illustration in Sprinkle,'The Book of the Covenant,' 167.

3. Treatment of the Poor in Exod 22:24–26 [Eng. 22:25–27]

   - Instructions: Do not demand interest from the impoverished. Return essential items taken as collateral before nightfall.
   - Rationale: Demonstrate compassion, recognizing shared humanity. Fear divine retribution for injustice.

4. Conclusion: Broader Ethical Posture in Exod 22:27 [Eng. 22:28]

   - Uphold reverence toward divine moral authority.
   - Show decorum for earthly moral authority.

"In vv. 23 [24] and 26 [27]," Sprinkle concludes, "God warns that he himself will take up the case of an oppressed orphan, widow, or poor man. Verse 27 [28] forms a conclusion to this thought: 'Do not take me lightly, nor show contempt for a leader of your people.'"[96]

More specifically, the collateral cloak law belongs to a subunit of laws pertaining to the handling of loans and interest as they relate to the involvement of the poor. This correlation is made clear in 22:24, "If you lend money to one of my people, the poor among you, you must not be to them as a creditor; you must not exact interest from them" (see Sprinkle's "Group C" above).[97] Van Wijk-Bos finds the phrase "my people, the poor among you" to be of special significance to the understanding of this subunit: "It could be that we should read this as the poor who are members of the community (i.e. 'my people'). At the same time, 'the poor with you' may be understood as an elaboration of 'my people.' That is to say, the poor in the community constitute in a special way God's people."[98] It bears repeating here that God's laws are not meant to set up a system that oppresses those who are less needy; rather, the aim is to address the reality that it is the poor that are often the ones experiencing injustice and oppression. The laws regarding loans and interest are no exception to this understanding.

---

96. Sprinkle, *'The Book of the Covenant,'* 168. For further support of the inclusion of v. 28 as a summarizing passage, see Brichto, *The Problem of 'Curse' in the Hebrew Bible*, 118–79; and Keil, *The Pentateuch*, 143.

97. Similar laws regulating lending are stated in Lev 25:35–38 and Deut 23:20–21, the latter allowing for interest payment in the case of foreigners.

98. Van Wijk-Bos, *Making Wise the Simple*, 188. See also Baentsch, *Exodus, Leviticus, Numeri*, 202; and Seeligmann, "Loan, Guarantorship and Interest in Biblical Law," 198.

> The proper interpretations of this law would seem to be, not that it fixes any special behavior towards the poor, but that it speaks in terms of the actuality of events as he [the legislator] understands them; to use the phrase used by the sages, 'Scripture spoke in terms of that which happens'. That is, since those who need loans are generally poor, the legislator imposed certain limitations upon creditors, such as that against acting like a creditor towards the poor or the prohibition against taking interest.[99]

Interestingly, Marshall suggests that the BC's insistence upon preventing undue oppression of the poor may have unwittingly increased their oppression as the wealthy may have refused to lend to the poor at all due to the serious warnings and conditions mentioned. This situation, should it have indeed been an issue, would later be addressed by Deut 15:7–8.[100]

The collateral cloak law in Exod 22:25–26 benefits from its inclusion within the larger segment of laws in Exod 22:20–26 in two primary ways. First, as Garrett points out above, its emphasis on preserving the dignity of the oppressed party—the cloak owner in this case—is made more apparent. Second, it becomes attached to the common issue of privileged or more powerful parties taking advantage of the poor and needy via loans and interest. The practical goal, then, is to address the situation in such a way where both sides rightfully benefit from the agreed-upon arrangement. The cloak owner must still offer up their garment as collateral, and the receiver of the pledged cloak must not be overbearing, remembering instead to treat others in a dignified and compassionate way. Deeper still is the lesson that the pledger is their neighbor (22:25) and regarded as precious by the Lord (22:24, 26).

Exod 22:25–26 and Deut 24:10–13

The Deuteronomic Laws (DL) are in the habit of more explicitly unpacking the underlying ethos of the BC, especially when it comes to repeated laws such as the one regarding the collateral cloak. The emphasis on the preservation of human dignity, for example, is further brought to light by the requirement to not enter into the pledger's home for retrieval of their pledged item. "Poverty robs a person of so much," C. J. H. Wright opines, "but the poor should be allowed to control what they still own and should

---

99. Brin, *Studies in Biblical Law*, 86.
100. Marshall, *Israel and the Book of the Covenant*, 148n28.

be given respect in their own homes . . . they [the DL] seek to mitigate the harshness of that reality by including an ethos of compassion and respect, which, while not a matter of enforceable legislation, insists on preserving the human dignity of every member of the community."[101] It has also been pointed out that this addition to how pledges should be handled may prevent undue conflict in the home.[102] Additionally, it highlights the plausible mentality that under no circumstance should pledged items be retrieved forcefully. Jewish interpreters of the law determined, after all, that distraint by force of any kind was oppressive, making distraint an action that must be permitted by the court.[103]

Other notable differences include the range of pledged items and the direct identification of the pledger as poor or needy. Regarding the former, Tigay points out that Jewish interpretation "construes the law broadly, holding that all objects that are permissible to distrain but necessary to the debtor must be returned to him daily when he needs them, such as a pillow at night and a plow and tools of his trade by day."[104] Regarding the latter, Christensen posits that the phrase "if he is poor" (24:12) could be read as "if he is a man of the poor," metaphorically referring to Israel itself as the poor, afflicted, or pious one (e.g. Ps 10:17; 22:26; 25:9; 34:2; etc.).[105] Observing that this bears some similarities to the address in Exod 22:24, many understand this law in Deuteronomy as having been influenced by the Exodus account. This opinion is furthered by the use of רעך "your neighbor" instead of the expected word אח "brother."[106]

Perhaps the most significant difference between the Exodus and Deuteronomy accounts of the collateral cloak law can be seen in Deut 24:13, "Be sure to return the pledge to him by sundown so that he may sleep in his cloak and bless you, and it will be accredited to you as righteousness before Yhwh your God." The command to return the cloak by sunset remains consistent, but the threat of punishment in Exod 22:26 is replaced with the positive motivation of a promised blessing. "The promise and the warning," Tigay explains, "rest upon the conviction that God is the ultimate patron of the powerless . . . they may also imply that human government was not well-equipped to protect their rights and

---

101. C. J. H. Wright, *Deuteronomy*, 257.
102. Tigay, *Deuteronomy*, 255.
103. Tigay, *Deuteronomy*, 255.
104. Tigay, *Deuteronomy*, 255.
105. Christensen, *Deuteronomy 21:10—34:12*, 583.
106. Christensen, *Deuteronomy 21:10—34:12*, 583.

that God was virtually their only recourse."[107] Should the more privileged party be overbearing and keep the pledge during the poor person's time of need, God will "certainly hear their cry" (Exod 22:22, 26); but should they choose to imitate the character of their God and show compassion by returning the cloak, it will be accredited to them as righteousness (Deut 24:13).

Exod 22:25–26 and the Yavne-Yam Ostracon

Especially conspicuous to any research surrounding the collateral cloak law is a certain ostracon unearthed in a fort's guard room just south of Yavne-Yam (modern-day Minet Rubin). Dating rather reliably back to the seventh century BC (perhaps during the reign of King Josiah, specifically 629/628 BC),[108] this ostracon details the petition of a worker whose task was to submit a specified amount to the local granary. According to Hoshayahu, son of Shobay, he had not fulfilled his quota as required, thus leading to the seizure of his cloak until the work was complete—a claim that the worker sought to contest. The complaint, written in typical biblical Hebrew, is as follows:

Lines 1–14

ישמע אדני השר את דבר עבדה קצר היה עבדך בחצר אסם ויקצר עבדך
ויכל ואסם כימם לפני שבת כאשר כל עבדך את קצר ואסם כימם ויבא
הושעיהו בן שבי ויקח את בגד עבדך כאשר כלתי את קצרי זה ימם לקח
את בגד עבדך וכל אחי יענו לי הקצרם אתי בחם השמש אחי יענו לי אמן
נקתי מא שם ועת ישב נא את בגדי ואמלא לשר להשב את בגד עבדך
ותתן אלו רחמם והשבת את בגד עבדך ולא תדהמני

May my lord, the official, listen to the word of his servant! Your servant was harvesting in Ḥaṣar Asam. Your servant harvested, measured, and stored in the granary, per the usual, before the Sabbath[109] As usual, your servant measured his harvest and gathered it a few days ago, but then came Hoshayahu, son of Shobay, and he took your servant's garment. All of my fellow workers, those who harvest with me in the heat of the sun, will

---

107. Tigay, *Deuteronomy*, 226.

108. Aḥituv, *Echoes from the Past*, 156–57. See also Lindenberger, *Ancient Aramaic and Hebrew Letters*, 111; and Reviv, *A Commentary on Selected Inscriptions*, 52.

109. The translation of לפני שבת as "before the Sabbath" is the subject of debate. For a comprehensive treatment of this issue, see Renz, *Handbuch der althebräischen Epigraphik*, 318. See also Aḥituv, *Echoes from the Past*, 161.

answer for me. They will confirm my testimony that I am innocent of guilt. So now, please return my garment. If it is not [the obligation] of the official to return the garment of your servant, then consider it out of mercy! Do not leave me as one dismayed . . .[110]

Should the worker's claim be true, then Hoshayahu, the overseer, was either negligent or purposefully abusing his authority, putting himself at odds with the Torah's teachings.

While some commentators are reluctant to associate this juridical plea with the precepts found within the BC or DL, one cannot help but wonder if the worker in question wrote this complaint with the collateral cloak law in mind given how "on-the-nose" some of its expressions come across. One critical element that may complicate this connection is the relationship between the worker and Hoshayahu. Naveh, for example, claims that the worker's garment was seized as payment due to his supposed failure to complete the task at hand as a hired worker, thus distancing this case from the Exodus and Deuteronomy accounts which more specifically discuss agreements regarding loans and interest.[111] Cross disagrees with this assumption, claiming that the author of the complaint indeed owed a debt as it would otherwise be difficult to see why a pledge was taken to begin with.[112] Milgrom, largely in agreement with Cross, goes a step further by highlighting the expectation that the garment should be returned nightly whether or not the worker was successful at his task. He states, "[The notion] that Hosaiah [Hoshayahu] was in fact a creditor may be inferred from the plaintiff's plea that even if he is not innocent the garment should be returned . . . an expectancy that is plausible only in the light of the pentateuchal law of distraint, Exod. 22:25–26 [22:26–27]. Indeed, if the complaint were not a debt what would lead him to expect the return of the garment?"[113] The logic that the worker is appealing to the Law of Moses is bolstered by his initiative to provide witnesses (Exod 20:16; Deut 19:15),[114] but his claim that he is "innocent of guilt" is not a requirement within the collateral cloak law itself.[115]

110. Translation my own.
111. Naveh, "A Hebrew Ostracon from the Seventh Century B.C.," 135.
112. Cross, "Epigraphic Notes on Hebrew Documents," 46.
113. Milgrom, *Cult and Conscience*, 96.
114. Aḥituv, *Echoes from the Past*, 162.
115. For a Jewish understanding of the worker's plea, see Tigay, "A Talmudic Parallel to the Petition from Yavneh-Yam," 329–30.

Given the Torah's clear position on how to treat the poor and needy, it should not come as a surprise to see the worker desperately ask for the official to show mercy (רחמם). Aḥituv notes that this request sets the tone for the whole appeal; the entire letter is an attempt to garner empathy. He states, "When the syntax and rhetoric of these clauses are properly understood, the text is imbued with intense emotion and deep pathos."[116] Whether or not the worker was indeed thinking of the Law of Moses in his appeal, the Torah had situations such as his in mind when it was written. To rule out the collateral cloak law as significant to the Yavne-Yam Ostracon based on technicalities alone (was he a hired worker or a borrower?) would be to miss the forest for the trees. The request for mercy, along with the assertion of his innocence ("I am innocent of guilt")[117] and a plea for justice ("do not leave me as one dismayed"),[118] portrays an instance of "crying out" (Exod 22:26) that will ultimately expose the official's humanitarian motivations. Will the official acknowledge the request or ignore it like those portrayed in the book of Amos? If he acknowledges it, will he do so out of obligation or out of his fear of the LORD? The lack of resolution to this finding presents the opportunity to reflect on this unnamed worker's plight and consider how his situation might be playing out in various ways today.

Literary Expressions in Exod 22:25–26

The collateral cloak law, though brief, contains an abundance of literary expressions that causes it to stand out within the legal genre. Sprinkle, for example, goes as far as to say that this passage may be more appropriately labeled as literary art rather than legal precision, calling it "essentially moral rather than legal in nature."[119] Sprinkle's enthusiastic assessment is no doubt influenced by the presence of the cloak law's constant shifts between persons (I/me/you/he), poetic connections with its surrounding context ("when he cries out"), and profound layers of motivation and persuasion. Such elements have caused some to label this section of laws as being distinctly set apart from the rest of the BC, perhaps even as a

---

116. Aḥituv, *Echoes from the Past*, 162.
117. Cf. Num 5:31 and Ps 19:14.
118. Cf. Jer 14:9.
119. Sprinkle, 'The Book of the Covenant,' 170.

later addition or redaction.[120] It is important to remember, however, that the Torah is in the habit of combining certain genres and literary features at different times with the aim of instructing and persuading. Additionally, the laws in particular have been noted by a variety of scholars to house a strategic placement of hortatory addresses and motive clauses.[121] Therefore, the BC and, by extension, the cloak law were not authored with only one literary tradition or style in mind.

Manner of Address and Repetition

Exod 22:25–26 ultimately contains two forms of address. The first includes the use of all three persons/points of view: first-person ("me/I"), second-person ("you"), and third-person ("he"). The second further identifies the third-person as the second-person's רעה "neighbor," a label which harkens back to the Decalogue and signifies an expected solidarity between the two parties. Moreover, the repetition of the line "when they cry out" connects the third-person with the situations of the widow and the fatherless in vv. 22–23, suggesting that the stipulations of the cloak law may not be exclusive to just the poor.[122] With regard to the three points of view, there is an interesting progression beginning with the responsibility of the reader (second) and concluding with the authority and standard that is God, the lawgiver (first). Both the reader and the lawgiver have their attention placed on the treatment and concerns of the disenfranchised party in the middle (third). Any reader of this law is able to identify with either the second-person or third-person, both of which look toward the first for instruction. Those belonging to the second party, the one holding the cloak in this case, are called to pay attention to the situation and keep their ethical values in line with the speaker's.[123] As Gane notes, the use of second-person address in biblical law is meant to establish a "direct link between the speaker and the hearer/reader" and "makes it clear that the hearer is the one responsible for keeping the law."[124]

---

120. See, for example, D. P. Wright, *Inventing God's Law*, 52, where he states that the laws of Exod 22:20–30 are "legal miscellany." He labels this body of laws "string I," ultimately asserting that their order can only be understood through comparison with 23:9–19, "string II." See also Doorly, *The Laws of Yahweh*, 18.

121. Watts, *Reading Law*, 62.

122. Cf. Deut 24:17.

123. Gilmer, *The If-You Form in Israelite Law*, 47.

124. Gane, *Old Testament Law for Christians*, 84.

Those belonging to the third party, the one who pledged their cloak, are reminded that there is a higher-than-human authority to appeal to when the second party misaligns their values.

Structure and Motivational Elements

"If you do 'X' to them, then you should do 'Y' for them." This grammatical structure, often referred to as an "if-you" formulation, introduces the cloak law and establishes a moral/ethical undertone which carries through to its conclusion. These formulations can include a variety of agents and actions, both situationally expected or by coincidence, but all of them generally contain a conditional circumstance followed by an expectation for the reader.[125] Such constructions are very often accompanied by motive clauses and aim to convince the second party to take a more considerate course of action. This is especially observable when the party being protected by the law in question includes oppressed classes (the poor, slave, foreigner, widow, orphan, etc.) or those lacking a strong family/adequate finances for their security as is the case here.[126] According to Sonsino, these cases, which he designates as "humanitarian admonitions and rules of moral conduct," constitute roughly 35 percent of all of the motivated laws within the BC (and 37 percent of all the prescriptions which are of moral/humanitarian nature).[127]

The cloak law contains only one motive clause proper, "because that is the only covering your neighbor has," but this is far from the only motivational element found within this passage.[128] Present also are appeals for sympathy: "it is a garment for his skin" and "what else will he sleep in?" This doubling-down of rationale provides two basic insights. First, it shows that God, through his compassion, possesses legitimate care for people's basic needs. To deprive someone of the essentials would be beyond legalistic; it would be cruel. On this, Kaiser notes that "to take

---

125. Here it is important to distinguish between a typical casuistic law and an "if-you" law. While both contain a protasis (if . . .) and apodosis (then . . .), the former requires the mention of a specific penalty. If-you laws, however, are "not laws in the strictly juridicial sense, for they do not describe a case subject to legal action (what is), nor do they prescribe penalties (what shall be)" (Gilmer, *The If-You Form in Israelite Law*, 46).

126. Gilmer, *The If-You Form in Israelite Law*, 48.

127. Sonsino, *Motive Clauses in Hebrew Law*, 88–89.

128. For a conversation on the specifics of what makes a motive clause, see Sonsino, *Motive Clauses in Hebrew Law*, 65–69.

a man's cloak or poncho, which doubled as his blanket for the night, was striking at the very being and essentials of personhood and so it was ruled illegal."[129] Second, it emphasizes how preposterous it would be to view the situation any differently as a covenant reader. To retain someone's cloak after sunset would be antithetical to God's character. "This is between God and the community," states Van Wijk-Bos. "'You,' as a covenant partner, are not to victimize those who are already weak and vulnerable because of their position in society."[130] So egregious is this misstep that, in the name of abundant clarity, God inserts himself directly into the situation: "When he cries out to me, I will hear, because I am compassionate." Van Wijk-Bos continues, "it is of the utmost significance that precisely at this juncture, where groups appear that are weak by their social position and therefore potentially victims of abuse, God enters the picture, not only in the first-person, but with a statement about God's inclination toward the ones who cry out to God."[131] Should the reader of this law indeed hold a proper fear of the LORD (Deut 31:12), then no further motivation should be necessary for adherence to its principles.

Theo-Ethical Overview

The collateral cloak law did well in implementing guidelines and practices that created "guardrails" against abuse in ancient Israel, but it would be shortsighted to limit it to mere situational application. Practically speaking, "by forcing a creditor to restore a poor man's garment every night, it erected a hindrance to the practice by the fact of sheer inconvenience. However," ventures Childs, "the actual motivation in the law goes beyond the legal stipulation and appeals to the compassion of the creditor."[132] Such compassion originates and emanates from the lawgiver, creating a triangular relationship between the borrower, the lender, and God. This dynamic is poetically depicted in Jewish commentary:

> "If you take [your neighbor]'s garment in pledge, etc." Said the Holiness, blessed be He: You, how much do you owe me? You sin before me and I wait for you, and your soul ascends to me every night, and gives accounting, and you owe me, but I return

---

129. Kaiser, *Toward Old Testament Ethics*, 109.
130. Van Wijk-Bos, *Making Wise the Simple*, 187.
131. Van Wijk-Bos, *Making Wise the Simple*, 187.
132. Childs, *The Book of Exodus*, 479.

it to you even though you owe. So to you, even though he owes, "you must return it to him before the sun sets."... "Therefore, if he cries out, etc." Why? For he complains before me and says: I am a mortal and he is a mortal. He sleeps on his bed, but I have nothing to sleep in.[133]

Put simply, why should the covenant reader (the second party) receive compassion from God if he or she is not willing to show compassion to others? It is not too farfetched to equate one's failure to do this with sinful action, as Deuteronomy states: "Do not take advantage of a hired worker who is poor and needy ... pay them their wages each day before sunset because they are poor and are counting on it. Otherwise, they may cry to the LORD against you, *and you will be guilty of sin*" (Deut 24:14–15). Proverbs 14:21 affirms that this is the case: "Whoever despises his neighbor is a sinner, but blessed is he who is kind to the poor."

Childs concludes that the collateral cloak law builds its stipulations on three grounds. First, Israel by this point should be well aware of what it is like to be taken advantage of and oppressed. (The beginning of this section of the BC, Exod 22:20, offers a stark reminder of this for good measure.) Second, the requirement to return the cloak by sunset so that the pledger is able to sleep is the only option that makes sense in light of God's compassionate character. Third, taking advantage of the lesser privileged through pledge is not a new development (Job 22:6; 24:3), but the fact of a covenant with God (22:24, "my people") rules out the possibility of exploitation with this relationship.[134] God's solidarity with the poor is more explicitly stated in Prov 19:17, "kindness to the poor is a loan to the LORD, and he will repay the lender" (see also Matt 25:40).

Exod 22:26 ultimately bears two important messages—one for the pledger and the other for the pledge holder. To the former, it provides a reminder that human lament draws out the compassion of God; he will hear the cry of the poor and respond with grace. Interestingly, "the structure of the [cloak] law corresponds with the psalms of lament in which the gracious attitude of God toward Israel is also the foundation for humans to entreat God in lament."[135] (Psalm 4:1 states, for example, "Show me compassion [חָנֵּנִי] and hear my prayer!") To the latter, it more than implies that one's treatment of others has serious and lasting ramifications.

---

133. *Midrash Tanhuma (Buber) Mishpatim* 9. See also T. Novick, "Social Justice in Rabbinic Judaism," 543–44.

134. Childs, *The Book of Exodus*, 479.

135. Dozeman, *Exodus*, 547.

Gane notes that laws like this one "contribute significant ethical progress by requiring the Israelites to provide for and protect needy individuals in specific ways as part of their covenant obligations, for which they are accountable to YHWH. Therefore, whether or not they treat such persons with kindness affects their individual and corporate well-being and fate."[136]

The Enemy's Donkey in Exod 23:4–5

"You have heard it said, 'love your neighbor and hate your enemy.' But I tell you, love your enemies and pray for those who persecute you so that you may be children of your Father in heaven." For those well-acquainted with the regulations of the Law of Moses, these verses from the Sermon on the Mount (Matt 5:43–45) may feel familiar. While Christ is presenting a "fuller expression" of the law in his discourse,[137] the laws regarding one's enemy's donkey (or ox) contain very similar requirements, namely to provide service and care for one's enemy in their time of need, even if they "hate you" (Exod 23:4–5). The enemy in question is remarkably not the only party benefiting from the practice of this law; their donkey/ox is also receiving humanitarian care and attention that alleviates its suffering. Such treatment of one's enemy and their property both provides rescue from imminent harm (a requirement that is unprecedented even in modern law)[138] and enforces a form of "creation care," a concept that will be seen again in the upcoming segment regarding the sabbath laws. Overall, the importance of understanding and obeying the enemy's donkey laws is perhaps best represented by Christ's summarizing statement regarding the command to love one's enemies: "Be perfect, therefore, as your heavenly Father is perfect" (Matt 5:48).

---

136. Gane, "Social Justice," 21. See also Unterman, *Justice for All*, 83–84.

137. Averbeck, "The Law and the Gospels, with Attention to the Relationship between the Decalogue and the Sermon on the Mount/Plain," 413. Here, Averbeck appropriately notes that "the relationship between the law of Moses and the life and teachings of Jesus has been a complicated matter since the first century" (409). With the understanding that there are a myriad of opinions and perspectives on this topic, this study will adopt Averbeck's position that Christ's "fulfillment" of the law (Matt 5:17) means that "he will teach and live it fully so the people see and learn what it looks like to live the law the way one should" (413).

138. Hiers, *Justice and Compassion in Biblical Law*, 21.

The Enemy's Donkey in Context

It would be an understatement to say that there is bewilderment surrounding the inclusion of Exod 23:4–5 within the larger framework of 23:1–9, a grouping that mostly concerns itself with ethical court procedure. Much of this conversation centers around redaction criticism given how different the enemy's donkey laws are, both in content and in structure, compared with the more judicial proceedings around it. For example, 23:1–3 and 6–8 are comprised of apodictic formulations while 4–5 have been labeled by some as being "quasi/pseudo-casuistic."[139] Moreover, the issue of encountering a wandering or fallen animal is seemingly estranged from the concerns of trial regulations. Why is this law so intrusively placed? Some scholars, such as McKay, argue that 23:4–5 is not a part of Exod 23's original layout and therefore opt to read vv. 1–3 and 6–8 in tandem to the overt exclusion of the enemy's donkey laws. McKay goes as far as to assert the possibility of a decalogue of sorts using 23:1–3, 6–8 as a basis,[140] though one would be hard-pressed to elevate this suggestion above the realm of speculation.[141] Others, such as Driver, posit that vv. 4–5 may have been displaced from their original location, most likely, in his opinion, following 22:23 or 22:26.[142] Finally, some even openly confess to being unsure of what to do with the placement of the enemy's donkey laws.[143]

Those willing to advocate for the placement of Exod 23:4–5 are left with the challenge of understanding the rationale behind its inclusion within its larger legal framework. Scholars such as Cassuto and Frey separately discuss the possibility that vv. 1–3 are directed at witnesses and 6–8 are directed at judges.[144] This distinction is helpful in that it suggests

---

139. D. P. Wright, *Inventing God's Law*, 308; Marshall, *Israel and the Book of the Covenant*, 154.

140. McKay, "Exodus XXIII 1–3, 6–8," 311–12. His proposed decalogue is as follows: 1. You shall not bring up false rumors. 2. You shall not make common cause with the wicked. 3. You shall not follow the multitude with intent to do evil. 4. You shall not answer with the majority with intent to pervert justice. 5. You shall not be partial to a great man in his suit. 6. You shall not turn aside the poor man in his suit. 7. You shall not slay the innocent and the righteous. 8. You shall not acquit the wicked. 9. You shall not utter a lying word. 10. You shall not take a bribe.

141. For another slightly more complicated redactional history of Exod 23:1–9, see Schwienhorst-Schönberger, *Das Bundesbuch (Ex 20,22—23,33)*, 379–88.

142. Driver, *The Book of Exodus*, 237.

143. Jacob, "Die altassyrian Gesetze," 319–87.

144. Cassuto, *Commentary on Exodus*, 296–99; Frey, "Das Ineinander von Kirche

vv. 4–5 are not interruptions; rather, they bridge the gap between the two parties. In response to this, Childs comments that "verses 4–5—whatever the historical reasons for the present position might be—expand the subject of justice in the court for the poor and the stranger to include one's exposed enemy. Indeed, the verses illustrate the extent of the demand by choosing an example lying outside of the court and one which is chiefly under the control of the conscience."[145] Childs's statement echoes the opinions of scholars like Noth and Hyatt, but not all are willing to yield to such reasoning.[146]

In more recent scholarship, Gane suggests that Exod 23:1–8 is literarily held together by the overarching theme of impartial justice. He illustrates this point through his observation that these eight verses form a chiasm (depicted below) with compassionate treatment toward one's enemy acting as the center point:[147]

A. Do not subvert impartial legal justice (vv. 1–2)
    B. Do not be partial to *the poor in his lawsuit* (v. 3)
        C. Return *your enemy's* lost animal to him (v. 4)
        C′. Assist *your enemy* in helping his animal (v. 5)
    B′. Do not subvert impartial justice against *the poor in his lawsuit* (v. 6)
A′. Do not subvert impartial legal justice (vv. 7–8)

Rather than counting the enemy's donkey laws as something which awkwardly stands out from its surrounding context due to its strange inclusion of animal treatment, Gane finds it more appropriate to focus on the treatment of the enemy. "At first glance," he states, "the brief laws in these verses appear to interrupt the theme of legal justice to put an anticlimax in the center of the chiasm . . . however, the point is not about the animals but the enemies who own them."[148] Further, he asserts that vv. 4–5 are an intensification of what preceded and what follows. "The issue is still impartial justice, but in an even more challenging form: away from judicial accountability and involving the choice to help or not help

---

und Welt," 43–44.

145. Childs, *Exodus*, 480–81.

146. See, for example, Marshall, *Israel and the Book of the Covenant*, 154, where he states, "This position is unconvincing because both form and subject matter are unrelated to the immediate context."

147. Gane, *Old Testament Law for Christians*, 223.

148. Gane, *Old Testament Law for Christians*, 224.

a person whom one could regard as having forfeited their right to receive aid."[149] This study finds Gane's take to be the most compelling explanation of Exod 23's framework and will therefore assume literary unity of this text moving forward. This is largely due to two reasons. First, as Sprinkle opines, the propositions relating to Exod 23's redaction and reconstruction are, put charitably, complex and lacking consensus.[150] Second, the notion that caring for one's enemy is tied to one's sense of justice mirrors well the description of God's חנון character in part one of this chapter, namely that mercy and justice constitute "two sides of the same coin."

Exod 23:4–5 and Deut 22:1–4

When comparing laws, it is important not to read concepts from one law into another, even when they are in parallel. This being said, the comparison between Deut 22:1–4 and Exod 23:4–5 provides valuable insights as to their shared underlying value structures.[151] Gane notes two significant similarities in this respect. First, the account in Deuteronomy refers to an ox and a sheep while Exodus mentions an ox and a donkey. While this might initially seem like a difference rather than a similarity, the point is that the listed animals serve as simple examples of animals that might be caught wandering off.[152] Ultimately, it does not matter which animal is discovered; the law applies all the same. This point is bolstered by the elaboration in Deut 22:3, "You shall also do this with his donkey or his garment, or with any lost thing belonging to your brother, which he loses and you find." Second, both Exodus and Deuteronomy employ a strong rhetoric which emphasizes the importance of returning the lost property—whatever it may be—but neither of them state a specific penalty for violating this requirement. Some take the lack of penalty in this context to mean that the law is upholding a moral standard,[153] while others claim that, whenever this is the situation, the implied penalty is the death sentence.[154] Whatever the case, both laws seem much more concerned with

---

149. Gane, *Old Testament Law for Christians*, 224.
150. Sprinkle, 'The Book of the Covenant,' 179.
151. Gane, *Old Testament Law for Christians*, 226.
152. Gane, *Old Testament Law for Christians*, 224.
153. Sprinkle, 'The Book of the Covenant,' 185.
154. Marshall, *Israel and the Book of the Covenant*, 155.

the well-being of the third party and the return of their property than with enacting punishments on the second.

Perhaps the most obvious difference between the two accounts is the use of the word "brother" in Deuteronomy as opposed to "enemy" in Exodus. It is important to note here that the former is not stated to the exclusion of the latter, as "brother" is most likely being used in a broad sense to mean "fellow Israelite," a category which may house both friends and enemies for the adherent of this law (cf. Exod 2:11; Lev 19:17; Deut 15:12; 17:15). Deuteronomy is therefore extending the range of influence initially set up in Exodus in the same way it clarifies the range of applicable lost properties. Woods explains further:

> The motivational element for keeping this law is the term *brother* (used six times in verses 1–4), and the description even extends to those who are non-local and personally unknown (v. 2). This may suggest that this law was difficult to enforce in practice, but in lifting the law from the original judicial context of Exodus, Deuteronomy now extends its application to all Israelites at any time, and appears to ignore any danger of the rescuer being accused of theft.[155]

Finally, Deuteronomy expounds upon the humanitarian treatment of the lost or burdened animal: "And if he [your brother] does not live near you and you do not know who he is, you shall bring it [the animal in question] home to your house, and it shall stay with you until your brother seeks it" (22:2b). As Gane notes, this implies that the finder is obligated to expend resources, time, and energy for the animal by giving it food, water, shelter, and protection.[156] Such a requirement may also explain the use of the word "brother" rather than "enemy" since it would be impossible to know if the owner of the animal was an enemy in this case.

Exod 23:4–5 and LE §50

Earlier, it was stated that the enemy's donkey laws have no ANE legal parallels. This is true in the direct sense, but some have noted the importance of reviewing LE §50 as it relates to the intentions of the one who

---

155. Woods, *Deuteronomy: An Introduction and Commentary*, 237. See also C. J. H. Wright, *Deuteronomy*, 240.

156. Gane, *Old Testament Law for Christians*, 225n5.

encounters a lost animal and is subsequently charged with returning it to its owner. The law reads as follows:

> If a military governor, a governor of the canal system, or any person in a position of authority seizes a fugitive slave, fugitive slave woman, stray ox, or stray donkey belonging either to the palace or to a commoner, and does not lead it to Eshnunna but detains it in his house and allows more than one month to elapse, the palace shall bring a charge of theft against him.[157]

According to Marshall, LE §50 suggests that "Exod 23:4 is probably concerned with preventing accusations of theft rather than with humanitarian concerns."[158] This opinion is most likely founded on Exod 23:4's immediate requirement to return the animal to its owner so as not to risk the appearance of keeping the animal for one's self, thus avoiding the charge of theft. D. P. Wright's insistence that this law may have been directly influenced by the LE provides further backing for Marshall's hypothesis.[159]

While the connection between the BC and the LE on this account is certainly worthy of mention,[160] the speculation that the second party in Exod 23:4 is focused more on preserving their good name than on the well-being of their enemy is just that: a speculation. When one takes into consideration the following verse (23:5) and the parallel found in Deut 22:1–4, the grounds for Marshall's claim become shaky. There is no reason to believe that the helpful and caring mentality required in Exod 23:5 is absent in 23:4.[161] If the DL habitually expound upon the implicit ethics of the BC, as this study professes, then the notion of bringing someone else's animal home would only be considered a humanitarian action. There is no deadline like the one mentioned in the LE since the animal will be cared for as long as it takes to return it to the owner. Such precepts are enforceable when Yhwh is assumed to be the ultimate judge

---

157. Translation taken from Roth, *Law Collections from Mesopotamia and Asia Minor*, 66–67.

158. Marshall, *Israel and the Book of the Covenant*, 154n58. He goes on to admit, however, that "Exod 23:5 seems to have no other purpose than a humanitarian one."

159. See D. P. Wright, *Inventing God's Law*, 307–8.

160. Cf. HL §§71, 75, and 79.

161. A minority view, based on an alternative translation of the verb עזב, suggests that Exod 23:5 is actually encouraging the reader to *stay away* from their enemy's animal. For more on this, see Cooper, "The Plain Sense of Exodus 23.5," 1–22. For a critique of this view, see Sprinkle, 'The Book of the Covenant,' 182.

as opposed to a local governing body (Exod 23:7, "I will not acquit the guilty").[162]

Literary Expressions in Exod 23:4–5

The enemy's donkey laws find themselves included within a larger subcategory of laws that many consider to be a separate division within the BC. This is primarily due to the fact that this supposed division (Exod 22:17—23:9) is mostly comprised of apodictic structures and contains exhortative formulations calling for divine justice.[163] On one hand, Exod 23:4–5 fits in with this assessment in that it, too, houses exhortations; but on the other hand, as noted above, it disrupts the apodictic format. Given that the collateral cloak law is also found within this same division, yet acts as a formulaic disruption like the enemy's donkey laws, this study will remain skeptical concerning claims that the BC is comprised of segregated parts based on literary expression, notwithstanding redactional analyses. Instead, the assumption moving forward will be that different formulations—apodictic or otherwise—are organically (or intentionally) intermixed, as they are often complementary in nature.[164]

Manner of Address and Structure

The enemy's donkey laws refer directly to only the second and third-persons. Since vv. 4–5 are playing a more specific role within the larger framework of vv. 1–9 in that they are presenting an example of how one should treat their legal opponent outside of court, the expected appeal to the first-person, God, comes two verses later. Overall, there are two third parties being discussed, the animal(s) belonging to the reader's enemy and the enemy himself, thus creating two beneficiaries for humanitarian aid. The theological richness of this law is undoubtedly the result of the stipulation to assist a person who is explicitly identified as an enemy,[165] but it is also significant to note that animals are deserving of kindness

---

162. Gane, *Old Testament Law for Christians*, 221–22.

163. E.g., Doorly, *The Laws of Yahweh*, 11–12; Marshall, *Israel and the Book of the Covenant*, 141.

164. For a brief conversation on how apodictic and casuistic formulations can complement each other, see Averbeck, *The Old Testament Law for the Life of the Church*, 162.

165. Gane, *Old Testament Law for Christians*, 219.

as well (cf. Matt 6:26a). "Indeed, the principles of fairness and compassion [extend] even to working animals, such as the laden donkey and the threshing ox."[166]

Like the collateral cloak law, the enemy's donkey laws are made up of humanitarian if-you formulations. According to Gilmer, this is largely due to their protected subjects: both the enemy and his animal. The cloak law made it a point to protect the oppressed/insecure, but humanitarian if-you clauses are also identified by the desire to serve one's own peers (those with whom one might have everyday exchange) and animals which are at a disadvantage due to unfortunate circumstances.[167] The way in which these if-you clauses interrupt their surrounding constructions is also worthy of comment. Put simply, a series of absolute proscriptions (23:1–3 and 6–7) is broken up by two positive laws (more on this below) having to do with an animal that is lost or overburdened.[168] "The change in style goes together with a sharpening of focus," Van Wijk-Bos explains. "Here the recipients of the action are not a general group, 'the majority,' 'the wicked,' 'the poor,' 'the innocent and righteous,' but an animal and its owner, more specifically, 'your enemy' and 'one who hates you.'"[169]

Positive Commands and Motivational Elements

The enemy's donkey laws contain a striking mixture of positive commands and exhortations which display a strong recognition of the need for persuasion.[170] The first and last of these injunctions are reinforced by infinite absolutes, further emphasizing their authoritative appeal. These are often rendered in various ways: "You shall surely return it to him" (NASB; cf. NKJV); "Be sure to take it back to him" (NIV); "You must take it back to him" (NJPS); etc. Positive formulations like these are meant to more directly express the principles of the author and, by their very nature, create prohibitions. For example, "Honor your father and your mother" (Exod 20:12) implies a prohibition against dishonoring them (cf. Exod 21:15, 17; Deut 21:18–21).[171] In similar fashion, the positive

---

166. C. J. H. Wright, *Old Testament Ethics*, 160.
167. Gilmer, *The If-You Form in Israelite Law*, 48.
168. Van Wijk-Bos, *Making Wise the Simple*, 190.
169. Van Wijk-Bos, *Making Wise the Simple*, 190.
170. Gane, *Old Testament Law for Christians*, 221.
171. Gane, *Old Testament Law for Christians*, 81.

commands in the enemy's donkey laws prohibit the reader from ignoring the animal, as simply doing nothing could result in harm to it or its complete loss to one's enemy.[172] In the event that this law fails to invoke empathy for the enemy's situation, further motivation can be found in the expectation that the reader will follow through anyways, even if they would prefer to "refrain from helping it" (Exod 23:5 [NKJV]). As such, there are no punishments listed; God, as the ultimate judge of the situation, remains aware of one's obedience or lack thereof. "The fact that only God would know explains why the law lacks a clause specifying a penalty for violation administered by the community,"[173] Gane elaborates, "including it in covenant instructions for which the Deity makes his people accountable to himself is intended to motivate you to do the right thing even when you don't feel like doing so."[174]

Theo-Ethical Overview

As outlined in part one of this chapter, relational growth is a priority for those seeking to imitate God's חנון character. Being non-discriminate in one's loving service, after all, is a mark of being a child of the Father (Matt 5:43–45; Eph 5:1–2; 1 John 2:6); as such, the beneficiary of Exod 23:4–5 should not come as a surprise to those who seek to learn the LORD's ways (Exod 18:20; Isa 55:8–9). Dozeman adds that relational progression can even be seen at play within the laws themselves, pointing out that "the first requires the return of an enemy's ox or donkey if it wanders away (v. 4)," while "the second may go further, demanding all Israelites to aid someone who may hate them (v. 5). According to this interpretation," he concludes, "there is progression in the two laws. The second goes beyond the simple return of an animal to an enemy to require more personal assistance."[175] Sprinkle adds that "an Israelite is to do everything in his power to end any hostility between himself and his neighbor. He cannot force another man to cease to be hostile towards him, but an act of kindness to his enemy could well become the first step towards reconciliation,

---

172. Gane, *Old Testament Law for Christians*, 221.
173. Cf. Exod 22:8; Lev 6:3–4.
174. Gane, *Old Testament Law for Christians*, 220. Cf. Exod 19:5; 21:1; 24:3–4, 7–8.
175. Dozeman, *Exodus*, 548.

and societal harmony."[176] Nothing, not even a legal conflict, should intervene in the humanitarian treatment of another.

Gane highlights three ethical/moral qualities instilled within the enemy's donkey law worthy of consideration.[177] First, it shows how actions which seem significant can point toward a larger perspective with profound significance (Matt 25:31). Second, it helps reveal logical relationships between actions that can assist one in making decisions. Rather than needing to legislate every step necessary to provide aid, for example, the laws simply need to use words like "return it" (23:4) and "help him" (23:5).[178] Logic can inform the reader as to what steps are needed in order to lovingly satisfy these commands. Third, it aids in informing the reader how to approach other situations in life that no law specifically addresses by emphasizing the value in choosing to love one's enemy, even if one may not feel so inclined in the moment.

The Sabbath in Exod 23:10–12

With special appearances and variations located in all of the Torah's legal collections, the regulations regarding the Sabbath are perhaps the most layered and multifaceted laws into which this study has ventured thus far. The Sabbath has been said to be "a cornerstone of Israelite religious practice"[179] and an illustration of "a genial marriage of social and cultic legislation."[180] It is a feast day of which the meaning harkens back to the creation (Exod 20:11), outward to the social context (Exod 23:12; Deut 5:14), and into the history of the Hebrew people as a liberated group (Exod 31:12–17; Deut 5:15).[181] Much can therefore be said about the Sabbath's theological implications and interconnectedness with other significant biblical concepts.[182] As evidenced by the previous two case studies, however, this section will seek to highlight and unpack the humanitarian values and motivations within Exodus' sabbath laws while simultaneously

176. Sprinkle, 'The Book of the Covenant,' 186.
177. Gane, *Old Testament Law for Christians*, 227.
178. For more on the relationship between legislation and the Torah, see J. Berman, *Inconsistency in the Torah*, 115–16.
179. Glatt and Tigay, "Sabbath," 888.
180. Plaut, *The Torah*, 548.
181. Van Wijk-Bos, *Making Wise the Simple*, 52.
182. For a helpful study on such matters, see Swiderski, "Sabbatical Patterns in the Book of the Covenant."

appreciating their rich theological import. On this, Stuart's commentary is helpful: "The Sabbath, whether of years or days, was intended by God to provide restoration and well-being for God's people, not merely a cessation of all activity."[183] Those struggling with such explanations would do well to pay attention to Christ's clarification in Mark 2:27, "The Sabbath was made for man, not man for the Sabbath."

The Sabbath Laws in Context

There are, in general, two outstanding discussions relating to the positional inclusion of the sabbath laws in the BC. The first relates to the possible parallels between Exod 23:10–12 and Exod 22:24–26 [25–27]. Originally proposed by Carmichael in 1972, this textual connection, should it indeed be present, suggests that the BC's regulations were deliberately (re)organized with the intent to relay topical coherence to the reader for easier comprehension.[184] The second relates to the sabbath laws in their original state as being a part of a larger legal framework which emphasizes the historical deliverance of the Hebrew people from slavery out of the land of Egypt. The presence of such a sabbatical framework would then influence how one reads the entirety of the BC, especially as it relates to the humane treatment of the foreigner.[185] This study finds the latter of these two to ultimately be more compelling and will endeavor to unpack it further in chapter 3 given its broader historical-critical, literary, and theological implications. The former, with its more limited scope and immediate relevance to the text at hand, is below.

Carmichael's work, at its most broad, analyzes the potential parallels between Exod 20:21–31 and 23:1–19, a range which includes the sabbath laws' pairing with Exod 22:24–26. He argues that these two segments of the BC contain very similar themes and structures and therefore may be related, ultimately suggesting that the verses in chapter 23 were intentionally (re)arranged to mimic the ones in chapter 22.[186] The similarities can be observed as follows:

183. Stuart, *Exodus*, 530.
184. Carmichael, "A Singular Method," 19–25.
185. Averbeck, *The Old Testament Law for the Life of the Church*, 163–64. See also Averbeck, "The Egyptian Sojourn, 143–75. Other works that reference the existence of a sabbatical framework include Morrow, *An Introduction to Biblical Law*, 78; and Watts, *Reading Law*, 78.
186. Carmichael, "A Singular Method," 22–23.

1. Exod 22:20-23 [21-24] and 23:1-9

   Both texts contain prohibitions against oppressing a sojourner with nearly identical wording. Other protections are also included.

2. Exod 22:24-26 and 23:10-12

   Both advocate for protection of the poor. Ch. 22 protects them from interest on loans and from oppressive pledging while ch. 23 offers both produce for the poor and sabbath rest for the bondmaid's son and sojourner.

3. Exod 22:27 and 23:13

   The former demands respect for human and divine authority; the latter demands obedience for all that has been said and contains the stipulation to have no other gods.

4. Exod 22:28-29 and 23:14-19a

   The former includes offerings regarding harvest and vintage, one's firstborn son, and one's firstborn oxen and sheep; the festivals mentioned in the latter contain such themes as well.

5. Exod 22:30 and 23:19b

   The former discusses the requirement to not eat flesh torn by beasts while the latter talks about not cooking a kid in its mother's milk.[187]

Some have pointed out that Deuteronomy appears to acknowledge the above parallels. Deut 14:21, for example, seems to combine the rulings found in Exod 22:30 and 23:19; in similar fashion, Deut 15:1-15 looks to be bringing together Exod 22:24-26 and 23:10-11.[188] Moreover, Hyatt, in line with Carmichael's thinking, argues that Exod 23:13 may have originally come after 23:19 but was later moved in order to better parallel 22:27 [28].[189] Such observations are no doubt interesting and worthy of mention; but given the speculative nature of these redactional claims, it would be precarious to insist on them too heavily. Durham sums up the risks well: "Intriguing though these and other speculations like them are, we must not fail to take seriously the text as it stands. For some compiler(s),

---

187. Parallels adapted from Carmichael, "A Singular Method," 19-25. See also B. S. Jackson, *Studies in the Semiotics of Biblical Law*, 219-21; and Sprinkle, *'The Book of the Covenant,'* 190-91.

188. Sprinkle, *'The Book of the Covenant,'* 191.

189. Hyatt, *Exodus*, 247.

the present order of Exod 23 was the one to be transmitted, and v. 13 may best be seen in its present sequence not as dislocated or the parallel of some other sequence, but as the conclusion of at least a subsection within the larger compilation that is the Book of the Covenant."[190] Indeed, the placement of the sabbath laws within the BC contributes to a larger picture than what Carmichael's hypothesis allows. As will be discussed in more detail later on, the positioning of Exod 23:10–12 was penned with the entirety of the BC's structure in mind.

Exod 23:10–12 and Lev 25:1–7

The sabbath laws found within Exodus, both in the Decalogue and in the BC, are revisited several times throughout the Torah (cp. Exod 20:8–11 with Deut 5:12–15 and Exod 23:10–12 with Lev 25:1–7). In surveying these relationships, it is helpful to think of the sabbath laws in Exod 23:10–12 as having two topical parts. Part one, consisting of vv. 10–11, centers its humanitarian concerns on the handling of one's land and produce. Part two, consisting of v. 12, accomplishes its humanitarian goals through a wide-spread, scheduled prohibition on work in general. Benefiting from the first part are the "poor among your people" and the wild animals in that they are able to eat. Benefiting from the second are the domesticated animals, slaves, and foreigners in that they receive rest and refreshment. While there are certainly other worthy topics to discuss relating to the Sabbath, such as the year of Jubilee and the issues surrounding the release of slaves, the comparative discussion here will remain centered on humanitarian concerns as they are expressed in Exod 23:10–12 and how biblical texts elsewhere expound upon, complement, or modify them.

Lev 25:1–7 is a close parallel to part one of the BC's sabbath laws (23:10–11), focusing all of its attention on the handling of one's land, working it for six years and allowing it to remain fallow on the seventh. There has been some debate, however, regarding the specifics of this timetable. To some, the account in Exodus seems to imply that each field contains its own individual rotation while Leviticus appears to speak of the seventh year in a corporate sense.[191] The supposed rationale for this is

---

190. Durham, *Exodus*, 332.

191. See Hartley, *Leviticus*, 430. For the suggestion that Israel mimicked Joseph's agricultural solution in order to eat during the seventh year, see Carmichael, *The Origins of Biblical Law*, 204–6.

that Exodus was primarily motivated by a concern for the poor (23:11), and allowing each field to have its own independent rotation would better serve them on a consistent basis.[192] According to de Vaux, however, Exodus must also be referring to a fixed schedule given the way Deut 15:1–18 repeats the BC's debt slave laws and includes a more direct enforcement of a universal cycle for their release (cf. Deut 31:10–11). This, along with Leviticus' assertion that the land itself requires a fixed sabbath rest year (25:2 and 26:34), suggests that the scheduling of the 6/7 cycle must be harmonious across all accounts. "The sabbatical year was marked by a rest for the land *and* the setting free of Israelite slaves."[193]

Some have pointed out what they believe to be a decisive difference between Exod 23:10–12 and other biblical passages referring to the Sabbath, namely that the Exodus account does not speak of a "Sabbath day" proper at all. Rather, it is simply referring to the cessation of work for the purposes of economic, agricultural, and physical rest. Ultimately, this assertion reduces Exod 23:10–12 to being purely practical and non-religious in nature. Marshall explains the rationale behind this distinction:

> The fallow law and seventh day rest law are often categorized as sabbath observances. However, the designation "sabbath" is not given to these practices in the BC context. In 23:10–11, the law requires the people to שמט (drop) the land and נטש (leave or permit) the land for the poor. The verb שבת (stop, desist, rest) is used in 23:12, but the name "sabbath" is not given to the seventh day. Also, despite being present in other fallow year and seventh day rest regulations, the cultic element is absent in the BC version of these laws . . . In BC, this is essentially a secular law with explicit humanitarian motivations.[194]

While it is true that Exod 23:10–12 does not mention a "Sabbath day" like in Lev 25:1–7, the claim that the humanitarian concerns within this law are purely "secular" (and thus in line with general humanitarianism as

---

192. Stuart goes further, stating that Lev 25 also does not enforce a nationwide fallow year on the basis that such an ordinance would be impractical and cause more harm than good (Stuart, *Exodus*, 531). This conclusion, however, may not be fair to Leviticus since it clearly mentions provisions for the poor in Lev 19:9–10 and 23:22. For more on this discussion, see Milgrom, *Leviticus: A Book of Ritual and Ethics*, 312; and Morrow, *An Introduction to Biblical Law*, 183.

193. De Vaux, *Ancient Israel*, 174, emphasis added. See also Levine, *Leviticus*, 170.

194. Marshall, *Israel and the Book of the Covenant*, 157–58. See also Andreasen, *The Old Testament Sabbath*, 135; Cazelles, *Études sur le Code de l'alliance*, 92–95; and Robinson, "The Idea of Rest in the Old Testament," 32–42.

opposed to חָנּוּן humanitarianism) can only be supported through a willful removal of its surrounding context. In the scenario that Leviticus is simply updating Exod 23:10–12 to include cultic practice, this still leaves the precedent established in Exod 20:8–11 that the "seventh day is a sabbath to the LORD your God." Should one exclude even this, the basis for the 6/7 cycle remains to be pondered. The Sabbath simply cannot be seen as being anything other than a religious ordinance because "its essence is a cyclical commemoration of an event in the past: God's cessation from completion of creation on the seventh day of the creation week (Gen 2:2–3; Exod 20:11; 31:17)."[195] Practicing the Sabbath is therefore a form of imitation and worship that promotes well-being.

EXOD 23:12 AND NUM 15:32–36

While not a direct legal parallel to Exod 23:10–12, Num 15:32–36 narratively illustrates the importance of taking the sabbath laws seriously. Since this passage directly depicts someone violating part two of the BC's sabbath decrees by working (picking up sticks) on the seventh day and because there has been little discussion on the humanitarian values at work in this situation to date, it will be briefly reviewed here. The majority opinion amongst commentators relating to why the Israelites took the offender into custody (15:34) rather than immediately implementing the death penalty as dictated in Exod 31:12–17 rests on whether or not the gatherer intended to make a fire (see Exod 35:2–3).[196] Such a conclusion synergizes well with the message from Christ's sermon that one's intent or desire matters as much as the action itself (Matt 5:21–27). As Stubbs states, "The ruling from God is that the man should be punished [Num 15:35], even though he has not yet lit a domestic fire. Given this reconstruction, the ruling shows that God is just as interested in a person turning away from him in their heart as in the final crossing of the legal line."[197]

Without necessarily being at odds with the above sentiments, it is beneficial to explore how the gatherer's actions may have affected others' observance of the Sabbath. In the event that he was in possession of an ox, donkey, or slave or if he was host to a foreigner, then his decision to

---

195. Gane, *Old Testament Law for Christians*, 250.

196. See, for example, Ashley, *The Book of Numbers*, 291; Cole, *Numbers*, 254; and Budd, *Numbers*, 175–76.

197. Stubbs, *Numbers*, 141.

work on the Sabbath would have impacted them as well.[198] "Work for six days but you shall rest on the seventh day," states Exod 23:12, "*so that your ox and your donkey may rest and the son of your maidservant and the foreigner may be refreshed.*" While the owner/host benefits from both parts of the sabbath laws in the BC in that he is able to rest, emphasis is consistently placed on those under him since their needs are in many ways contingent upon his obedience to the sabbath requirements (cf. Deut 5:14). With this in mind, the covenant reader must then "do what they need to do to prepare themselves, their family, their workers, and even their animals to enjoy the Sabbath day rest."[199]

Literary Expressions in Exod 23:10–12

Given the cultic nature of Scripture's sabbath laws at large, traces of religious and moral overtones within Exod 23:10–12's literary expressions are to be expected (the 6/7 motif, the consistent concern for the well-being of the poor and disenfranchised, etc.). Such elements only complement the more explicit humanitarian practices enforced in these laws. (Provisions for physical rest and refreshment in Exod 23:12 are, for example, connected to the covenant stipulations outlined in 31:13–17.)[200] Interestingly, Sprinkle notes that the sabbath laws in Exodus are made more "religious and humanitarian in character" as opposed to being strictly "legal" due to what is *not* detailed within them.[201] Like the collateral cloak and enemy's donkey laws, there are no punishments specified for non-compliance. Moreover, there are no specifics on how to go about enacting or enforcing their decrees, hence the aforementioned confusion surrounding timetables and scheduling. "This brevity is possible because the author knows that other passages, both previous and subsequent, fill in more of the details on how the sabbaths and pilgrim feasts are to be observed," he opines, concluding that "the present regulations are more exhortations to do homage to deity than laws."[202]

---

198. For a conversation on how the foreigner may have been seen as a dependent in the familial sense, see Boecker, *Law and the Administration of Justice*, 139.

199. Averbeck, *The Old Testament Law for the Life of the Church*, 131. Cf. Deut 8:18; Prov 12:10.

200. Watts, *Reading Law*, 73.

201. Sprinkle, '*The Book of the Covenant,*' 193–94. Emphasis added.

202. Sprinkle, '*The Book of the Covenant,*' 194.

Manner of Address and Motivational Elements

Exod 23:10–12 harbors several literary expressions which have already been discussed in the segments regarding Exod 22:25–26 and 23:4–5 such as positive/negative commands and apodictic/casuistic structures (see table 2). Additionally, like in the previous two case analyses, the sabbath laws continue to address the needs of the poor and even the well-being of animals. Different addressees, however, very conspicuously include slaves and foreigners.[203] The handling of these third parties in particular is critical in understanding the humanitarian values behind the sabbath commands, both within the Exodus account and elsewhere in the Bible, since the Israelites were themselves slaves and foreigners in the land of Egypt (Gen 15:13; Exod 20:2; 22:20; 23:9; Lev 19:34; Deut 5:15; 10:19; 15:15; 24:18).

While there is no question that slaves were dependent upon their masters for humanitarian provisions, there has been some debate concerning the reliance of foreigners on their hosts. Spina's definition of גר is helpful here: "*ger* in the Hebrew Bible refers to people who are no longer directly related to their original setting and who have therefore entered into dependent relationships with various groups or officials in a new social setting. The *ger*... was without customary social protection or privilege and of necessity had to place himself under the jurisdiction of someone else."[204] In light of this description, it is not a coincidence that the foreigner is included as a beneficiary in Exod 23:12 since they, like slaves, would have no direct ties with an economic subsistence and power base, making them susceptible to abuse and oppression.[205] "Depicting the alien as a person who now occupies the position that their forebears had occupied serves to close the gap between the alien and the Israelite," Van Houten explains, "It does not allow the Israelites to hold the alien at arm's length. The memory of their stay in Egypt mitigates the apparently universal exclusivism common to all social, political and religious communities."[206] In other words, this historical connection, made explicit in 23:9, was meant to invoke a theological and humanitarian feeling of

---

203. Both of these groups, along with all other beneficiaries in Exod 23:10–12, are found within motive clauses which Sonsino categorizes as being cultic or sacral in nature. See Sonsino, *Motive Clauses in Hebrew Law*, 88.

204. Spina, "Israelites as *Gerim*," 325.

205. Marshall, *Israel and the Book of the Covenant*, 149.

206. Van Houten, *The Alien in Israelite Law*, 54. See also Blenkinsopp, "Yahweh and Other Deities," 354–66.

sympathy which influenced how the Israelites observed these sabbath decrees.[207]

The sabbath laws' use of the second-person also contains some intrigue. Like in the collateral cloak and enemy's donkey laws, the second-person in vv. 10–12 refers to the singular covenant reader, "you." Some have pointed out, however, that Exod 23:10–12 is directly preceded and followed by second-person plural verbs, thereby "sandwiching" the individual addressee between appeals to the corporate body of the Hebrew people. Verse 9 sets up the sabbath laws by encouraging group solidarity with the foreigner: "You [pl.] know what it is like to be a foreigner because you [pl.] were foreigners in the land of Egypt."[208] Verse 13 then proceeds to cite the authority of the Lawgiver: "Pay close attention to everything which I have said to you [pl.]." This framework (plural to singular to plural) can be seen as underscoring the central principles on which the particulars of the sabbath decrees are based,[209] namely that "each member of the covenant community is to have compassion for such a disadvantaged person because all of them *together* have known the experience of his plight" (23:9),[210] and that the identity of the Hebrew people is rooted in their obedience to Yhwh alone (23:13) whom they imitate through their observance of the Sabbath.

Theo-Ethical Overview

It can be said that the Torah offers four different rationalizations of the principle of sabbath rest, all of which overlap with other important biblical concepts to some degree.[211] First, it is an acknowledgment of the 6/7 pattern which God established during the act of creation as a model for imitation (Gen 1:31—2:3); second, it serves as a sign of God's covenant with Israel (Exod 31:13–17); third, it is a recollection of the exodus from the land of Egypt (Deut 5:15); and, fourth, it acts as a form of social legislation on behalf of those who labor (Exod 23:10–12). This

---

207. Childs, *Exodus*, 482.

208. Some assert that Exod 23:9 serves as a conclusion to the BC's subsection on court rulings (23:1–9). Propp, however, sees this verse as transitionary. See his notes in *Exodus 19–40*, 280. See also Averbeck, *The Old Testament Law for the Life of the Church*, 164.

209. Sprinkle, 'The Book of the Covenant,' 191.

210. Durham, *Exodus*, 331; emphasis added.

211. Goldenberg, "Sabbath," 258.

sabbath refreshment is entirely inclusive, offering a moment of pause for the whole of creation—family members, the poor and needy, foreigners, slaves, animals, even the land itself—and was to be taken very seriously (Num 15:32–36; Isa 58:13–14; Jer 17:19–27).

Goldingay sees the ethical implications of the Sabbath day to be directly connected with how one relates to their work.[212] There are, for example, those who risk not being able to feed themselves or their families if they take time off. Then there are others, especially in today's Western culture, who may be in the habit of idolizing their work, choosing to labor continually because they do not want to stop. Exod 23:10–12 speaks to both of these. To the former, v. 11 offers assurance that provisions will be made for the poor and needy—for "God's people" (Exod 22:24)—by way of fallow fields, an act which harkens back to the manna provisions in Exod 16 where God personally saw to the needs of his people.[213] As such, "the Sabbath principle is first of all a lesson in trusting God, confident that he will provide for us."[214] To the latter, v. 12 offers the reminder that keeping the Sabbath as a day of ceasing from work is to "sanctify it as a day just for that, not for work and business, as if life amounts only to making worldly gain for oneself or one's family."[215] It also demands consideration of how other people may be affected as the result of an imbalanced work life. One's labor should never be at odds with humane and compassionate treatment of others.[216]

SUMMARY AND CONCLUSION

In this chapter, it was put forward that the BC contains a unique and inherent humanitarian outlook founded upon the character of its ultimate author, Yhwh. This claim was approached in two parts. Seeing that an understanding of God's character would be necessary in order to more appropriately understand the humanitarian values within the laws of the BC, part one centered its attention on his self-proclamation brought

---

212. Goldingay, *Old Testament Ethics*, 96.

213. Goldingay, *Old Testament Ethics*, 96. See also Gane, *Old Testament Law for Christians*, 254; and Rodd, *Glimpses of a Strange Land*, 220, where he states, "The implication seems to be that the fallow fields revert to Yahweh, to whose care the wild animals belong."

214. Garrett, *A Commentary on Exodus*, 533.

215. Averbeck, *The Old Testament Law for the Life of the Church*, 131.

216. Garrett, *A Commentary on Exodus*, 533.

about by his concern for the poor and needy in Exod 22:26: "I am compassionate [חַנּוּן]." God's compassionate nature was therefore assumed as the motive force behind proper obedience to his decrees. In order to more fully comprehend the nuances of this nature, consideration was given to Exod 34:6–7 where God further expounds on his compassionate disposition, identifying his inclination toward mercy (v. 6) and robust sense of justice (v. 7) as crucial components.

Having unpacked God's חַנּוּן character—that is, his solidarity with the poor and needy, inclination toward mercy, and robust sense of justice—attention was then given to how the covenant reader should respond to his revelation in Exod 22:26. The prophet Micah directly addresses this in his clarification that the BC relays God's command to imitate the above חַנּוּן qualities,[217] making God, as Barton puts it, "not only the commander but also the paradigm of moral conduct."[218] Humanitarian actions motivated by this *imitatio Dei* (or "חַנּוּן humanitarianism") are set apart from the traits of general humanitarianism outlined in chapter 1 in that they add three unique principles. They (1) seek relational growth, (2) are done with the expectation of repetition as needed, and (3) are considered acts of worship. Additionally, חַנּוּן humanitarianism consistently endeavors to renew human dignity, treating all people as made in God's image. Put simply, practicing biblical humanitarian principles means caring for others in a way that pleases God and reflects his revealed character.

Part two then sought to observe the theological and ethical values discussed in part one at play within the BC's laws; this was done with the aim of showcasing the harmony between the value claims of the author and the content of his commandments. With the understanding that such values tend to be implicit within the BC, Gane's method of revealing underlying value systems within legal writing was adopted. His approach involves the examination of key literary features such as positive and negative commands, repeating formulas, manners of address, apodictic and casuistic formulations, and motivational elements.[219] Additionally, Averbeck's advice to note style and grammar, textual comparisons, and the meaning of words, phrases, clauses, sentences, and paragraphs was heeded.[220] Three laws were chosen for such treatment: the laws regarding

---

217. Mic 6:8; cf. Lev 19:3; Psa 112:4; Luke 6:36.
218. Barton, *Understanding Old Testament Ethics*, 52.
219. Gane, *Old Testament Law*, 81. See also Watts, *Reading Law*, 61–88.
220. Averbeck, "Law," 133.

the collateral cloak (Exod 22:25–26), the enemy's donkey (23:4–5), and the Sabbath (23:10–12).

Examination of the above laws indeed displayed the unique humanitarian principles at work which were outlined in part one. First, both the collateral cloak and enemy's donkey laws expressed the importance of relational growth and solidarity despite factors like indebtedness and conflict wherein the remedies were compassion and love, respectively. While less conspicuous, the Sabbath day is also relational in that it contributes to the Israelites' identity through corporate adherence. Second, all three were to be unconditionally repeated as needed. The motivation for such repetition is always stated to be out of consideration for the well-being of others. Such persuasions include "what else will he sleep in?" (22:26), "be sure to help him" (23:5), and "so that [they] may be refreshed" (23:12). Third, all three are considered to be acts of worship. The compassionate treatment of the poor in the collateral cloak law is seen as direct service to the LORD (Prov 19:17; Matt 25:40); loving one's adversary in the enemy's donkey law exemplifies God's perfect attributes (Matt 5:43–48) as well as identifies one's devotion towards his ways (John 13:35); and participating in the Sabbath commemorates God's acts at creation (Gen 1:31—2:3) as well as displays trust that he will provide for the needs of his people.

While helpful in understanding the humanitarian undertones in the BC, the conversations begun in this chapter remain incomplete. In order to fully realize God's pronouncement in Exod 22:26, one must look to the example which he set during the exodus, namely the deliverance of the Hebrew people out of slavery in the land of Egypt. If a proper humanitarian outlook and appropriate obedience to God's laws is brought about through imitating his compassionate character, then a mere declaration of this character is not enough. In this larger picture of the exodus, God not only states that he is compassionate, but he also shows his covenant readers what it looks like to act compassionately.

3

The Deliverance from Slavery as a Basis for the Book of the Covenant

Be careful that you do not forget the Lord who brought you out of the land of Egypt, out of the house of slavery.

—Deuteronomy 6:12

There remains an experience of incomparable value. We have for once learnt to see the great events of world history from below, from the perspective of the outcast, the suspects, the oppressed, the reviled—in short, from the perspective of those who suffer. The important thing is that neither bitterness nor envy should have gnawed at the heart during this time, that our perception of generosity, humanity, justice and mercy should have become clearer, freer, less corruptible.

—Dietrich Bonhoeffer, *Letters and Papers from Prison*

God's deliverance of the Hebrew people from slavery out of the land of Egypt is directly referenced three times within the Book of the Covenant (see Exod 22:20 [21]; 23:9; and 23:15; cf. Exod 20:2 and 20:22). While citations like these aided the ancient Israelites in remembering their past bondage for the purpose of garnering empathy for others in unfortunate circumstances (see chapter 2), they also connect the BC to the narrative of the exodus. The significance of this connection cannot be overstated. Averbeck, for example, identifies the deliverance from Egypt as being the premise of the covenant made at Sinai, ultimately claiming that, without the former, the latter would not exist (Exod 19:4–6).[1] Moreover, the exodus event (Exod 1–18), which was motivated by God's previous covenant commitment to the patriarchs (Exod 2:23–25; 19:3; Deut 4:37; 7:8), continues to show up as the basic rationale throughout the BC and other areas of the Torah.[2] The deliverance from Egypt is therefore paramount to understanding what God means when he calls himself חַנּוּן "compassionate" in Exod 22:26 since his actions during the exodus not only paved the way for the ratification of the BC, but it also demonstrated his power, benevolent character, and concern for the freedom and well-being of all Israelites. "Having provided a powerful example," states Gane, he went on to require his covenant readers to "treat each other with similar justice and kindness."[3]

The historical claims put forward by the Torah about the exodus event have generated a lot of skepticism within the field of biblical studies, especially in recent years. Suspicion of the exodus' historicity is only encouraged by the lack of any contemporary record concerning Moses or the Israelites living in or leaving Egypt. Regardless, it is undeniable that the Hebrew Scriptures consider the exodus from Egypt as Israel's formative and foundational event.[4] As Hoffman observes, "The exodus from Egypt is the most frequently mentioned event in the O.T. apart from the story itself in Ex. i–xv. It is mentioned about 120 times in stories, laws, poems, psalms, historiographical writings and prophecies."[5] Since there is no reason to assume that ancient writers could not record accurately or comment knowledgeably about events that occurred long before their times, and since such an assumption would discredit other more widely accepted recordings of ancient historical events, the memories reported within the Bible deserve to be taken seriously.[6]

---

1. Averbeck, "The Egyptian Sojourn," 143–44.
2. Averbeck, "The Egyptian Sojourn," 155.
3. Gane, "Social Justice," 29.
4. Hoffmeier et al., *"Did I Not Bring Israel Out of Egypt?,"* ix.
5. Hoffman, "A North Israelite Typological Myth," 170.
6. Hoffmeier et al., *"Did I Not Bring Israel Out of Egypt?,"* x.

Given the ethical aims of this study, the dating of the exodus and whether or not the deliverance from Egypt is a verifiable, historical event will not be explored.[7] A proper sensitivity to the Hebrew text as it stands, however, indicates the need for some historical-critical considerations alongside this study's literary and theological measures. Much is at stake, for example, if it is assumed that the exodus story is mere folklore. How would the ramifications of this reality affect the understanding of OT law and how it applied to the lives of the ancient Israelites? Is Yhwh any less compassionate if he did not actively bring the Hebrew people "out of Egypt with a strong hand and outstretched arm, with terrifying power, and with signs and wonders" (Deut 26:8)? The implications of questions like these are weighty.

Helpful to the goals of this chapter is Averbeck's explanation that the biblical text contains three corresponding dimensions: literary, historical, and theo-ethical.[8] All of these are innately connected to the exodus event's permeation throughout the Torah. "As the text stands, these memories of slavery are essential to our understanding of the literary, historical, theological, and ethical dimensions of the Law."[9] As such, this chapter will set out to bring attention to the presence and influence of the BC's humanitarian context through a pertinent consideration of each of these dimensions. For example, from a literary point of view, the deliverance from slavery contributes to the literary structure and framework of the BC. It also connects the genres of law and narrative in such a way that, given due consideration, can "lead to a deeper understanding of the law as part of human culture and human life as a whole."[10] From a historical point of view, it perpetuates a cultural memory (or "mnemohistory") which contributes to the Israelites' collective identity as God's chosen people (Deut 7:6–8; 2 Sam 7:23–24; 1 Kgs 8:53; 1 Chr 17:20–21; Isa 43:1–3). This memory, in turn, influences the way in which the Israelites are to humanely treat others.

Finally, from a theological point of view, the fact that God delivered the Israelites from slavery before he gave them his covenant stipulations

---

7. For a concise list of scholastic issues relating to the study of the historical exodus, see Dozeman, *Exodus*, 26–31. For discussion regarding the archaeological and literary evidence from Egypt for the exodus, see Frerichs and Lesko, *Exodus: The Egyptian Evidence*; Hoffmeier, *Israel in Egypt*.

8. Averbeck, "Factors in Reading the Patriarchal Narratives," 116.

9. Averbeck, "The Egyptian Sojourn," 143.

10. Bartor, "Law and Narrative," 225.

at Sinai established an ongoing paradigm of compassion and mercy.[11] "Laws were not the means of salvation, but were guidelines for those already saved," Sprinkle clarifies: "Before the Mosaic law (Abraham), after the Mosaic law, and during the Mosaic law, salvation was and is a matter of God's grace rather than human merit."[12] Obedience to the laws within the BC (and elsewhere in the Torah) is therefore a celebration of God's great deeds (Exod 23:15) and a recognition of the opportunity to live and treat others in accordance with his compassionate ways (Psa 25; 103).

LITERARY CONSIDERATIONS

Literary approaches to Scripture often take on many different forms. They may, for example, incorporate the study of different genres such as prose and poetry and the relationships between them, they may involve more critical analyses regarding grammar, discourse, or how one goes about understanding the conveyance of meaning.[13] When it comes to biblical law, literary styles most frequently entail the identification of legal motifs within other biblical genres such as narrative,[14] or the motifs of other genres within legal collections.[15] Instead of adopting one of these approaches, this segment will seek to unpack the BC's literary bond with its preceding narrative, the exodus, with particular respect to how this connection may play a role in the BC's structural composition. If the format and contents of the BC are indeed inspired by the Israelites' deliverance from bondage, then this is a good place to begin articulating a rationale for its innate and prevalent humanitarian ethic.

The Composition of the BC

Scholars have expended much effort in the attempt to show how the BC (along with the Torah as a whole) was originally compiled. Source and redaction criticism have more often than not led the methodological charge in such endeavors, often prioritizing ways which aim to show

---

11. Gane, *Old Testament Law for Christians*, 47.
12. Sprinkle, *Biblical Law and Its Relevance*, 7.
13. Averbeck, "Factors in Reading the Patriarchal Narratives," 116.
14. See, for example, Barmash, "The Narrative Quandary," 1–16.
15. See Bartor, "Reading Biblical Law as Narrative," 292–311.

whether a given segment of the text comes from J, E, D, or P documents.[16] While there are increasing agreements from a variety of vantage points (including conservative ones) that the Torah is a complex and composite piece of literature that incorporates various kinds of writing, sources, and topics around a broad thematic unity, the "neat linear scheme of cleverly interwoven documents stretched out over Israel's reconstructed history" is becoming less and less convincing.[17] This decrease in confidence is largely being brought about for three reasons. First, and likely foremost, is the lack of scholarly consensus on the matter. With regard to just the book of Exodus, there has been much debate as to whether or not D even plays a role in composition,[18] whether J and E are both present or if one of them takes the place of the other,[19] and whether Exodus as a whole is better off being categorized as simply containing "P History" documents and "Non-P History" documents.[20] These are but a few of the fragmenting disagreements concerning Exodus' redactional composition.[21]

Second is the apparent lack of consultation with ANE law and its literary traditions. Garrett points out, for example, that the BC is widely regarded as a "collection of various laws from different times and places in the history of Israel," but that "this consensus was reached without any real reference to the analogies in ancient Near Eastern law."[22] Westbrook offers up a useful clarification on this point:

> Conventional wisdom regards the Covenant Code as an amalgam of provisions from different sources and periods, the fusion of which has left tell-tale marks in the form of various inconsistencies in the text . . . Interpreters of the Covenant Code need to come to terms with the fact that it is part of a widespread literary-legal tradition. The starting point for interpretation must therefore be the presumption that the Covenant Code is a

---

16. That is, "Yahwist" (J), "Elohist" (E), "Deuteronomic" (D), and "Priestly" (P).

17. C. J. H. Wright, *Exodus*, 4.

18. See, for example, Philips, "A Fresh Look at the Sinai Pericope, Part 1," 39–52; along with his "Part 2," 282–94; Dozeman, *God at War*.

19. For an explanation supporting the existence of both, see Propp, *Exodus 1–18*, 47–52. For an argument against this, see Dozeman, *Exodus*, 35–43.

20. Dozeman, *Exodus*, 48–51.

21. For a more exhaustive survey of the current state of scholarship on this matter, see Alexander, *From Paradise to the Promised Land*; and Van Seters, *A Law Book for the Diaspora*. For an innovative proposition combining the broader acceptance of the JEDP sources with a historical view of the exodus event, see Friedman, *The Exodus*.

22. Garrett, *A Commentary on Exodus*, 4.

coherent text comprising clear and consistent laws, in the same manner as its cuneiform forbears.[23]

The "widespread literary-legal tradition" that Westbrook mentions here is in reference to the cuneiform laws' static nature—that is, the understanding that cuneiform legal collections tend to resist change and gradual development and amendments over long periods of time.[24] Why, then, according to this rationale, would the BC be so different from its contemporaries? According to C. J. H. Wright, the use of documentary treatments on the BC feels somewhat forced and motivated by modern and Western conceptions of how ancient authors went about their work. Garrett agrees, labeling the practice as being stuck in a particular era of thought. Both conclude that such treatment of the BC is "dubious."[25] This call for a sincere consideration of ANE legal traditions is likely what led to D. P. Wright's innovative work that bases the entirety of the BC's composition on the Laws of Hammurabi (LH).[26] Notably, he even acknowledges that a winsome consensus on the BC's redaction history would likely endanger much of his research.[27] While this author is not in agreement with many of D. P. Wright's claims, his work regarding the composition of the BC is no doubt helpful in its literary explorations.

Third, and perhaps most relevant to the topic at hand, is the apparent struggle to fruitfully contribute to exegetical and hermeneutical tasks, or as C. J. H. Wright puts it, to discern the "meaning, intentions, and implications of the text for anyone who comes to it as in some sense authoritative Scripture with a view to understanding and communicating its message today."[28] Commentaries have been in the habit, for example, of spending pages discussing the proposed sources and the scholastic discussions on their arrangements without saying much about why such matters are pertinent to the text as it stands. It bears repeating here,

---

23. Westbrook, "What is the Covenant Code?," 36.

24. Westbrook, "What is the Covenant Code?," 21–22. This is not without exception. The Hittite Laws (HL), for example, display various changes in pricing over time. Westbrook argues that this minor adjustment in cost is economic and not relating to the HL's compositional history. If anything, in his view, this serves as further evidence that if there were more substantial redactions, they would likely be observable. See also Otto, "Interdependenzen zwischen Geschichte," 366–67.

25. C. J. H. Wright, *Exodus*, 4; Garrett, *A Commentary on Exodus*, 18–19.

26. D. P. Wright, *Inventing God's Law*.

27. D. P. Wright, *Inventing God's Law*, 352.

28. C. J. H. Wright, *Exodus*, 4–5.

however, that the biblical text *is* in many ways compiled by separate sources; but as Averbeck notes, it is crucial to differentiate between what is believed to be true and what can be shown to be true. Such a process needs to start by "turning the text of the Hebrew Bible back upon itself in order to allow it to tell us about its own composition."[29] In other words, what does a biblically driven compositional study reveal about the Scriptures? Such refocusing enables exegetical explorations without abandoning the important, critical treatments of the text.[30]

With the above hesitancies in mind regarding source-driven methodologies, scholars have discovered more reasons to assume greater literary unity between the BC and its immediate narrative context (Exod 19–24, the Sinai narrative)[31] and its extended narrative context (Exod 1–15, the deliverance of the Israelites from Egypt).[32] D. P. Wright, for example, asserts that the BC cannot be separated from its narrative context compositionally, as doing so would remove the rationale for both the narrative and the Law.[33] J. D. Hays further emphasizes the connection between the Law and its context by appealing to the whole as a "theological narrative." Before using the placement of the BC as a key example of this, he opines,

> The Old Testament legal material does not appear in isolation. Instead, the Mosaic Law is firmly embedded in Israel's theological history. It is an integral part of the story that runs from Genesis 12 through 2 Kings 25. The Law is not presented by itself, as some sort of disconnected but timeless universal code of behavior. Rather it is presented as part of the theological narrative that describes how God delivered Israel from Egypt and then established them in the Promised Land as His people.[34]

Additionally, Morrow adds that the Bible's legal collections are more than just extensions of their narratives; they also participate in the narrative process. "Law has always had a narrative function," he states, "in that it

29. Averbeck, "The Exodus, Debt Slavery, and the Composition of the Pentateuch," 30.

30. For more on this topic, see Garrett, *Rethinking Genesis*.

31. See Alexander, "The Composition of the Sinai Narrative," 2–20; and esp. Sprinkle, '*The Book of the Covenant*.'

32. C. J. H. Wright, *Exodus*, 8–11.

33. D. P. Wright, *Inventing God's Law*, 149–51, 322–23, 327, 332–45, 353, and esp. 356. See also Averbeck, "The Egyptian Sojourn," 157–58.

34. J. D. Hays, "Applying the Old Testament Law Today," 24.

'tells a story' about what a particular society values, about who is an insider and who is an outsider, how the society is organized, and what it does when faced with certain forms of social disruption."[35] These literary observations—the contextual connections, theological threads, and story elements of the Law, amongst others—do more than simply validate some form of strategic placement of the BC; they play a significant role in its literary makeup. Indeed, the story of the exodus "constitutes the point of crystallization of the great Pentateuchal narrative in its entirety."[36] What follows is therefore a survey of some of the prominent ways in which the deliverance of the Hebrew people from slavery can be seen influencing the literary composition of the BC.

Emphasis on Slave Laws

"Alongside the history of sacrifice and the festival calendar," states Levinson, "the question of the sequence and relation of the laws concerning manumission of slaves has been essential to any larger attempt to construct a history of Israelite religion and a compositional history of the Pentateuch."[37] It is therefore not surprising to see several scholars pointing out that the BC's collection of laws begins with matters concerning debt-slavery (Exod 21:2–11).[38] To some, the reasoning for this is arbitrary.[39] To others, it is obvious: slavery was a serious topic that deserved fronted attention because the LORD delivered his people from Egypt in order for them to be free (Lev 26:13). The Torah therefore seeks to safeguard those who fall into servitude for reasons such as losing their financial independence.[40] The rationale for the primacy of the debt slave laws is also supported textually. C. J. H. Wright explains, "There are good grounds for

---

35. Morrow, *An Introduction to Biblical Law*, 43.

36. Noth, *A History of Pentateuchal Traditions*, 51, which is a translation of *Überlieferungsgeschichte des Pentateuch*, 54.

37. Levinson, "The Manumission of Hermeneutics," 281.

38. For example, Averbeck, "Law," 133; Sprinkle, "Law and Narrative in Exodus 19–24," 244; D. P. Wright, *Inventing God's Law*, 149; Garrett, *A Commentary on Exodus*, 495–96, to name a few.

The preceding altar laws in Exod 20:22–26 are rightly considered by many to be a part of the BC's composition. As will be discussed in the pages to follow, these laws contribute to the BC's "cultic framework," with the more formalized listings following Exod 21:1, "These are the ordinances you are to set before them."

39. Greengus, *Laws in the Bible*, 9.

40. Gane, "Social Justice," 23.

seeing the prioritizing of this law about Hebrew servants as intentional, since the exodus is referred to twice in the following sections as primary motivation for exercising justice for the vulnerable (22:20 [21]; 23:9)." Consideration of Deuteronomy's version of this same law only reinforces these sentiments: "Remember that you were slaves in Egypt and the Lord your God redeemed you. That is why I give you this command today" (Deut 15:15).[41]

When compared with its ancient legal contemporaries, the positioning of the slave laws so near the beginning of the BC seems especially unusual, as no other ancient legal collection begins with this topic.[42] On this, Sprinkle notes that "slave laws end rather than begin the Laws of Hammurabi (§§278–82), and the Laws of Eshnunna place its most substantial slave laws at the end (§§49–52). Middle Assyrian laws only rarely deal with slaves at all."[43] This difference between the BC and other ANE legal collections is notable in that it highlights the unique value hierarchy of the Torah (more on this in chapter 4) and prominent concerns of their respective intended audiences.[44] More simply put, the BC addresses matters of slavery first because its covenant readers were slaves, whereas other ANE legal collections tend to open up with matters regarding personal property or retributive justice with the foremost goal of assuring a stable and orderly society, thus legitimizing their respective kings' influence and right to rule (more on this in chapter 5).[45]

Literary Framing of the BC

While some are in the habit of excluding the altar laws (Exod 20:22–26) and/or the messenger epilogue (Exod 23:20–33) in their treatments of the BC, both play important functions within its composition, especially as the BC relates to the exodus narrative and theme of deliverance. As illustrated below, the BC is comprised of several "frames" beginning with the "narrative frame" which is outlined by these two passages.[46]

41. C. J. H. Wright, *Exodus*, 395.
42. Garrett, *A Commentary on Exodus,* 495; Averbeck, "Law," 133.
43. Sprinkle, "Law and Narrative in Exodus 19–24," 244. It is worth noting that the HL contain some references to slaves within their initial decrees, but these are sporadic and their primary focus varies from law to law.
44. Hess, "Structure of the Covenant Code," 126.
45. Walton, *Introducing the Conceptual World of the Hebrew Bible*, 273–77.
46. For a more detailed illustration of the BC's framework, see Averbeck, "The

Figure 1. The Structure of the Book of the Covenant

```
20:22-23  ◄─────────────────────────────►  23:20-33
                    Narrative Frame

   20:24-26  ◄──────────────────────►  23:14-19
                    Cultic Frame

      21:2-11  ◄────────────────►  23:10-13
                  Sabbatical Frame

         21:12  ◄──────────►  23:9
                  Casuistic &
                  Apodictic Frames
```

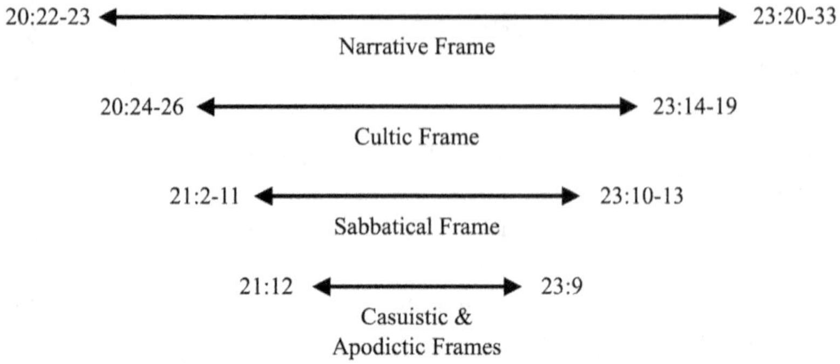

The Narrative Frame

The demarcation of a narrative frame for the BC is not common since Exod 20:22–23 is usually considered to be a part of the cultic frame (see above). Even so, scholars often highlight Exod 20:22 in particular as initiating a changeover from narrative genre to legal genre.[47] It does this by reminding the listener of God's presence and past actions: "You yourselves have seen that I have spoken to you from heaven." In turn, this reminder acts as a motive force for the hearer to earnestly listen to what is about to be said next and is further illuminated by 20:22's connection with two previous passages. The first connection includes the Ten Commandments which God himself literally "spoke from heaven" only a few verses prior before the people requested Moses as an intermediary. The second is Exod 19:4–5a which 20:22 seems to be echoing, the Hebrew being identical: "*You yourselves have seen* what I did to Egypt and how I carried you on Eagles' wings and brought you to myself. Now therefore obey me fully and keep my covenant." The rationale behind both of these passages is the deliverance from bondage (see 20:2 and 19:4). Exod 20:22 is therefore invoking the exodus narrative as a rationale for the laws which follow.

Like its preceding verse, Exod 20:23 also links back to the Ten Commandments in that it offers a reminder to worship and obey only Yʜᴡʜ:

Egyptian Sojourn," 157; and Averbeck, *The Old Testament Law for the Life of the Church*, 163.

47. Sprinkle, '*The Book of the Covenant*,' 36. See also Van Houten, *The Alien in Israelite Law*, 44–46.

"Do not make gods of silver to rival me; do not make gods of gold for yourselves" (see Exod 20:3–6). God's opening words to Moses in Exod 20:22–23 therefore narratively connect the whole next section of the book with the previous key texts, the Ten Commandments and the introduction to the Mt. Sinai narrative. As such, C. J. H. Wright appropriately submits the conclusion that Exod 20:22–23 "anchor[s] the whole collection of laws and exhortations backwards, as it were, in what has already been done and said in the story."[48] Everything that follows in the legal sections, beginning with Exod 20:24, depends on the people remembering who they were and what God has done for them.

The messenger epilogue in Exod 23:20–33 bookends the BC's narrative frame in the same way it was opened: by aiding in the transition back from legal genre to narrative genre and by offering motivation to worship and obey Yhwh alone, namely in the promise that he will now deliver the Israelites to the place he has prepared (23:20). As Dozeman notes, "the style of this section changes from legislation to a more sermonic discourse, when God promises to give the Israelites the land of Canaan in exchange for obedience to the law."[49] This frame of the BC can therefore be seen as referencing and supporting the following narrative progression:

Deliverance (19:4, 20:2, 22) ⟶ Obligations (20:23–23:19) ⟶ Promises (23:20–33)
"What happened?"   "What now?"   "What's next?"

While many tend to incorporate Exod 20:22–23 as part of the BC's cultic frame (and by extension consider 23:20–33 to be a stand-alone epilogue), it is important to understand these verses as carrying a weighty narrative function.[50]

The Cultic Frame

If the goal of the narrative frame is to point towards God's previous (and upcoming) actions in the exodus story as motivation to worship and

---

48. C. J. H. Wright, *Exodus*, 392.
49. Dozeman, *Exodus*, 554.
50. The intention here is not to deny the cultic nature of Exod 20:22–23; scholars are right to see these verses as operating within the cultic frame. This study, however, finds value in their unique interactions with the surrounding narrative and how they aid in interlacing the BC with that narrative.

obey only him, then the cultic frame can be understood as handling the conversation on what appropriate worship and obedience looks like in light of this story. Additionally, as Boecker points out, there is a significant theological dynamic at play within the cultic frame. "Laws designed to promote proper person to person relationships are sandwiched, in the [BC], between laws intended to promote a proper relationship of man to God," he explains. "We can also say that ordered observance of the law is possible, on the OT understanding of things, only if the relationship to God is right first."[51] This arrangement is not circumstantial, seeing as the Torah's other legal collections contain similar cultic frameworks.[52]

Both ends of the cultic frame (Exod 20:24–26 and 23:14–19) are grounded in the deliverance from Egypt. While some aspects of the altar laws in 20:24–26 can be a bit more confusing, thus eluding scholastic consensus,[53] the types of offerings listed in 20:24 are generally understood as supporting a means of expressing thankfulness for what God has done and a joyful celebration of his presence. C. J. H. Wright clarifies: "The burnt offering, in which the whole animal was consumed, seems to have primarily been an act of thanksgiving and praise to God, while the fellowship offering, where the meat was consumed by the family or community, would have been an occasion of joyful horizontal communion in the accepting presence of God."[54] This is notably the first mention of burnt offerings and fellowship offerings in the OT; the next time they are mentioned is in the ceremony of covenant ratification in Exod 24:5.[55]

The three festival regulations found in Exod 23:14–19 are much more straightforward in their connection to the exodus event, including a motive clause which directly references the Israelites' deliverance from Egypt: "Celebrate the Festival of Unleavened Bread . . . at the appointed time in the month of Aviv, *because you came out of Egypt in that month*" (23:15).[56] Like the altar laws in Exod 20:24–26, these festivals were intended to facilitate times of celebration and rejoicing, linked as

---

51. Boecker, *Law and the Administration of Justice*, 138.

52. Boecker, *Law and the Administration of Justice*, 145.

53. For example, there are several differing perspectives on the prohibition of cut stones in v. 25 and the caution against nakedness in v. 26. For a survey of some of these perspectives, see Childs, *The Book of Exodus*, 466–67.

54. C. J. H. Wright, *Exodus*, 393.

55. C. J. H. Wright, *Exodus*, 393.

56. While the instructions for the three festivals are a bit brief in the BC, there are more details provided in Lev 23:4–22, 33–43; Num 28:16–31; and Deut 16:1–17.

they were to God rescuing his people out of slavery and blessing them in a land of their own.⁵⁷ While the notions of celebration and rejoicing are appropriate—and even commanded (see Deut 16:11, 14)—it is also important to note that the word "celebrate" (NIV) for each of the three festivals in vv. 15–16 comes from the Hebrew word שמר which more generally means "keep," "observe," or in some cases, "be careful," or "pay attention."⁵⁸ In this light, the festivals served the purposes of both thanksgiving and meaningful worship. Never are the people to forget the ways the LORD has provided for them, as this is critical to a proper understanding and observance of the Law.

Verses 17–19 go on to provide further details regarding appropriate worship procedures. Of these, none have been more perplexing than the command to not "cook a young goat in its mother's milk" (19b; cf. Exod 34:26 and Deut 14:21). Some popular explanations have included the avoidance of a potential Canaanite custom,⁵⁹ a call to refrain from mixing life and death (the slaughtering of a young goat and then using its own mother's life-giving milk for cooking),⁶⁰ and the prohibition of certain mixtures in food preparation common in modern Jewish kosher regulations.⁶¹ More recently, Averbeck has put forward that Exod 23:19b is not just a standard regulation, but serves as a type of motto or proverb that appeals to the natural created order—what some would refer to as the laws of nature. "From the first mention of humanity in the Bible," he notes, "God made it our specific responsibility to rule over and manage the animal world in his image as his likeness (Gen 1:26–28). Those who have lived close to nature, as ancient Israel did, realize the primary importance of this."⁶²

In adding to the list of possible meanings, this author sees some merit in connecting this law with the regulations enforcing proper apportionment (the giving of one's "first fruits" or "firstborn" to the LORD). Given that all three instances of this prohibition are paired with laws of apportionment (Exod 23:19, 34:26; Deut 14:21–23) and given that each finds itself within the context of worship/cultic regulations, it may

---

57. C. J. H. Wright, *Exodus*, 438.

58. C. J. H. Wright, *Exodus*, 438.

59. See Childs, *Exodus*, 485–86, where he mentions the discovery of an Ugaritic text describing the process of cooking "a kid in milk, a lamb in butter."

60. C. J. H. Wright, *Exodus*, 439.

61. For more on these views, see Sarna, *Exodus*, 147.

62. Averbeck, *The Old Testament Law for the Life of the Church*, 158–59.

serve as a motto or idiom (as Averbeck points out) supporting sincere, worshipful giving. Not cooking a young goat in its mother's milk could, for example, be speaking toward an inappropriate mixing of last year's leftovers with the current year's offering, thereby "padding" it to meet a quota or promote the appearance of a larger, more generous gift. Such a practice of mixing "young and old generations," so to speak, would be insincere and far from the command to give of one's "first fruits." This explanation serves to further highlight the goals of the festivals—that is, sincere worship and thanksgiving following the deliverance of the Israelites from bondage (cf. the sentiments in Acts 4:32—5:11).

The Sabbatical Frame

As discussed above, the BC's judicial regulations unsurprisingly begin with matters of debt-slavery (Exod 21:1–11). Alone, these laws no doubt aid in the counter-cultural treatment of slaves as dignified human beings, but many have also pointed out their "chiastic relationship" with the sabbath laws in Exod 23:10–12 due to the presence of the 6/7 motif.[63] According to Swiderski, however, this relationship is built on much more than a mere number of parallels. He emphasizes that "this sabbatical connection constructs a frame within which the BC then unfolds," pointing out that "frequently this frame is understood only or mainly based on its numerical 6/7 patterns, whereby the properly 'sabbatical' nature of the frame is neglected."[64] In other words, the formula of "six years . . . but on the seventh" requires one to reflect on the concept and implications of the Sabbath rather than just its presence—a notion that Cardellini calls the "Sabbath idea."[65]

Such reflections contain strong theological implications for how one goes about understanding and interpreting the BC for both its ancient and modern readers. The sabbatical frame is significant, for example, in that it reminds the BC's covenant readers of how God compassionately delivered

---

63. See, for example, Crüsemann, *The Torah*, 182; Averbeck, *The Old Testament Law for the Life of the Church*, 163–64; Dohmen, *Exodus 19–40*, 149–50, 186; Levinson, "The Manumission of Hermeneutics," 321; W. Janzen, *Exodus*, 312; and Osumi, *Die Kompositionsgeschichte des Bundesbuches Exodus 20, 22b–23, 33*, 150–51.

64. Swiderski, "Sabbatical Patterns in the Book of the Covenant," 137.

65. Cardellini, *Die biblischen "Sklaven"-Gesetze im Lichte des keilschriftlichen Sklavenrechts*, 245n21. See also Sprinkle, '*The Book of the Covenant*,' 200, where he labels the presence of a "Sabbath principle."

them from slavery out of Egypt and, in turn, gives them the opportunity to imitate that compassion in their treatment of others. It is only fitting, then, that this frame is enclosed within the cultic frame and its guidelines for worship. C. J. H. Wright's explanation captures well this line of thought:

> Having established the first "vertical" priority for the people—that they must worship the LORD and worship him alone, and that in doing so they will continue to enjoy God's promised coming and blessing—what is the first "horizontal" priority in this society that worships this God? Most significantly and intentionally, they must reflect Yahweh's character and do for others what he had done for them. Just as God had looked on them with compassion as oppressed Hebrews in Egypt and brought them out, so they must deal justly with those who have fallen into a similar plight in their own society by providing a means for them to "go out."[66]

The beginning of the judicial section of the BC, with its focus on the release of debt-slaves, therefore corresponds to the larger story of the book of Exodus and is significantly influenced by (and even patterned after) the "Sabbath idea."[67]

Slaves are a priority concern in the entirety of the BC; regulations regarding their treatment are not limited to the initial "slave laws" section (see Exod 21:20–21, 26–27, 32; 23:12; and more if one includes the laws regarding foreigners). This has prompted many to speculate on alternative frameworks. Chirichigno, for example, claims that the slave laws organize Exod 21:2–27, with 2–11 and 26–27 (the laws of release) constituting the outer frame and 20–21 (with the law on the assault of slaves) at the center.[68] Otto broadens the scope, interpreting the protection of debt slaves (21:2–11) and the protection of the resident alien and poor (22:20–24) as a frame for the first half of the BC.[69] Despite suggestions like these, the numerous connections present between Exod 21:1–11 and 23:10–12 reinforce these two passages as bracketing the BC's inner contents.[70] As Dozeman concludes, "The repetition between the Sabbath

---

66. C. J. H. Wright, *Exodus*, 394. See also Van Seters, *A Law Book for the Diaspora*, 94–95; and Cassuto, *A Commentary on the Book of Exodus*, 301, where he opines that "Every Israelite resembles the Hebrew slave in this respect, that he, too, shall work for only six consecutive years, and after this period he also shall be freed."

67. Swiderski, "Sabbatical Patterns in the Book of the Covenant," 157.

68. Chirichigno, *Debt-Slavery*, 196.

69. Otto, *Rechtsgeschichte der Redaktionen im Kodex Ešnunna*, 7–14.

70. For a list of such connections, see Swiderski, "Sabbatical Patterns in the Book of

release of debt slaves (21:2–11) and the law of the Sabbath rest for slaves is striking (23:10–12), suggesting literary design in the composition of the Book of the Covenant."[71]

Casuistic & Apodictic Frames

It would be an understatement to say that the laws within Exod 21:12—23:9 have undergone a variety of treatments regarding their possible categorizations and frameworks.[72] Aside from the opinion that there might not be any logical arrangements,[73] there have been two general fields of thought as to how these laws might be organized. First is the suggestion that they form a chiastic structure (or contain a series of chiastic structures).[74] Second is the idea that they contain parallelisms; that is to say, there are internal repeating formulas using different headers or other associative reference points.[75] D. P. Wright, in a more recent example of this, posits that there are two "strings" of apodictic laws (Exod 22:20–30 and 23:9–19) which follow the casuistic listings (Exod 21:12—22:16) where each string bears parallels with the other. They therefore introduce two separate sections of law rather than acting as literary "bookends" for the laws between them.[76] Overall, the amount of scholarship regarding the literary structure of the BC is staggering, leading commentators like Crüsemann to exclaim that an interpretation of structure must "be the starting point for all further analysis."[77]

---

the Covenant," 142–56.

71. Dozeman, *Exodus*, 526.

72. Some of these treatments have already been discussed in chapter 2 (part two) as they relate to the placements and larger legal contexts of Exod 22:25–26; 23:4–5; and 23:10–12 in particular.

73. Childs, *Exodus*, 459–60; Alt, *Essays on Old Testament History and Religion*, 81–132.

74. Paul, *Studies in the Book of the Covenant*, 106–11; Otto, *Wandel der Rechtsbegründungen*, 9–11; Halbe, *Das Privilegrecht Jahwes Ex 34*, 10–26, 421; B. S. Jackson, "Modeling Biblical Law," 1779; B. S. Jackson, *Studies in the Semiotics of Biblical Law*, 218.

75. Carmichael, "A Singular Method," 19–25; Dohmen, *Exodus 19–40*, 150. For examples of each of these approaches, see Sprinkle, 'The Book of the Covenant,' 199–201.

76. Averbeck, "The Egyptian Sojourn," 156n28. See also D. P. Wright, *Inventing God's Law*, 10–16, 51–90. Wright's conclusions are notably based on his insistence that the BC is entirely dependent on the structure of the LH (the LH's "exhortatory block," in this case).

77. Crüsemann, *The Torah*, 113. See also Dozeman, *Exodus*, 501, for more details.

THE DELIVERANCE FROM SLAVERY AS A BASIS

Newer to this discussion is the notion that the literary framing of Exod 21:12—23:9, like the placement of the slave laws in 21:1–11, directly correlates with the theme of the Israelites' deliverance from bondage. Averbeck, for example, suggests that there are three frameworks in total which can be highlighted via the close correspondence between Exod 22:20 and 23:9:[78]

Exod 22:20 [21]

וְגֵר לֹא־תוֹנֶה וְלֹא תִלְחָצֶנּוּ כִּי־גֵרִים הֱיִיתֶם בְּאֶרֶץ מִצְרָיִם

You must not afflict a resident alien and oppress him, for you were resident aliens in the land of Egypt.

Exod 23:9

וְגֵר לֹא תִלְחָץ וְאַתֶּם יְדַעְתֶּם אֶת־נֶפֶשׁ הַגֵּר כִּי־גֵרִים הֱיִיתֶם בְּאֶרֶץ מִצְרָיִם

You must not oppress a resident alien, since you yourselves know the life of the resident alien, for you were resident aliens in the land of Egypt.

"Structurally, if we keep the cultic and sabbatical framing of the law in mind," he explains, "Exod 23:9 would conclude the unit that begins with [Exod 22:20]. Thus, Exod 22:20 through 23:9 would constitute a discrete unit of largely apodictic laws surrounded and framed by these two verses about the treatment of resident aliens in light of the people's own resident alien experience in Egypt."[79] The other two frames include Exod 21:12—22:16, which mostly contains casuistic laws, and 22:17–19, which exclusively contains apodictic laws that focus on capital crimes. Averbeck illustrates these frames as follows:[80]

---

78. Averbeck, "The Egyptian Sojourn," 156–57. Translation his.
79. Averbeck, "The Egyptian Sojourn," 156.
80. Adapted from a portion of the illustration in Averbeck, "The Egyptian Sojourn," 157.

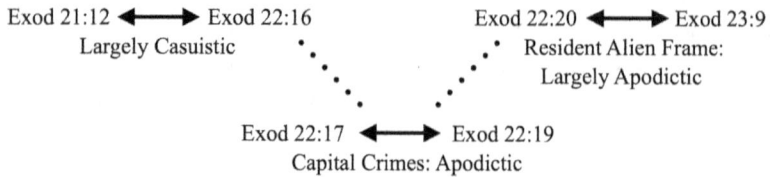

Figure 2. The Literary Framing of Exod 21:12—23:9

The beginning of the casuistic frame corresponds to the ending of the resident alien frame in that they are both connected to the sabbatical frame. Exod 23:9, for example, provides a transition into the sabbath laws (Exod 23:10–12), which, in turn, relate to the seventh-year release of debt slaves at the beginning of the casuistic section (21:1–11). "This is all part of the literary framing of the Book of the Covenant," Averbeck concludes, "Virtually at every turn, the rationale for the Law depends on the people's deliverance from slavery in Egypt and its implications for the way that they must treat the poor and disadvantaged in Israel, including the resident alien."[81]

HISTORICAL CONSIDERATIONS

Questions of factuality abound within historical approaches to the Bible. Whether a given text is describing people, events, or conditions, there is always an innate desire to "fact check" its claims and assumptions about reality. Such concerns are interrelated with the study of cultures in and around Israel in its ANE context and even the nature of history writing as a genre (i.e., historiography).[82] Biblical law, as has been established up to this point, contains several references to a historical exodus of the Israelite people out of Egypt. However, none of these references seem to be interested in unpacking the exodus' historicity—that is to say, while there are clear and resolute claims that the exodus indeed transpired (Exod 20:2; Lev 25:38; Deut 5:6; etc.), they do not delve into lengthy explanations with the aim of persuading the reader of that reality. Instead,

---

81. Averbeck, "The Egyptian Sojourn," 158. Averbeck qualifies the capital crimes unit as transitional, stating that its laws "initiate the apodictic unit, but they stand outside the resident alien unit and are distinctive" (157). For further discussion on Exod 22:17–19 and its role within the literary framing of the BC, see Sprinkle, 'The Book of the Covenant,' 160–65.

82. Averbeck, "Factors in Reading the Patriarchal Narratives," 117.

callbacks to the exodus event are often used to remind the Israelites of their identity, thereby tutoring them on how to behave or what decisions to make. Though there are legitimate discussions supporting a historical exodus, this segment will not seek to definitively date or prove the reality of the Israelites' delivery from bondage. Rather, it will examine the cultural memory, or "mnemohistory," of the exodus from Egypt and how the memory of this historical event lays out the foundation for the BC's theological and ethical implications.

History as Cultural Memory

Mnemohistory, more commonly referred to as cultural memory or collective memory, has enjoyed increasing attention since its introduction to biblical studies by Assmann in 1992.[83] Broadly stated, collective memory understands history as "the means by which a conscious sense of the past, as something meaningfully connected to the present, is sustained and developed within human individuals and human cultures."[84] According to Kofoed, mnemohistory is not as interested in the historicity of what is remembered, but in chasing the memory itself, how it is constructed using both historical facts and the imagination of the person or group who did the remembering, including how the memory produces the identity that it describes. More simply put, it is "the history and dynamics of the remembering of a given past."[85]

The concept of cultural memory analysis has not gone uncriticized. Some, for example, have seen it fit to label the practice as nothing more than a "rehash" of historical-critical form criticism and tradition history.[86] Others, such as Nora, preemptively dismissed the notion of combining history with the study of memory. He states: "Memory is life, borne by living societies founded in its name. It remains in permanent evolution, open to the dialectic of remembering and forgetting, unconscious of its successive deformations, vulnerable to manipulation and appropriation, susceptible to being long dormant and periodically revived. History, on

---

83. See Assmann, *Das Kulturelle Gedächtnis*; English trans. in Assmann, *Cultural Memory and Early Civilizations*.

84. Cubitt, *History and Memory*, 9.

85. Kofoed, "The Exodus as Cultural Memory," 178. See also Carstens, "The Torah as Canon of Masterpieces," 309.

86. Kofoed, "The Exodus as Cultural Memory," 185.

the other hand, is the reconstruction . . . of what is no longer."[87] Spencer astutely identifies the unsound rationale behind such opinions, explaining that "history and memory have often been positioned on different sides of a great divide between objective and subjective with history being understood as the dispassionate, disciplined area of scholarly pursuit and memory as the biased musings of groups with special interests."[88] Moreover, as Spencer goes on to point out, the insistence that memory and history are at odds with each other sidesteps Huizinga's reputable take that history is "the intellectual form in which a civilization renders account to itself of its past."[89] As such, the relationship between objectivity and subjectivity, and therefore history and memory, is best understood as being inseparable and even complementary.[90]

The complexities surrounding the broader relationship between history and theology is not to be minimized in the pursuit of innovative ways forward. Whether or not the historical events described in the Bible actually happened bears great import for how one interprets, understands, and applies the biblical text today. It may even, as Anderson notes, play a role in the trustworthiness of the entirety of Scripture. He states,

> It seems to me inescapable . . . that anyone who chanced to read the pages of the [Bible] for the first time would come away with one overwhelming impression—that here is a faith that 'does not understand itself to be the discovering and imparting of generally valid, timeless truths,' but that is firmly based on certain allegedly historical events—a faith which would be false and misleading if those events had not actually taken place, but which, if they did take place, is unique in its relevance and exclusive in its demands on our allegiance.[91]

G. E. Wright concurs, concluding that "in biblical faith everything depends upon whether the central events actually occurred."[92] The point of

---

87. Nora, "Between Memory and History," 8–9. See also P. Novick, *That Noble Dream*.

88. Spencer, "Remembering Sabbath," 8.

89. Huizinga, "A Definition of the Concept of History," 1–10. For more discussion on this, see Averbeck, "Sumer, the Bible, and Comparative Method," 88–125.

90. Spencer, "Remembering Sabbath," 8.

91. Anderson, *Jesus Christ: The Witness of History*, 14. Anderson's reflection here is in response to a reading of the New Testament, but it was not made at the expense or exclusion of the Old Testament. See also C. J. H. Wright, *Exodus*, 17–18.

92. G. E. Wright, *God Who Acts*, 126–27. The "central events" that Wright is referring to include, in his view, the reality of the exodus, "that the nation was established at

mnemohistory is therefore not to sidestep the importance of the Bible's historicity. Instead, it seeks to approach it from the vantage point of the ones recounting their own historical events. It also attempts to stray away from the over-stressing of the "event" in favor of appreciating the "event aspect" of revelation, or as Goldingay puts it, the understanding that "event and word are both part of revelation."[93] Whatever one's take on the prominence and provability of the Hebrew Bible's historicity, Tigay rightly establishes that "it is of interest to note that many historians agree that, despite the complex process through which the Pentateuchal narratives passed, the present form of the narratives has preserved some historical memories."[94]

Davies, in an attempt to address the above concerns and criticisms, offers a helpful summary of mnemohistory's unique contributions.[95] Some of these include (1) its utilization of both empirical and theoretical bodies of knowledge, (2) the ability to focus on the memory itself rather than the event it conjures, and (3) its insistence on understanding the identity of the group to which the memory belongs. These points mitigate the claims that cultural memory analysis is redundant with respect to other historical-critical methods or that it devalues empirical/archaeological data concerning an event's factuality. On the contrary, it aids in redefining the relationship between event and interpretation by affirming the Bible's historicity as a necessary condition for the truth of the Christian faith but that it is not a sufficient condition thereof.[96] In other words, as Long explains, "Faith does not require that the factuality of the biblical events be proven (such proof is, at any rate, seldom possible)," but at the same time, "faith can never entirely insulate itself from the findings of historical study."[97] Should it be conclusively shown that the exodus, for example, did not factually occur, then "not only would the veracity of the Bible be seriously undermined, but the fall of historicity

---

Mount Sinai, that it did obtain the land, that it did lose it subsequently, that Jesus did live, that he did die on a cross, and that he did appear subsequently to a large number of independent witnesses."

93. Goldingay, "The Patriarchs in Scripture and History," 37.

94. Tigay, "The Evolution of the Pentateuchal Narratives," 26. See also Eissfeldt, *The Old Testament*, 241, where he states that, "The important point is indeed, in the last analysis, not this or that individual dissection of the material, but the total outlook."

95. Kofoed, "The Exodus as Cultural Memory," 185.

96. Goldingay, *Approaches to Old Testament Interpretation*, 77.

97. Long, *The Art of Biblical History*, 99.

would inevitably bring down Christian faith with it."[98] Remembering and reminiscing about God's deliverance of the Israelites from Egypt, then, is an acknowledgment that the exodus event provides worthy grounds for faith and not the other way around.[99]

Remembering the Historical Exodus

The Torah is not shy when it comes to elevating the importance of the exodus from Egypt. On numerous occasions, it contains the explicit requirement to "remember" what happened (Deut 5:15; 6:12; 8:14) along with the command to pass on the exodus memory to the next generation (Exod 10:2; 13:14; Lev 23:43; Deut 6:21). The early prophets, who largely condemned the people's forgetfulness, also participated in the call to remember the exodus (Hos 2:15; 11:1; 13:4; Amos 2:10; 3:1; Mic 6:4; 7:15). This generational act of remembering, chronologically fashioned, accomplished three things. First, it maintained the identity of the Israelite people as an exclusive ethnocultural group founded on the covenant between the patriarchs and their deity; second, it sustained Israel's shared history of slavery in (and deliverance from) the land of Egypt as a part of their origin story; and, third, it legitimized Israel's national existence and rights to the land of Canaan as a result of the Mosaic covenant ratified at Sinai so long as they obeyed everything the LORD, their deliverer and God of their forefathers, had commanded them (Exod 23:20–33; 24:7). King Josiah's later assessment of Judah's predicament following generations of forgetfulness is therefore unsurprising: "Great is the Lord's anger against us because our predecessors have not obeyed the words of this book [the book of the Law][100] in order to do everything which is written about us" (2 Kgs 22:13b).

Israel's Ethnocultural Identity

It is something of a truism to point out that ethnicity has played an important role in the history of the Jewish people, both before and after the

---

98. Long, *The Art of Biblical History*, 99.

99. Goldingay, "The Patriarchs in Scripture and History," 37.

100. Cf. 2 Kgs 22:11. This is likely referring to the book of Deuteronomy. For more on this, see Konkel, *1 & 2 Kings*, 635.

events in Scripture.[101] Defining what is meant by "ethnicity" or "ethnocultural group" (Jewish or otherwise), however, has been a point of significant debate, with some labeling such terms as "extraordinarily elusive" and "very difficult to define in any precise way."[102] This study finds Barth's time-tested explanation on the matter to be compelling. He suggests that terms like "ethnicity," "cultural identity," and so on are general references to a social boundary that partitions population groups on the basis of one or more of the following distinctions: (1) genealogical characteristics; (2) cultural traits such as language, religion, customs, shared history; and (3) inherited phenotypical characteristics.[103]

Of Barth's three distinguishing traits, genealogical characteristics are generally regarded as the most important (followed closely by shared history). Sparks, for example, labels this trait as "the primary carrier of ethnic sentiment,"[104] and summarizes the overall topic of ethnicity as incorporating "a particular kind of sentiment about group identity wherein groups of individuals view themselves as being alike by virtue of their common ancestry."[105] This understanding is exemplified in the way the OT attaches the memory of the exodus event to the pre-existing covenant that God made with the Israelites' ancestors: "The Israelites groaned in their slavery and cried out, and their cry for help because of their slavery went up to God. God heard their groaning and he remembered his covenant with Abraham, with Isaac, and with Jacob. So God saw the Israelites, and God knew" (Exod 2:23b–25). Not only does God choose to deliver the Israelites from slavery on the basis of his promise to the patriarchs (Gen 15; 28:13), but he also references them in order to identify himself to Moses (Exod 3:5–6) before telling him to "say this to the people of Israel: 'The Lord, the God of your fathers, the God of Abraham, the God of Isaac, and the God of Jacob, has sent me to you'" (Exod 3:15). The Israelites were therefore an exclusive people group identified by a shared cultural memory regarding the historical and genealogical importance of Abraham, Isaac, and Jacob.

101. Sparks, *Ethnicity and Identity in Ancient Israel*, 1. See also Brett, "Interpreting Ethnicity," 11; and Williamson, "The Concept of Israel in Transition," 141–61.

102. Parsons, "Some Theoretical Considerations," 53.

103. Barth, *Ethnic Groups and Boundaries*. This is not to say that such terms are synonymous. Sparks rightly points out that there are subtle yet important nuances between them that may hold some consequence depending on their use in ethnicity studies. See Sparks, *Ethnicity and Identity in Ancient Israel*, 1–6, for more on this.

104. Sparks, *Ethnicity and Identity in Ancient Israel*, 3.

105. Sparks, *Ethnicity and Identity in Ancient Israel*, 1.

What gave the Israelites this idea of genealogical uniqueness? As some are in the habit of pointing out, claims like these tend to be connected to self-legitimization and the perpetuation of tradition.[106] According to Kofoed, however, "it is not likely that a memory of *allochthony*, 'foreign origin,' as expressed in the exodus tradition, developed into such a strong and long-lived 'official memory intrinsically related to power and tradition,' if it only pertained to a small group or a minor 'memory community.'"[107] Smith goes a step further, positing that "Those whose identities are rarely questioned and who have never known exile or subjugation of land and culture, have little need to trace their "roots" in order to establish a unique and recognizable identity. Yet theirs [Israel's] is only an implicit and unarticulated form of what elsewhere must be shouted from the roof-tops: We belong, we have a unique identity, we know it by our ancestry and history."[108] While the identity of the Israelite people prior to the exodus was contingent upon the memory of their common genealogical ancestry, it particularly relied on the memory of the relationship their ancestors had with "God Almighty" (Exod 6:2–3). (Note God's appeal to this memory in Exod 3:6a and especially Moses's reaction to this appeal in 3:6b.) Indeed, even in the midst of their groaning, the Israelites understood that it was characteristic of the God of their fathers to hear their plight and respond favorably to their situation (Exod 2:23–25; 3:16–18; Num 20:14–17).

Israel's Identity as Former Slaves

"The Old Testament Scriptures do not treat the sojourn-exodus-wilderness events as trivial matters," states Hoffmeier, "Rather, these events stand at the heart of Israel's religious life, as evidenced by the fact that these themes are ubiquitous throughout the Old Testament itself."[109] References to the Israelites' mnemohistory of deliverance from bondage within the Bible can be seen, for example, in its legal collections (Exod 22:20; 23:9; Lev 19:34; 25:42, 55; Deut 15:15; 24:17–18), hymnody (Exod 15:1–18, 21; Judg 5:4–5; Ps 66:5–6; 74:12–13; 77:19–20; 78, 105, 106), prophetic literature (Judg 6:8–10; 1 Sam 2:27–28; Hos 12:9; Isa 10:26;

---

106. See, for example, Faust's work *Israel's Ethnogenesis*.
107. Kofoed, "The Exodus as Cultural Memory," 192.
108. Smith, *The Ethnic Origins of Nations*, 2.
109. Hoffmeier, "Why a Historical Exodus is Essential for Theology," 156.

11:16; Jer 2:6; 7:22, 25; 16:14; 31:31–32; Ezek 20:5–10, 22–31; 23:19, 27; Dan 9:15; Hag 2:5), historical retrospectives (Exod 17:8–16; Num 20:14–17; Deut 25:17–19; 1 Sam 15:2, 6), and several other portions of the Text.[110] Some scholars are in the habit of dismissing these numerous references in favor of external data (particularly archaeological data).[111] In doing so, they further discount Huizinga's aforementioned point that civilizations are capable of rendering to themselves their own past. If such textual pervasiveness of a singular historical event as remembered by the Israelites has nothing to say of their own history, what does?[112]

The deliverance from slavery in Egypt became so critical to the corporate distinctiveness of the Israelite people that it grew to be a chief marker of their ethnocultural identity. Moses, for example, describes them in Exod 32:7 and 11 as "your people, whom you brought up out of the land of Egypt."[113] Even the way in which God discloses himself to the Israelites changed following their deliverance: "I am the LORD your God who brought you out of the land of Egypt" (Exod 20:2; Lev 19:36; 25:34; 26:23; Num 15:41; Deut 5:6; Ps 81:10; Hos 12:9; 13:4).[114] Hoffmeier notes that this act of identifying an ethnic group and their bond with their deity (or deities) in terms of a particular event is not seen among Israel's neighbors,[115] causing many to affirm the link between Israel and the exodus as a critical ethnic and theological identifier.[116] He concludes that "in a sense, every time 'my people' occurs in the Old Testament, it is a reminder to Israel that they are God's people, liberated by him from slavery in Egypt."[117] As will be seen in the next segment, the Israelites'

---

110. Hoffmeier, "Why a Historical Exodus is Essential for Theology," 112–32.

111. See, for example, Sparks, *God's Word in Human Words*, 11–14, 136–57.

112. According to Hoffmeier, the historicity of the Israelites enduring slavery in Egypt "has long been considered to have a ring of truth even for more skeptical scholars," going on to recount that, "Sir Alan Gardiner, the renowned twentieth-century Egyptologist and usually sharp critic of the historical value of the Old Testament . . . conceded 'that Israel was in Egypt under one form or another no historian could possibly doubt; a legend of such tenacity representing the early fortunes of a people under so unfavorable an aspect could not have arisen save as a reflection, however much distorted, of real occurrences'" (Hoffmeier, *Israel in Egypt*, 112).

113. Cf. Num 22:5, 11, "a people came out of Egypt."

114. Cf. Gen 15:7 where God, prior to the exodus event, discloses himself to Abraham as "I am the LORD who brought you out from Ur of the Chaldeans."

115. Hoffmeier, "Why a Historical Exodus is Essential for Theology," 113.

116. See, for example, Albertz, *A History of Israelite Religion*, 49; and Rendtorff, "The Concept of Revelation in Ancient Israel," 25–27.

117. Hoffmeier, "Why a Historical Exodus Is Essential for Theology," 113. For an

identity as belonging to God would later be formalized through his covenant with them at Sinai.

Israel's National Identity

Prior to the people's response to the reading of the BC at Sinai (Exod 24:7), the cultural memory of the Israelites maintained a type of "family identity" through their shared ancestry with Abraham and shared history as slaves in the land of Egypt.[118] So long as they "walked blamelessly" (Gen 17:1) and engaged in the act of circumcision as a sign of their ongoing covenant with God (Gen 17:9–14), they were to look forward to his blessings on them that would one day take the form of a prosperous national existence presiding over the land of Canaan (Gen 17:3–8). It was after their deliverance from slavery that these promises were formalized through the covenant at Sinai (Exod 23:20–33). Not only were the Israelites a more numerous family, but now they were also a theocratic nation with the newly given laws serving as their constitution. So long as they kept the covenant and obeyed God fully, they would enjoy a deeper and more explicitly defined relationship with him and go on to possess the Promised Land (Gen 15:7–21; Exod 19:5; Lev 26:40–46).[119]

Of particular significance to Israel's new national status is the relationship between the people's obedience to YHWH and their reception of the land, a topic which would be further expounded upon at the covenant

---

opposing view, see Hendel, "The Exodus in Biblical Memory," 601–22; and Hendel, *Remembering Abraham*, where he advances the notion that outsiders could (and almost certainly did) assume an Israelite identity by independent choice. He states, "The cultural boundaries of early Israel were, at least in part, constructed by the dissemination of stories about the deliverance of Israel from Egyptian bondage and birth of a free people in the Promised Land. It is important to note that even Israelite settlers who had never been slaves in Egypt could easily participate in this narrative memory, for Egypt had been the overlord of Canaan for several centuries previously . . . By adopting this story as their own, the villagers in the highlands became Israelites, and a mixed multitude crystalized its collective identity as the people of Yahweh."

118. Kofoed, "The Exodus as Cultural Memory," 194.

119. It would be an understatement to say that there has been a lot of discussion on the way biblical covenants function in relation to one another. This study adopts the view put forward in Averbeck, *The Old Testament Law for the Life of the Church*. Simply stated, the "redemptive covenants" (the Abrahamic, Mosaic, Davidic, and new covenants) "build one on the other so that none of them eliminates the Lord's previous covenantal commitments and expectations" (60) with each possessing "permanent promises and ongoing obligations" for the people of Israel (56–57; see esp. the helpful chart on 58).

renewal in Deuteronomy right before entering Canaan.[120] As Brueggemann states, henceforth "Israel's involvement is always with land and with Yahweh, never only with Yahweh as though to live only in intense obedience, never only with land, as though simply to possess and manage; always with land and with Yahweh, always receiving gifts from land, always being addressed by Yahweh."[121] So important are these three factors—God, Israel, and the land—that C. J. H. Wright labels them as "the three pillars of Israel's worldview," depicting their interdependence in triangular fashion. Tsai expounds on this depiction by including the central role of law along with the ramifications of obedience and disobedience:[122]

Figure 3. The Three Pillars of Israel's Worldview

YHWH, as the God of Israel
redeem / *own/give*

LAW
(obey/disobey)

revere / *reflect YHWH's satisfaction*

Israel, as an elect people   *live on* ⇄ *expel*   The land, as a gift and the
in unique relation to YHWH   concretization of the covenant

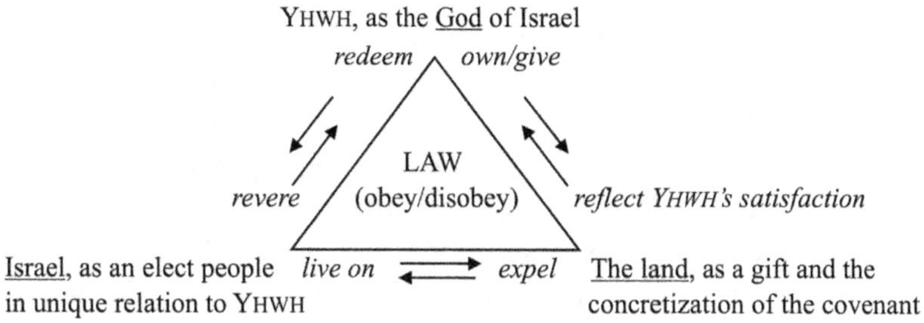

Daisy Yulin Tsai, *Human Rights in Deuteronomy.*
With Special Emphasis on Slave Laws, 36.

Those who are in tune with deuteronomic scholarship are well aware of the tendency to see Deuteronomy as something other than a record of a renewal of the Sinai covenant prior to the Israelites' entry into the Promised Land. Assmann, for example, promotes the view that while the memories in Deuteronomy may indeed be rooted in real historical events (at least to some degree), they were written much later, likely during the time of Josiah, with the goal of using the above theological reasoning

---

120. Given that Deuteronomy does not explicitly state that it is renewing the Sinai covenant, there is some debate as to whether it is describing a covenant renewal or establishing a new divine covenant altogether. For support of the former, see Averbeck, *The Old Testament Law for the Life of the Church*, 48. For support of the latter, see Greengus, "Covenant and Treaty in the Hebrew Bible," 91–126.

121. Brueggemann, *The Land*, 36.

122. Shown here is Tsai's variation of C. J. H. Wright's figure with an added emphasis on the central role of law; see Tsai, *Human Rights in Deuteronomy*, 36. For the original, see C. J. H. Wright, *Old Testament Ethics*, 19.

to bring about a "deuteronomistic revival." He states, "Deuteronomy was the manifesto of a group, 'movement,' or 'school,' which was the bearer of a new, spiritual form of identity that was based solely on the Torah, and through this one foundation possessed everything that other societies has to build up in visible form—territories, institutions, monuments and the trappings of power."[123] A major concern with such assertions is that their rationale, at least in terms of dating, is largely based on the discussions surrounding source critical methods and the documentary hypothesis (the shortcomings of which were highlighted earlier) and other similar redaction theories.[124]

Rather than seeing the "deuteronomistic program" as the theological radicalization of a later religious movement, it may instead be seen as a characteristic of the relationship between God, people, and land from the beginning.[125] As Spencer points out, Deuteronomy's inclusion of historical recitations, exhortations to remain obedient, and calls to remember through participation in mnemonic practices such as rituals and ceremonies all aid in conditioning the believing community as they prepare to enter the Promised Land.[126] The goal of this preparation is reminiscent of the exodus itself, namely that they must remember that their identity as foreigners persists in a land that ultimately belongs to God (Lev 25:23) and that all the good that is given to them is *also* given to the foreigner among them (Deut 26:11). "What it means to be Israel must be taught in the Liberation Boot Camp, where it is easy to learn," Kofoed opines, "so that it can be remembered in Canaan, where such an identity is difficult to maintain."[127]

THEO-ETHICAL CONSIDERATIONS

Theological and ethical approaches to Scripture very often go hand in hand. The former finds its center in the "foment over presuppositions

---

123. Assmann, *Cultural Memory and Early Civilization*, 192. See also Van Seters, "Cultural Memory and the Invention of Biblical Israel"; and Cross, "The Structure of the Deuteronomic History," 9–24.

124. Kofoed, "The Exodus as Cultural Memory," 190–91.

125. Kofoed, "The Exodus as Cultural Memory," 194. See also Hoffmeier, "Why a Historical Exodus is Essential for Theology," 113–16, for a discussion on Deuteronomy's historical placement using ancient Hittite treaty formulae.

126. Spencer, "Remembering Sabbath," 158.

127. Kofoed, "The Exodus as Cultural Memory," 194.

and beliefs, ancient and modern, regarding the nature of God, people, the world, the Bible, and the relationships between them"[128] while the latter encapsulates the subsequent human response and gratitude to such beliefs.[129] Birch labels the two as inseparable, stating "ethics in the Hebrew Bible is inextricably bound up with the entire theological witness of the biblical story to a god who becomes known in relation to the people of Israel."[130] The relationship between the historical exodus and the giving of the law at Sinai is in many ways representative of this dynamic. As Bartor explains, "Law is understood as a way in which the people *respond* to what God has done on their behalf. The law is an exegesis of the divine action, of the narrative."[131] This segment will therefore be handled in two parts. Just as God's deliverance of the Israelites came before their collective response in Exod 24:7, step one will identify the theological significance of the exodus memory before ultimately moving to its influence on the BC's promotion of humanitarian ethics.

Theological Reflections on the Exodus

Perhaps the most foundational theological observance to make regarding the exodus from Egypt can be seen in Exod 6:7 where God preemptively states, "I will take you as my people, and I will be your God. *You will know that I am the Lord your God*, who brought you out from the forced labor of the Egyptians."[132] In the previous section, some of the implications of the exodus memory on the Israelites' identity as a people group were surveyed, namely their connection with covenant-making ancestors, origin as now-delivered slaves in Egypt, and status as a land-owning nation under the auspices of the Mosaic Law. God did these things for them out of faithfulness to his own character and the promises he made to their forefathers (Exod 2:24; 3:6–8), all with the foremost intention of making himself known to his people.[133] What is there to learn about who God is through the exodus story? There are a variety of worthy answers to this

128. Averbeck, "Factors in Reading the Patriarchal Narratives," 116.
129. C. J. H. Wright, *Old Testament Ethics*, 25. See also Birch, *Let Justice Roll Down*, 37–41.
130. Birch, "Moral Agency," 24. See also Childs, *Biblical Theology in a Canonical Context*, 676.
131. Bartor, "Law and Narrative," 221; emphasis added.
132. Emphasis added. Cf. Deut 4:32–35.
133. C. J. H. Wright, *Old Testament Ethics*, 27.

question, but chief among them, as pointed out by the text, includes the specifics of his distinct identity and the rationale behind the sequence of his actions—both of which illuminate his compassionate character (see chapter 2, part one).[134]

God's Distinct Identity

It is not enough to simply acknowledge that there is only one god (Jas 2:19). While monotheism is no doubt a fundamental pillar in Judeo-Christian theology (Deut 6:4), the God of the historical exodus—of the entire Bible—was determined to make himself personally known. Deuteronomy perhaps makes this point best: "You were shown these things [the signs during the exodus] so that you might know that Yhwh [specifically] is God; besides him there is no other ... Acknowledge that Yhwh is God in heaven above and on the earth below. There is no other" (Deut 4:35, 39).[135] As C. Wright opines, "The acts of *this* God, Yhwh, proved who was truly God. It was not the gods of the Egyptians or the Canaanites. It was Yhwh who alone had done these things, uniquely as God and uniquely for Israel." The primary issue at hand, then, was not how many deities there were, but "the *identity and character* of the God who had done these amazing things in their history."[136] God himself made his personal pursuit of the Hebrew people abundantly clear in his statement, "I, Yhwh, your God, am a *jealous* God" (קַנָּא; Exod 20:5)—a Hebrew descriptor that many acknowledge as an emotional word rooted in the concepts of love and marriage.[137] This attribute is so central to God's character that it is later even used as his name (see Exod 34:14; cf. Deut 4:24; 5:9; 6:15; Josh 24:19; Nah 1:2).[138]

---

134. C. J. H. Wright, *Old Testament Ethics*, 23–30. See also Zimmerli and Brueggemann, *I am Yahweh*; and Boda, *The Heartbeat of Old Testament Theology*, where he identifies what he calls three "creedal expressions" which include God's historical action, active character, and relational identity.

135. Cf. John 20:31.

136. C. J. H. Wright, *Old Testament Ethics*, 25.

137. Tigay points out, for example, that the root meaning of קָנָא is "to become dark red" and is often used for "fiery passions such as love, anger, indignation, and jealousy." See Tigay, *Deuteronomy*, 65. See also Weinfeld, *Deuteronomy 1–11*, 295, where he suggests the alternative translation, "an impassioned God."

138. C. J. H. Wright, *Exodus*, 363.

God's Sequential Actions

Critical to a proper theological understanding of the exodus is the fact that it occurred prior to God's giving of the law. Israel's obedience was always meant to be a response to what God had already done for them, *not* as a means to earn deliverance. "This is the foundation not only of Old Testament ethics," asserts C. Wright, "but is indeed the principle running through the moral teaching of the whole Bible ... God's grace comes first; human response, second."[139] It is not surprising, then, that the Mt. Sinai event opens with God saying, "You have seen what I did to the Egyptians and how I carried you on eagles' wings and brought you to myself. *Now* if you will carefully listen to me and keep my covenant, you will be my own possession out of all the peoples" (Exod 19:4–5a).[140] What was formerly experienced as a vertical encounter with God in crucial historical moments (e.g., the Israelites' deliverance and reception of the laws) is now horizontally directed through texts to later generations.[141] Living out the reality of the exodus story as an authoritative source for ethical behavior is therefore expected of every member of the Israelite community moving forward.[142]

Ethical Reflections on the Exodus

The above theological reflections can be chronologically outlined as follows: initially, the Israelites have a unique experience of God's revelation and redemption. As a result of this, they come to possess a unique

---

139. C. J. H. Wright, *Old Testament Ethics*, 29.

140. Emphasis added. See Averbeck, "The Egyptian Sojourn," 144, where he points out that the sequential theme of deliverance-obedience-promise plays a central, unifying role in what he calls the "most inclusive frame for the Law" beginning with Exod 19 and going through Deut 26. In his view, this framework is identified by a three-fold pattern which includes the background history of the Lord's deliverance from Egypt (Exod 19:4), the call for the Israelites' commitment to keep the regulations of the covenant (5a), and the Lord's corresponding commitment to make Israel his "special treasure ... kingdom of priests and holy nation" (5b–6).

141. For example, "Remember that you were slaves" (Deut 15:15) and "Not with our ancestors ... but with us, who are all of us alive here today" (Deut 5:3).

142. Childs, *Biblical Theology*, 677–78. See also Birch, "Moral Agency," 27, where he states, "The community is formed ... by the belief that the narrative witnesses to the reality of the community-shaping encounter with God in historical time and space ... Israel's character is significantly formed by its remembering and reinterpreting of God's previous actions on its behalf."

knowledge of his identity. In turn, they receive a "unique responsibility to live in the midst of the nations in a manner that reflects in their own behavior the ethical character of the Lord as expressed in the commands he has given them for their own good."[143] In other words, the new revelation of God during the exodus gave birth to much more than a novel form of monotheism as a matter of "quaint religious preference." Rather, for Israel, "exclusive commitment to Yhwh as sole deity was part of a covenantal structure of life that impacted every dimension of their social, economic, judicial, and political existence."[144] Moving forward, the way they were to humanely treat slaves, women, enemies, the poor and needy, animals, and especially the foreigner was meant to look radically different from the ways of the surrounding nations (Exod 23:31–33; Num 23:9). It is no wonder, then, that the BC makes such stark references to God's mighty acts of deliverance. Knowledge of the historical exodus and thoughtful meditation on its memory are presupposed by its laws in such a way that without them one cannot fully grasp their implications.[145] "The practical outcome of [following biblical law] is humanitarian," concludes C. J. H. Wright, "but the origin and motive are theological, and this is what is ethically most significant about it. It is here that we see . . . that a wholehearted covenant commitment to God requires that his people reflect his character, as revealed in his actions on their behalf."[146]

Understanding the Life of a Foreigner

The BC champions what many describe as a "protection motif." Van Wijk-Bos, for example, asserts that any conversation regarding the BC's ethos must begin with its requirements "to protect those who are most vulnerable in the society and to refrain from pushing them further to the margins and exploiting their weakness."[147] Among those who qualify for

---

143. C. J. H. Wright, *Old Testament Ethics*, 53–54.

144. C. J. H. Wright, *Old Testament Ethics*, 55.

145. See Rodd, *Glimpses of a Strange Land*, 115, 148–49; Gamoran, "The Biblical Law Against Loans on Interest," 127–34; and esp. Birch, "Moral Agency," 34, where he states, "The legal materials reflect an understanding of Israel as a community that was initiated by the saving activity of God and that continued in ongoing covenant relationship with God."

146. C. J. H. Wright, *An Eye for an Eye*, 157–58.

147. Van Wijk-Bos, *Making Wise the Simple*, 191.

protection as the "most vulnerable" (such as slaves and the poor)[148] is a special emphasis on the protection of foreigners, the only social group to be referenced twice (Exod 22:20 and 23:9).[149] Additionally, per the discussion in chapter 2, the foreigner is mentioned as a group who benefits from the sabbath rest (Exod 23:12). As directly pointed out by the verses in question, such an emphasis only makes sense in light of what the Israelites experienced. "Since the Israelites themselves had been oppressed as resident aliens in Egypt, they must be sure to avoid oppressing resident aliens when they themselves are in charge."[150]

The call to heed the plight of the foreigner is not limited to the realm of empathy. Careful consideration of the BC's previously discussed literary composition and mnemohistory point toward the identity of God as being the foundational element. "The opening and closing sections [of the BC]," Van Wijk-Bos explains, "concern the issue of worship and shape a framework around the various directives for the social life of the community."[151] In other words, the Israelites were indeed able to "understand the life of a foreigner" (Exod 23:9) as a result of their shared historical experience as foreigners in Egypt, but the motivation to care for them following their deliverance from slavery was based on the nature of their God. Rather than simply "paying it forward," care for the foreigner was to be a compassionate act of worship in its reflection of the one who cared for them first. "An interesting use of historical events is tied to the concept of *imitatio dei*—imitation of divine deeds," states Bartor, "The law does not draw an analogy between different human behaviors, but between divine and human behaviors, basing the legal norm on acts performed by God."[152] The difference between these two analogies (acts imitating human behaviors as opposed to acts imitating divine ones) in many ways marks the distinction between humanitarian acts and חנון humanitarian acts. The former, in this case, would be more akin to mere pity while the latter is worship.

---

148. This is not to say that the BC excludes others from being protected. All parties, for example, are protected from violence against their persons (21:12–36), against their property (21:37—22:14), and perhaps even against behaviors which threaten their relationship to God (22:27–30). See Van Wijk-Bos, *Making Wise the Simple*, 182–83.

149. Van Wijk-Bos, *Making Wise the Simple*, 188.

150. Averbeck, "The Egyptian Sojourn," 162. Cf. Lev 19:33–34.

151. Van Wijk-Bos, *Making Wise the Simple*, 181.

152. Bartor, "Law and Narrative," 221.

Hearing the Ones Who Cry Out

The above sentiments are only made more consequential by the LORD's declaration that he will certainly hear the cry of the oppressed, empathize with their suffering, and intervene on their behalf (Exod 22:22–23).[153] Such a statement should not be surprising, however, since this is precisely what God did for the Israelites in Exod 3:7–8. He states, "I have *seen* the affliction of my people in Egypt, and I have *heard* them crying out because of their oppressors. I *know* their suffering, and I have come down to *rescue* them from the power of the Egyptians and to *bring them out* from that land to a good and spacious land, a land flowing with milk and honey."[154] The first-person verbs spread across these verses (I have seen, I have heard, I know, I have come down to rescue/bring them out) give tremendous weight to God's declaration of attention and intention.[155] When it comes to the oppressed/vulnerable, God's inclination to listen, empathize, and act is grounded in his summarizing statement that "when they cry out to me, I will hear, because I am compassionate" (22:26).

The parallels between God's account of his actions in favor of Israel in Exod 3:7–8 and how he portrays himself in the BC against Israel (should they opt to not follow the law's instruction) reveal the multifaceted nature of his compassionate disposition:

---

153. "'I am powerless *not* to react' God seems to say, 'once the abused party cries out to Me,'" Kugel, *The God of Old*, 110.

154. Emphasis added. Cf. Exod 2:23–25.

155. C. J. H. Wright, *Exodus*, 102. There exists a tendency to translate יָדַעְתִּי אֶת־מַכְאֹבָיו as "I am concerned about their suffering" (e.g., NIV). Such a translation "seems too weak for the more intense 'I know (*yada'*) their suffering,'" states Wright; "The Hebrew suggests not just that God is cognitively aware of what is being inflicted on his people in Egypt but that he, in some sense, experiences it himself. He knows it from the inside, as it were" (C. J. H. Wright, *Exodus*, 102–3). See also Fretheim, *Exodus*, 60; and Fretheim, *The Suffering of God*, 127–30.

Table 3. Compassion in Exod 3 vs. Exod 22

	Exod 3:7–8 (Mercy)	Exod 22:22–23 (Justice)
Listen	"I have seen/heard"	"I will certainly hear"
Empathize	"I know their suffering"	"My anger will be aroused"
Act	"I have come to rescue"	"I will kill you with the sword"

The Israelites had two options to consider in response to what God did for them when it comes to their treatment of the vulnerable. They could either imitate Yhwh and show compassion, or they could imitate Egypt, their former oppressors. On this, Van Wijk-Bos opines:

> This is between God and the community. "You," as a covenant partner, are not to victimize those who are already weak and vulnerable because of their position in society. It is in "my," God's, character to pay attention to the cry of the oppressed. As I once heard "your" cry, children of Israel, when you were abused in Egypt, and held the Egyptians accountable, so you will be held accountable if you mete out similar treatment to the disadvantaged among you.[156]

SUMMARY AND CONCLUSION

The BC's references to the deliverance of the Israelites from Egypt, which are no doubt useful in matters of ethical conduct, connote a deeper and more consequential connection with the narrative than some may realize. In the effort to further explore the relationship between the historical exodus and the BC, namely the dependence of the latter upon the former, this chapter launched a "three dimensional" discussion which includes literary, historical, and theo-ethical considerations.[157] Should an acknowledgment of God's tangible actions during the exodus be seen as anything other than necessary for sound interpretation and application of his law, then his compassionate character risks losing its merit, and the way his covenant readers are commanded to treat others would be based solely on proclamation without action (Deut 15:15).

---

156. Van Wijk-Bos, *Making Wise the Simple*, 187.

157. See Averbeck, "Factors in Reading the Patriarchal Narratives," 116; and Averbeck, "The Exodus, Debt Slavery, and the Composition of the Pentateuch," 26–27.

The literary considerations revealed that the BC belongs and contributes to the theological narrative and cannot simply be seen as an external document which was written in isolation and inserted into the text in a tactical way. So strong is the BC's integration with the biblical story that its very composition reflects the contents and lessons of the exodus event. This can be seen in the way it prioritizes the well-being of slaves (an ordering which is not seen elsewhere in the ancient world) and the manner in which it frames its contents. These frames—narrative, cultic, sabbatical, and casuistic/apodictic—constitute the overall structure of the BC (Exod 20:11—23:33) and contribute to a larger theological picture. For example, the narrative frame encloses the entirety of the BC within the exodus story (the prior deliverance from Egypt and the upcoming possession of the land of Canaan). Following this, the cultic frame outlines appropriate ways in which to worship God alone and express thanksgiving for what he has done (and will do). The sabbatical frame then provides opportunities for the BC's covenant readers to reciprocate God's loving acts for the benefit of others, especially for the poor, the needy, and the foreigner (and even animals), all the while imitating the model which he established at creation (Gen 2:2–3). Finally, the casuistic and apodictic frames outline specific scenarios and express direct concerns relating to the everyday life of the newly established Israelite nation in light of their covenant relationship with God.

The historical considerations displayed that even though the exodus cannot be empirically proven to have transpired, evidence for its historicity can be satisfactorily observed through the Israelites' recorded cultural memory. This "mnemohistory" established the identity of the Israelite people as an exclusive, ethnocultural group founded upon the covenant which God made with their ancestors; sustained their shared history as slaves in Egypt; and legitimized their national existence and rights to the land of Canaan as a result of the Mosaic covenant ratified at Sinai so long as they remained obedient to Yhwh, the one and only God who delivered them from bondage. This cumulative memory of the historical exodus, in turn, served as a type of "vertical" reference point (what God did for his people) that would go on to influence Israel's "horizontal" lifestyle (how they proceeded to treat others in light of God's actions). "God twice draws Israel's attention to the undeniable facts of their historical experience (Exod 19:4; 20:22). All that follows in the legal sections depends on them remembering who they were and what God had done for them."[158]

---

158. C. J. H. Wright, *Exodus*, 400.

The theo-ethical considerations identified the primary goal of the exodus as being relational, namely that the Israelites would come to know their God more personally (Exod 6:7). God is not only "one" (Deut 6:4), but he is also "jealous" for his people (Exod 20:5) and distinctly different from every other god (Deut 4:35). The fact that God delivered his people from oppression prior to the giving of the law is perhaps the most glaring example of his distinct character. He is a God that is eager to show grace, compassion, and mercy (Isa 30:18). Seen in this light, the law becomes celebratory rather than rigid, a gift rather than a burden, and a source of freedom rather than bondage. Having been the object of God's compassion, the Israelites were then called to imitate his example by caring for the foreigner (Exod 22:20; 23:9) and hearing the cries of the vulnerable (Exod 22:22–23). The exodus, then, serves as a practical illustration of how to best reflect God's compassion.

The above literary, historical, and theo-ethical angles all point toward the BC as being directly dependent upon the exodus event for its rationale. Moreover, had the Israelites never, in fact, been delivered from slavery out of the land of Egypt, the BC would not exist.[159] Such a conclusion rejects the general understanding that the law is simply an expression of ideals or timeless truths which are then enforced to define the Israelite people. This would imply that the BC stands alone as an authoritative end in itself, practically detached from the story which surrounds it. Instead, it is more accurate to understand the Israelite community as having already been defined by their relationship to Yhwh through his actions and revelations during the exodus. The law, then, becomes a source for "guidance and instruction in apprehending and living out the implications of such a community."[160] Patrick adds,

> [During] the period which the legal tradition was in formation, the law of God was an unwritten Law. It was the sense of justice and right shared by the legal community and sharpened by lawgivers and judges ... The precepts and judgements of the codes were not prescriptions with statutory force but testimony to God's just and righteous will ... The law books were intended not for judicial application but for instruction in the values, principles, concepts, and procedures of the unwritten divine Law.[161]

---

159. Averbeck, "The Egyptian Sojourn," 143–44.
160. Birch, "Moral Agency," 34.
161. Patrick, *Old Testament Law*, 189–90, 198.

Any interpretation or application of the BC without an informed knowledge of its author as revealed in the exodus would be akin to reading only the middle section of a book. It is only with the pretext that the ultimate goals of the BC can be adequately understood, namely that the reader learn the ways of the Lord, walk blamelessly before him, and seek him with their whole heart (Ps 119:1–8). Such sentiments are fundamentally what set biblical law apart from its ANE contemporaries, a topic that will be further explored in the next chapter.

4

The Book of the Covenant's "Scale of Values" in Light of Its ANE Contemporaries

What other nation is so great as to have such righteous decrees and laws as this body of laws I am setting before you today?

—Deuteronomy 4:8

Truly he taught us to love one another; his law is love, and his gospel is peace. Chains shall he break for the slave is our brother; and in his name, all oppression shall cease.

—*O Holy Night*

"From the broadest perspective, the laws of a society may serve as a window into its values."[1] What is permitted, and what is forbidden? Who benefits from each decree, and who is at fault? What does punishment look like? What motivations are provided for obedience? Which

---

1. C. B. Hays, *Hidden Riches*, 138.

situations do the laws try to prevent or promote?[2] While modern presuppositions and sensibilities can make questions like these difficult to answer, passages like 2 Tim 3:15–17 stand as constant reminders that the laws of the OT remain "useful for training in righteousness." Such training, according to C. J. H. Wright, is hard to take seriously without recourse to some form of principled approach to discerning what ethical values God intends his people in every age to learn.[3]

C. J. H. Wright's take is only complemented through acute comparisons with other ancient legal collections, as the practice of comparing and contrasting texts very often brings focus to their respective theological and ethical features. Such a practice is more than just helpful, however—it is necessary. "Even complex concepts like justice, goodness, and beauty turn out to be relative," states C. B. Hays, "and our comprehension and appreciation of them are dependent on comparison."[4] It is certainly true that nothing can replace the careful reading or meditation of an individual text (as the previous chapters aim to illustrate), but comparison with other writings becomes inevitable the moment similar texts are introduced.[5] It is also worth repeating that the laws of the OT were not written in a vacuum; they, in many ways, echo the culture of the ANE at large and utilize several of the traditions seen in other pre-existing legal collections.[6] Expanding the scope to include biblical law's ANE contemporaries can therefore only be regarded as a beneficial and illuminating process. As such, this project shares in C. B. Hays's enthusiasm:

> What does it mean to give proper attention to the ancient Near Eastern nature of the Hebrew Scriptures? Minimally, it means reading other ancient Near Eastern texts. The Scriptures are exceedingly "respiratory": they breathe in the culture of their times, and breathe it back out in a different form. To the reader who learns to breathe the same air . . . it is increasingly hard to

---

2. C. B. Hays, *Hidden Riches*, 138. See also C. J. H. Wright, *Exodus*, 426.

3. C. J. H. Wright, *Exodus*, 426n28. See also Averbeck, *The Old Testament Law for the Life of the Church*, 290, where he states that "even near the end of his life, the apostle Paul highlighted the importance of these Old Testament Scriptures that Timothy had been learning since he was a little child . . . The apostles could expect that those who would read their inspired New Testament writings would have the inspired Old Testament as their Bible—and that they would know it well."

4. C. B. Hays, *Hidden Riches*, 5.

5. Malul, *The Comparative Method*, 1–2.

6. See Morrow, "Legal Interactions," 13; Frahm, *Babylonian and Assyrian Text Commentaries*, 364–68; and Walton, "Biblical Texts," 573–85.

believe that he or she once read the Bible without it. Reading the Hebrew Scriptures in context is intoxicating, like breathing pure oxygen: everything is clearer and sharper, and the energy is immeasurably higher.[7]

With the above in mind, this chapter will seek to highlight the Book of the Covenant's unique and proper humanitarian values through a comparison of its debt-slave laws (Exod 21:2–11) and goring ox laws (21:28–32) with their cuneiform counterparts (primary examples include LH §§117–118; LU §§4–5 and LH §§250–252; LE §§53–55, respectively).[8] These laws were chosen for two reasons. First, both have been the subject of many ongoing scholarly conversations due to their remarkable similarities with laws found in cuneiform collections, especially the Laws of Hammurabi.[9] Second, situations regarding slavery and injury/death brought about by neglect were commonplace in the ancient world and lend themselves well to ethical deliberation.[10] Many first-time readers are shocked to discover that the Bible contains regulations regarding slavery and punishment by retaliation, or *lex talionis*, but by interpreting such laws in light of their ANE backdrop, it becomes easier to identify the BC's compassionate agenda present within the harsh realities of its time.[11]

It would be an understatement to say that the debt-slave and goring ox laws have received much scholastic attention. This is no doubt due to their complex textual transmission histories, insights regarding everyday life in the ancient world, and clear delineations of differing social classes.[12] This study will seek to unpack topics like these as necessary, but the

7. C. B. Hays, *Hidden Riches*, 4.

8. For a broader list of suggested comparisons, see D. P. Wright, *Inventing God's Law*, 9.

9. For some recent and reputable resources on the similarities and differences between biblical and ANE law, see D. P. Wright, *Inventing God's Law*; Greengus, *Laws in the Bible*; Barmash, "Ancient Near Eastern Law," 17; and S. Jackson, *A Comparison*.

10. According to Westbrook, the laws found in both biblical and cuneiform legal collections by and large deal with matters of power abuse, revenge and the application of the talionic principle, maltreatment of slaves, and theft. Together, the debt-slave and goring ox laws cover most of these prominent issues. See Westbrook, *Studies in Biblical and Cuneiform Law*.

11. Morrow, *An Introduction to Biblical Law*, 98. For an explanation on how texts contain the potential to create something not previously known to the reader by utilizing materials at hand, see Kristeva, *Semeiotiké*, 144.

12. Morrow, for example, considers these two laws to be optimal case studies for understanding many of the finer points of ancient jurisprudence as a whole. See Morrow, *An Introduction to Biblical Law*, 86–90 and 96–105.

primary focus will be on the value judgments present within the laws themselves. Instead of attempting to draw out every moral implication within the debt slave and goring ox laws, however, both sides will be read in light of C. J. H. Wright's proposed "scale of values," a process which largely concerns itself with the text's implicit value hierarchy regarding matters of life and property, persons and punishment, and needs and rights.[13] Given that laws can be seen as expressions of their author's character (their principles, values, etc.), the ramifications of such an analysis are ultimately personal. In other words, comparing laws can essentially boil down to comparing authors. What values might the BC's author, Yhwh, prioritize over against human writers/compilers?[14]

TOWARD A SCALE OF VALUES

As chapter 1 briefly touched on, what is meant by "principle" in this volume is an objective, changeless truth that governs human nature and relationships (e.g., "You shall not murder").[15] A "value," on the other hand, places ideas on a scale/hierarchy of relative worth or importance, as contrasted with things that are less valuable or rejected (e.g., it is *better* to preserve life *rather than* harming or taking life). Value hierarchies often prioritize what is good over what is evil, but they can also prioritize the relative importance of good principles. Matt 23:23 states, for example, "Woe to you, scribes and Pharisees, hypocrites! For you tithe mint and dill and cumin, but have neglected the *weightier matters* of the law: justice and mercy and faithfulness. These you ought to have done without neglecting the others." While human values occasionally change based on newly learned information or fresh experiences, divine values, much like principles, remain objective and changeless.[16] They are "preferences for what is regarded as right, appropriate, and beneficial. As such, they tend to shape attitudes and behaviors and to serve as benchmarks for

---

13. See C. J. H. Wright, *Old Testament Ethics*, 307–14. See also Tsai, *Human Rights in Deuteronomy*, 23, where she points out that "laws that share the same subject matter ... may differ fundamentally in their legislative spirits, ethical values, social-economic motivations, political intentions, or theological rationales."

14. For a discussion on how Yhwh is the ultimate source of the BC without the need for a human monarch, see J. Berman, *Created Equal*, 40–44.

15. See Gane, *Old Testament Law for Christians*, 20–23.

16. Gane, *Old Testament Law for Christians*, 22–24.

measuring outcomes."[17] OT law in particular often serves as a catalyst for ethical and moral growth through the way it seeks to persuade people to adopt its own clearly expressed principles and encourages them to bring their personally held values into alignment with divine ones.[18]

The idea of discerning fundamental values in biblical and ANE law is a recent development in the field of biblical studies.[19] Greenberg's groundbreaking essay in 1960 serves as the formal entry point into the conversation in its assertion that any interpretation of biblical law must take into account its "key concepts" and "value judgments" since law is ultimately "an expression of underlying postulates or values of culture." Moreover, he states that any comparisons made between biblical law and other ancient legal collections must consider such values as they are represented by each side.[20] "Much of the comparative work done in Israelite-Near Eastern law has been content with comparing individual laws rather than law systems or law ideologies," he opines, "but until the values that the law embodies are understood, it is a question whether any individual law can be properly appreciated, let alone profitably compared with another in a foreign system."[21]

Although Greenberg faced some opposition to his conclusions,[22] his work paved the way for later publications to delve deeper into the subject of fundamental values in ancient legal collections. In 1970, both Paul and Philips took up the mantle,[23] each advancing the idea that there are "char-

---

17. Gane, *Old Testament Law for Christians*, 23.

18. Gane, *Old Testament Law for Christians*, 23. It is worth noting at this point the difference between "ethics" and "morality." According to Rae, "Most people use the terms *morality* and *ethics* interchangeably. Technically, morality refers to the actual content of right and wrong, and ethics refers to the process of determining right and wrong. In other words, morality deals with moral *knowledge* and ethics with moral *reasoning*... Morality is the end result of ethical deliberation, the substance of right and wrong." See Gane, *Moral Choices*, 15.

19. For some of the earlier works leading up to this topic, see Speiser, "Law and Civilization," 871–76; Goetze, "Mesopotamian Laws and the Historian," 119; and David, *Der Rechtshistoriker und seine Aufgabe*, 13–17.

20. Greenberg, "Postulates," 5–28. For examples of earlier discussions on some aspects of Greenberg's study, see Loewenstam, "Din hano'ef wedin haroẓeaḥ," 55–59; and Weinfeld, "Litefiṣat haḥoḳ beyisrael umeḥuẓah lo," 58–63.

21. Greenberg, "Postulates," 8.

22. See, for example, B. S. Jackson, *Essays in Jewish and Comparative Legal History*, 25–63, where he lists what he understands to be some of the important shortcomings and "serious dangers for the unwary" regarding Greenberg's methodology and general assumptions.

23. Paul, *Studies in the Book of the Covenant*; and Philips, *Ancient Israel's Criminal*

acteristic traits" or "leading features" which distinguish biblical law from the legal culture of the ancient Near East.[24] Their work, in turn, spurred on J. J. Finkelstein to further develop aspects of Greenberg's work. He states, "The Laws of the Bible and the 'Code' of Hammurabi belong to two utterly disparate universes of classification and conceptualization."[25] In the decades to follow, the discourse evolved, taking on a more theological and ethical tone as it transitioned from focusing on "what" to exploring "why" and "who." Scholars not only scrutinized the value and reliability of comparative endeavors, but they also investigated the underlying ethics and intentions associated with the authorities behind the writings. What are the reasons for readers to comply with the author's demands, and to whom precisely are they pledging their allegiance?

While some of the points mentioned above will receive further attention in chapter 5, it is worth briefly elaborating on the notion that the author's character and values significantly influence one's overall comprehension of their respective legal collections. Every writer of law, whether divine or human, embeds their values in their works, albeit in different forms. Disregarding the author's character and motivations thus impairs one's capacity to thoroughly grasp the nuances of their decrees. "The OT laws manifest the justice of their divine lawgiver," states Gane, "just as the ANE collections can demonstrate the justice of the human rulers who sponsored them."[26] One's perspective on the significance of biblical law therefore hinges on whether they accept or reject its distinguishing feature: its divine origin and authority. "Without divine authority, the laws may be good and helpful in many ways, like some other human laws, yet would lack Yhwh's wisdom, and Yhwh would not hold people accountable to them or bless their obedience. Such a toothless Torah can neither bite nor smile."[27] Brueggemann goes a step further, opining that the text is meant to "give a particular account of reality with this God as agent and as character at its center . . . a Holy Character who is given us on the lips of Israel," and any scholarship that refuses to acknowledge this is "'tone deaf' to the voice of the text . . . for when the Holy Character is deleted

---

Law, respectively.

24. Paul, *Studies in the Book of the Covenant*, 25.

25. See Finkelstein, "The Goring Ox," 269. See also Malul, *The Comparative Method*, 68–75 for a discussion on important issues in comparing ancient texts.

26. Gane, *Old Testament Law for Christians*, 127.

27. Gane, *Old Testament Law for Christians*, 21.

from the calculus of meaning, not much that matters remains."[28] Understanding God's character is therefore crucial in examining his value system, how these values are reflected in his laws, and even how they can guide contemporary moral behavior.[29]

C. J. H. Wright, with God's compassionate character in mind, presents three criteria or "scales" with which to better understand the value system present within biblical law in comparison to ANE law. These criteria include: (1) the preservation of life and property, (2) the treatment of peoples and the administration of punishment, and (3) attending to needs and upholding rights. C. J. H. Wright asserts that biblical law consistently prioritizes the first aspect in each category (life, people, and needs), whereas ANE law, being of human authorship, can at times be observed prioritizing the second (property, punishment, and rights).[30] Gane notes: "It seems clear that OT laws were formulated with awareness of ANE legal traditions. However, the Bible presents OT law as promulgated by and carrying authority from the Deity Yhwh, whose distinctive set of values is represented by his commandments. Thus OT law has utilized and thereby affirmed some existing legal concepts that are in harmony with Yhwh's values."[31] Put differently, while biblical law upholds certain existing ANE traditions that align with God's "scale of values," it provides alternative guidance where human laws emphasize different priorities. Moreover, it does this while speaking practically into the time and place of the Israelites, always taking into account the harsh realities of the ancient world.[32] "Doubtless all of these arrangements were vulnerable to abuse," C. Wright concludes, "but the attitude and principle behind them seems clear and important: the law inculcates an ethos in which even the law itself, and the rights and claims it gives to people, yield[s] to the realities of human need."[33]

---

28. Brueggemann, "The Role of Old Testament Theology," 78, 83. For an overview of this topic along with a survey of scholars in opposition to these sentiments, see C. J. H. Wright, *Old Testament Ethics*, 447–54.

29. For an opinion expressing doubts about the fruitfulness of searching for values and principles within biblical law, see Walton and Walton, *The Lost World of the Torah*, 167–82.

30. See C. J. H. Wright, *Old Testament Ethics*, 300–314.

31. Gane, *Old Testament Law for Christians*, 129.

32. Gane, *Old Testament Law for Christians*, 214–18.

33. C. J. H. Wright, *Old Testament Ethics*, 314.

CASE STUDIES IN THE BC

The examination of the BC's debt slave and goring ox laws will be conducted in three stages. The first step will involve an introduction to the case in question, providing necessary definitions and addressing any relevant concerns in order to establish a solid foundation for what comes next. Step two will observe the laws in the BC as they stand before comparing and contrasting them with similar texts from both the Bible and the ANE, all the while following the basic principles of comparison previously discussed in chapter 1.[34] Step three will then offer a theo-ethical overview with the purpose of unpacking how the respective laws from each side (biblical and ANE) may exhibit an inherent and compassionate humanitarian ethic using C. J. H. Wright's proposed "scale of values" as a frame of reference.

The Case of the Debt Slave

Before embarking on a more thorough examination of the debt slave laws in the BC, it is important to unpack the topic of slavery within the context of the ancient world. First, and perhaps most helpful to the outset of this conversation, is the differentiation between slavery in the ANE and the form of slavery prevalent in early American (New World) history. As Averbeck emphasizes, "The type of slavery familiar to New World studies, where entire populations were seized and transported from their native land with the explicit purpose of laboring in another country (or on a different continent), is absent in the ancient Near East, including the Bible."[35] Moreover, systematic ANE slavery was not linked with any kind of racial distinction. By unwittingly projecting New World history into the topic of slavery in the Bible, as some conversations in recent decades have done,[36] it can be easy to overlook important details. For example, the BC provides a way for Israelite slaves to return to their original household (see Exod 21:2–11; cf. Deut 15:12–18), and even non-Israelite slaves were granted certain protections and the possibility of advancing in social status (see Exod 21:20–21, 26–27, 32).[37] More crucially, while the BC

---

34. See Younger, "The 'Contextual Method,'" xl; Averbeck, "Sumer, the Bible, and Comparative Method, 88–125; and Averbeck, "Law," 130–31.

35. Averbeck, "Slavery in the World of the Bible," 423.

36. See Patterson, *Slavery and Social Death*.

37. Averbeck, "Slaves and Servants in Ancient Israel." See also Averbeck, "Slavery in

categorizes a slave as belonging to the master as property (Exod 21:21), it consistently endeavors to uphold their dignity as a fellow human being. In doing so, it puts forward an implicit challenge with which the covenant reader must grapple: Does the human institution of slavery align with and reflect the character of God?

Second, it is essential to clarify certain commonly used terms, namely the Hebrew word for "male slave/servant" (עֶבֶד) along with the various categories of slaves that existed in the ancient world.[38] With regard to the former, עֶבֶד has a very wide range of meanings in the OT, causing its usage to feel unclear at times. At its most broad, it can simply mean "worker," a term that even applied to Pharaoh's government officials (Gen 41:38). It is also occasionally used in titles; Moses, for example, is called the "servant [עֶבֶד] of the LORD," as is Israel (Isa 41:8–9).[39] More specifically, עֶבֶד can refer to a person who sold himself into slavery to a creditor to pay off a debt or to a person who was acquired to be a slave (more on this below). C. Wright sums up well the translational difficulties that accompany this Hebrew word:

> The trouble is that our polite English word "servant" does not quite say enough, since servants are not necessarily in bondage, lacking legal freedom. But our English word "slave" says too much, since it carries the whiff of the appalling history of African slavery and, indeed, of modern human trafficking and slave labor still rampant all over the world. We should remove such pictures from our minds when considering what it meant to be an 'ebed [עֶבֶד] in Israel.[40]

While there seems to be several differing statuses among עֲבָדִים in the ancient world,[41] there are ultimately two types of slaves outlined in the OT: debt slaves and chattel slaves. In short, "debt slave" (as the name implies) refers to an individual who became a slave in order to cover family debt. This status was largely temporary pending the repayment of the debt,

---

the World of the Bible," 424–29.

38. There are distinctions to be made between male slaves (עֶבֶד) and female slaves (אָמָה) in the BC. Such differences will be further discussed in the pages to follow as they relate to the laws themselves.

39. C. J. H. Wright, *Exodus*, 395.

40. C. J. H. Wright, *Exodus*, 395.

41. For more on this, see Lemche, "Ancient Near East and Hebrew Bible," 303, where he offers up a general definition for the Hebrew meaning of "slave/servant" regardless of the specific circumstances at play: "Technically speaking, the term 'slaves' referred to persons without freedom who were subjected to masters."

the coming of the year of release (Exod 21:2), or the decision of the debt slave to remain in servitude (Exod 21:5–6). Chattel slavery, on the other hand, was a more permanent status exclusive to non-Israelites who were purchased via the slave trade, inherited from family, or taken through warfare (Lev 25:44–46).[42] Even though the same term is used for both of these types of slaves in the BC, they can usually be discerned in their respective contexts using these qualifications.[43] This study understands the topic of debt slavery to be treated in Exod 21:2–11 while more general rules regarding the handling of slaves, including chattel slaves, can be seen in Exod 21:20–21, 26–27, 32.[44]

Finally, and perhaps most relevant to the current issue, is the conflict between the supposed compassion of God and the persistence of slavery in Israelite society. The opening line of the BC, "When you acquire a Hebrew slave . . ." (Exod 21:2), is immediately jarring to contemporary sensibilities. How could Yhwh, a God known for his compassion (Exod 22:26 [27]), appear to endorse the ownership of another human being in any form?[45] It is undeniable that slavery in the ancient world, even within ancient Israel, could be characterized as harsh, dehumanizing, and lacking in full human dignity.[46] Even the most optimistic interpretation is faced with the reality that the God of the Bible permitted his people to be "unfree" in certain circumstances and for certain durations.

According to Averbeck, the confusion often brought about by the juxtaposition of slavery with the reality of God stems from a misunderstanding of the purpose and function of the OT laws. He states, "The biblical provisions are not designed to provide for an ideal society, but rather to provide wisdom for Israel to live in covenant relationship to Yahweh in their time and place. The Old Testament law has fine ideals within it, but the regulations discussed here, and many others, are meant to apply these ideals in realistic ways in the world of ancient Israel."[47] In

---

42. Averbeck, "Slavery in the World of the Bible," 424–25. See also Westbrook, "Slave and Master," 162–65; Chirichigno, *Debt-Slavery*, 30; Williams, "'Slaves' in Biblical Narrative and Translation."

43. According to Averbeck, the same cannot always be said of the types of slaves referred to in other ANE legal collections (Akkadian *ardu*) since such qualifications are oftentimes absent (Averbeck, "Slavery in the World of the Bible," 428).

44. Averbeck, "Slavery in the World of the Bible," 429.

45. See Noll, "Battle for the Bible," 20–25, for a conversation on how the church has historically used the Bible's slave laws to justify owning slaves in modern times.

46. Averbeck, "Slavery in the World of the Bible," 430.

47. Averbeck, "Slavery in the World of the Bible," 430.

other words, the laws regarding slavery do not aim to depict an ideal way of life; they instruct the covenant reader on how to embody God's compassion within an already established (and undesirable) system. Morrow elaborates further, stating that biblical law possesses a unique plan of action which is meant to "make readers uneasy about the ethics of slave-owning." He goes on to explain, "these laws represent an early strategy for raising readers' conscience about the institution of slavery and (implicitly) calling it into question. Overall, their tactics reflect an ethic of concern for the vulnerable, a major theme in the Torah."[48] As previous chapters demonstrated, even the most perplexing decrees are to be read in light of the laws which call covenant readers to empathize with the less fortunate (Exod 23:9) and to fear taking advantage of the compassion that was shown to them (cp. Exod 3:7–8 with 22:22–23).

Exodus 21 is typically regarded as housing a strong emphasis on the value of human life.[49] For this reason, amongst others already discussed in previous chapters, it only makes sense that its initial focus centers on the case of the debt slave. "This group is certainly one of the most vulnerable of the society," states Van Wijk-Bos, "There is in the entire Bible not a word uttered against the principle of slavery as an institution . . . Yet, we note the significance of the primary place of this particular set of laws, extending at least a measure to this vulnerable group mitigating the evil effects of the practice."[50] The debt slave laws in the BC, outlined in Exod 21:2–11, are categorized into two distinct sections. Verses 2–6 specifically deal with the conditions of male slaves, while vv. 7–11 are applicable to female slaves. These laws are detailed as follows:

Exod 21:2–6

כִּי תִקְנֶה עֶבֶד עִבְרִי שֵׁשׁ שָׁנִים יַעֲבֹד וּבַשְּׁבִעִת יֵצֵא לַחָפְשִׁי חִנָּם אִם־בְּגַפּוֹ
יָבֹא בְּגַפּוֹ יֵצֵא אִם־בַּעַל אִשָּׁה הוּא וְיָצְאָה אִשְׁתּוֹ עִמּוֹ אִם־אֲדֹנָיו יִתֶּן־לוֹ
אִשָּׁה וְיָלְדָה־לּוֹ בָנִים אוֹ בָנוֹת הָאִשָּׁה וִילָדֶיהָ תִּהְיֶה לַאדֹנֶיהָ וְהוּא יֵצֵא בְגַפּוֹ
וְאִם־אָמֹר יֹאמַר הָעֶבֶד אָהַבְתִּי אֶת־אֲדֹנִי אֶת־אִשְׁתִּי וְאֶת־בָּנָי לֹא אֵצֵא
חָפְשִׁי וְהִגִּישׁוֹ אֲדֹנָיו אֶל־הָאֱלֹהִים וְהִגִּישׁוֹ אֶל־הַדֶּלֶת אוֹ אֶל־הַמְּזוּזָה וְרָצַע
אֲדֹנָיו אֶת־אָזְנוֹ בַּמַּרְצֵעַ וַעֲבָדוֹ לְעֹלָם

(2) When you buy a Hebrew slave, he shall serve[51] for six years; then, in the seventh, he shall go out as a free man without paying

---

48. Morrow, *An Introduction to Biblical Law*, 98.
49. Garrett, *A Commentary on Exodus*, 495.
50. Van Wijk-Bos, *Making Wise the Simple*, 181–82.
51. Several other documents expand "serve" to "serve you." Despite this, the

anything. (3) If he comes in single, he shall go out single; but if he comes in married, then his wife shall go out with him. (4) If his master gives him a wife and she bears him sons or daughters, the wife and her children belong to her master, and the man must leave alone. (5) But if the slave declares, "I love my master and my wife and my children and do not want to go free," then his master must take him before the judges. He shall be brought to the door or the doorpost; and his master shall pierce his ear with an awl; and he shall serve him forever.

Exod 21:7–11

וְכִי־יִמְכֹּר אִישׁ אֶת־בִּתּוֹ לְאָמָה לֹא תֵצֵא כְּצֵאת הָעֲבָדִים אִם־רָעָה בְּעֵינֵי
אֲדֹנֶיהָ אֲשֶׁר [לֹא] (לוֹ) יְעָדָהּ וְהֶפְדָּהּ לְעַם נָכְרִי לֹא־יִמְשֹׁל לְמָכְרָהּ בְּבִגְדוֹ־
בָהּ וְאִם־לִבְנוֹ יִיעָדֶנָּה כְּמִשְׁפַּט הַבָּנוֹת יַעֲשֶׂה־לָּהּ אִם־אַחֶרֶת יִקַּח־לוֹ
שְׁאֵרָהּ כְּסוּתָהּ וְעֹנָתָהּ לֹא יִגְרָע וְאִם־שְׁלָשׁ־אֵלֶּה לֹא יַעֲשֶׂה לָהּ וְיָצְאָה חִנָּם
אֵין כָּסֶף

(7) When a man sells his daughter as a slave, she is not to go out like male servants do. (8) If she does not please her master, who designated her for himself,[52] then he shall let her be redeemed; he shall have no right to sell her to foreigners because he has broken faith with her. (9) If he designates her for his son, he must treat her with the same rights as a daughter. (10) If he takes another wife for himself, he must not deprive the first one of her food, clothing, and marital rights. (11) If he does not do these three things for her, then she is to go out for free, without any payment of money.

---

translation offered here favors the shorter reading presented by the MT. This logic also applies to v. 4 ("if" rather than "and if"), but not to v. 5 ("But if" rather than "if") since the *waw* in this case is likely serving a larger syntactical role (discussed later on) and since there is only 1 other text containing this variant.

52. The *ketiv-kere* presented here (לֹא to לוֹ) has been the source of lengthy debate. If translated as-is, the text would read as, "did not designate for her." With the suggested correction, it would instead read as, "who designated her for himself." Propp adds: "The textual situation here is far more complex than the BHS [Biblia Hebraica Stuttgartensia] suggest. Some Versions read *lō(')* 'not'; other read *lô* 'for himself' (thus generating contradictory interpretations); some read *y'dh*; others read *h(w)'dh*. All four possible combinations may be attested" (see Propp, *Exodus 19–40*, 119, along with his extensive notes on this topic). Contra to Propp, the translation here rules in favor of the ketiv-qere since this interpretation appears to make the most logical sense.

The Male Debt Slave in Exod 21:2–6

All of the laws found within Exod 21:2–6 are to be read with the opening conditional clause in mind, "When you buy a Hebrew slave" (כִּי תִקְנֶה עֶבֶד עִבְרִי). Having already introduced some of the complexities surrounding the Hebrew word for "male slave" (עֶבֶד), it is only appropriate to ponder the significance of the inclusion of the word "Hebrew" (עִבְרִי). The presence of this term in the introduction of the debt slave laws is particularly noticeable when compared to how the people are described in other significant parts of Exodus. For instance, the opening line of the book (Exod 1:1) as well as the mention at the proposal of the Mosaic covenant (Exod 19:6) both label them as the "children of Israel" (בְּנֵי יִשְׂרָאֵל). According to C. J. H. Wright, while these two addresses can oftentimes be interchanged, they are far from being synonymous, stating that the word "Hebrew" tends to have a "derogatory ring."[53] Supporting this take is the increased use of the term in Exodus during the oppression of the Israelites in Egypt as well as when they were under the control of the Philistines. More on the nose, however, is the moment in which Potiphar's wife condemns Joseph as "that Hebrew slave" (Gen 39:17).[54] "So even if Hebrews were ethnic Israelites," he concludes, "when Israelites get called 'Hebrews,' it usually implies a lowly status, in a state of despised oppression."[55] Such a statement is likely meant to promote a feeling of solidarity with the newly bought slave given the history of the Hebrew people, including the slave owner.[56]

It is also worth briefly noting here the connection that some scholars have made concerning the word "עִבְרִי" with another (Akkadian) word used the describe a lower class of people who make an appearance in several ANE documents: the *habiru/hapiru*. In short, the term *habiru* "seems to describe landless and somewhat migrant groups who lived by selling their labor into various 'markets.' Sometimes they appear as mercenary soldiers. Sometimes as troublemakers in the realm. Sometimes as slaves."[57] Aside from the similarities in pronunciation, this description

---

53. C. J. H. Wright, *Exodus*, 396. See also Na'aman, "Ḥabiru and Hebrews," 271–88.

54. Na'aman, "Ḥabiru and Hebrews," 271–88.

55. Na'aman, "Ḥabiru and Hebrews," 271–88. See also Garrett, *A Commentary on Exodus*, 496.

56. For a conversation on how the Israelites ideally should not possess slaves at all given their time as slaves in Egypt, see Phillips, "The Laws of Slavery," 51–56.

57. C. J. H. Wright, *Exodus*, 396.

lends itself well to the Hebrew people prior to the exodus event, causing some to believe that the term *habiru* is indeed a direct reference to the Hebrew people.[58] Others, however, have pointed out that this is unlikely using a variety of methods like comparative linguistics,[59] cultural and economic analysis,[60] and comparisons of Exod 21:2 with Deut 15:12.[61] C. Wright adopts a neutral stance, claiming that the point is to handle the slave with an "unprecedented dignity" regardless of their origin. "The subject of the instructions in Exodus 21:2–6 may have been a non-Israelite 'Hebrew'—*hapiru*—who had been 'acquired,'" he explains, "or he may have been an Israelite who had descended to such a level of impoverished dependency that he could be labeled a 'Hebrew' as a description of his parlous socioeconomic status."[62] While there is ethical merit to C. Wright's stance, Exod 21, in particular, seems to be referring to fellow Israelites (cf. "brother" in Deut 15:12 and Lev 25:39).

Exod 21:2–6 ultimately seeks to answer three questions: (1) how long should a Hebrew slave remain in servitude; (2) what becomes of his family when his time in servitude ends, if he has one; and (3) what exceptions might there be to the above questions?[63] The first question is answered in v. 2 directly following the opening conditional clause, "When you buy a Hebrew slave," and plainly states that "he shall serve for six years; then, in the seventh, he shall go out as a free man without paying anything." As discussed in previous chapters, this verse contains both theological and historical import. It is theological in that it utilizes the 6/7 motif, thereby commemorating God's act of rest following his six days of labor and promoting the imitation of this cycle as an act of worship.[64] It is historical in that the slave's "going out" (יצא) is reminiscent of God "bringing the Hebrew people out" (יצא) of bondage from the land of Egypt (Exod 6:6).[65] Adding to these layers of significance is the

58. See, for example, C. J. H. Wright, *God's People in God's Land*, 253–59.

59. See, for example, Hess, "Alalakh Studies in the Bible," 205–8.

60. See D. P. Wright, *Inventing God's Law*, 125–26.

61. See Averbeck, "The Egyptian Sojourn," 154–55.

62. C. J. H. Wright, *Exodus*, 396–97. For helpful overviews of this topic in more detail, see Sprinkle, 'The Book of the Covenant,' 62–64; and Chirichigno, *Debt-Slavery*, 200–206.

63. Garrett, *A Commentary on Exodus*, 496.

64. Gane, *Old Testament Law for Christians*, 250.

65. C. J. H. Wright, *Exodus*, 394. See also Paul, *Studies in the Book of the Covenant*, 47–48, where he describes the Hebrew verb "to go out" as being a legal term for the release from slave status.

implementation of what some term the "sabbatical principle" within the slave's employment agreement. Regardless of the magnitude of the slave's debt or the harshness of his master, there was a limit to his servitude. His freedom was assured in due course.[66]

Following the "sabbatical principle" outlined in Exod 21:2 are four qualifying possibilities (vv. 3a, 3b, 4, and 5).[67] Each begins with "if" (אִם) and aims to address the remaining two questions outlined above, starting with the frequently misunderstood situation concerning the slave's family in the event of his release. Verse 3 introduces the topic in a straightforward fashion: if an עֶבֶד entered into debt servitude single, then he goes free single; if he entered while married, then his wife goes free with him at the time of his release. These seemingly reasonable stipulations are further limited, however, by the more detailed conditions included in the following verse. If an עֶבֶד entered into debt servitude single, but then he later receives a wife from his master, then he still goes free single, leaving his wife behind. Moreover, if they had children during his time in servitude, they remain behind as well.

These regulations may appear inequitable by contemporary standards, even appearing to conflict with the significance the Torah assigns to marriage in other passages (e.g., Gen 2:24). Does the BC truly prioritize economic concerns like sustaining a workforce and safeguarding property over the institution of marriage? Initially, it might seem so; but before drawing such a conclusion, there are several aspects that warrant consideration. As C. J. H. Wright notes, the master may well have made a considerable financial investment in providing the wife, especially if a dowry was involved, that he would be reluctant to have walk out the door.[68] Crüsemann adds that while the debt slave laws were largely meant to protect the well-being of the more vulnerable party (the slave), it also considered fairness unto the master. He states, "The slave laws of the Mishpatim [the BC] mediated between the interests of the ones who purchased or owned the slave and those of the slaves and their families. They placed boundaries on both sides of the law."[69] Garrett, in portraying

---

66. C. J. H. Wright, *Exodus*, 397.

67. For more on the sabbatical principle, see Cardellini, *Die biblischen "Sklaven"-Gesetze*, 245n21; Sprinkle, '*The Book of the Covenant*,' 200; C. J. H. Wright, *Exodus*, 397; and chapter 3 of this volume.

68. C. J. H. Wright, *Exodus*, 397.

69. Crüsemann, *The Torah*, 158. See also Averbeck, *The Old Testament Law for the Life of the Church*, 151; and Alexander, *Exodus*, 474, where he points out, "A slave who wished to ensure his own freedom and that of his wife and family could always

the generosity of the lawgiver, interestingly puts forward the idea that "the law only stipulated the slave's rights; it did not imply that the owner was obligated to separate the family; he might go beyond the demands of the law and free the wife as well."[70] The above considerations are no doubt helpful, but more immediate are the distinctive and unprecedented exceptions found in the next two verses.

In Exod 21:5–6, provisions are made for a ceremony that may occur if a slave (and not his master) requests it upon being released. If he expresses "love" for his master, wife, and children, and decides not to leave, then his master must bring him before הָאֱלֹהִים and perform an ear-piercing ritual at the doorpost, signifying that he will serve his master for life (21:6b).[71] This declaration of "love" is unique to biblical law and, according to C. J. H. Wright, gives remarkable insight regarding the nature of Israelite debt slavery, especially given the addition in Deut 15:16 that "he [the slave] is well off with you [the master]." He states, "The servant is taking up this option because he recognizes it is in the long-term good interest of himself and his family to stay and work in this household—something that further helps us understand that 'slavery' in ancient Israel was not the horror that it has been and still is in other contexts."[72] This forever bond was ceremonially cemented through a piercing of the slave's ear—a type of "receipt" that prevented either side from later making false claims regarding the relationship.[73]

The Female Debt Slave in Exod 21:7–11

Like the Hebrew term for "male slave," the word for "female slave" (אָמָה) is seen as having a range of meanings. Within this context, an אָמָה could be seen as something in between a mere female slave and a normal wife.[74]

---

postpone marriage until after his release in the seventh year."

70. Garrett, *A Commentary on Exodus*, 497. The idea of "going beyond the demands of the law" is more explicitly present in the goring ox laws and will be discussed later on in this chapter.

71. There is some dispute concerning the translation of הָאֱלֹהִים in this instance. Some translate it as "before God" while others translate it as "before the judges" (see the NIV). For arguments for the former, see Falk, "Exodus XXI:6," 86–88; and Viberg, *Symbols of Law*, 77–87. For an explanation of the latter, see C. J. H. Wright, *Exodus*, 398.

72. C. J. H. Wright, *Exodus*, 398.

73. Cf. LH §282.

74. The term אָמָה is often compared with the Hebrew word שִׁפְחָה which bears a very similar range of meanings. Many consider these two to be interchangeable, though

She bears the status of "servant," but she has been acquired, or will be assigned, as a sexual partner within the person's household (21:7a).[75] Some go as far as to use the term "concubine,"[76] but there are a few issues to note with this perspective. First, employing this term might imply a scenario involving multiple sexual partners in a harem-like setting; there is no reason to believe this is the case in this context.[77] Moreover, according to Averbeck, the possibility of becoming a "daughter" (21:9), along with the inclusion of marital language in v. 10 (אִם־אַחֶרֶת יִקַּח־לוֹ), indicates that she is indeed taking on the role of someone's legal wife.[78] Such will be the assumption moving forward.

Verse 7 introduces the case of the female slave through a comparison with the rights of the male slave: "She is not to go out [יצא] like male servants do." While this may seem unfair, it is very likely that this stipulation is to protect the female slave from adopting the life of a widow or divorced wife. "A woman who was purchased ... and cast off would be wretched indeed," states Garrett, "Her owner/husband would have 'broken faith' with her."[79] Like in the case of the male debt slave, however, the following verses outline further possibilities and exceptions to this overarching principle with the express purpose of protecting her from abuse. What if the purchaser changes his mind? What if he takes another אָמָה for himself? What if he ends up being incompetent or spiteful? The BC does not leave matters like these up to speculation.

Verse 8 handles what was likely the largest concern for an אָמָה: what if her buyer is not pleased with his purchase? Is she to be discarded or left without autonomy? According to the BC, the only recourse is for the buyer to let her be redeemed, most likely by her own family, since selling her to a foreigner would further objectify her and could promote the practice

---

the former seems to be more legal or formal in nature while the latter may be more informal or referring to a lower class (e.g., Ruth 2:13 and 1 Sam 25:41). For more on this, see Marsman, *Women in Ugarit and Israel*, 447–49. See also the discussion in Younger, "Two Comparative Notes on the Book of Ruth," 126–27.

75. C. J. H. Wright, *Exodus*, 399. See also Pressler, "Wives and Daughters, Bond and Free," 162.

76. See, for example, Westbrook, "The Female Slave," 149–74.

77. C. J. H. Wright, *Exodus*, 399.

78. Averbeck, "Slavery in the World of the Bible," 427. Here, Averbeck notes that the verb "takes," when combined with "another woman" is the usual verb for marriage. See also B. S. Jackson, *Studies in the Semiotics of Biblical Law*, 193–97.

79. Garrett, *A Commentary on Exodus*, 498.

of sex trafficking.⁸⁰ The concluding motive clause, בְּבִגְדוֹ־בָהּ "because he has broken faith with her," only reinforces this understanding by speaking of their relationship in marital terms.⁸¹ Key to this interpretation is the Hebrew verb בגד, about which Erlandsson states, "The verb expresses the unstable relationship of man to an existing established regulation and can be translated 'to act faithlessly (treacherously).' It is used when the OT writer wants to say that a man does not honor an agreement, or commits adultery, or breaks a covenant or some other ordinance by God."⁸² Like in the male debt slave laws, the institution of marriage is to never be devalued, even within the unideal reality of slave ownership.

Further protections are offered up in v. 9: if the owner selects her for his son, he must treat her with the same rights as a daughter (כְּמִשְׁפַּט הַבָּנוֹת יַעֲשֶׂה־לָּהּ). There is some discussion about whether this verse is connected to the consequences outlined in v. 8. For example, it could signify that if her family does not redeem her, she is to be given to a son of the purchaser,⁸³ or it might refer to a distinct circumstance. In any case, the intention of this verse is to ensure the well-being and status of a woman acquired for marriage to a son. She is not treated as a "slave" in this context.⁸⁴ Paul adds that the legal ramifications of being granted the "rights of a daughter" lead to being henceforth treated as a free(-born) woman.⁸⁵

Finally, vv. 10–11 offer guidelines for if the purchaser decides to acquire another servant-wife (אִם־אַחֶרֶת יִקַּח־לוֹ). In this case, "he must not deprive the first one of her food, clothing, and marital rights" (21:10).⁸⁶ Should he fail to provide "these three things,"⁸⁷ then she is to "go out

---

80. C. J. H. Wright, *Exodus*, 499.

81. For the opinion that other (Israelite) parties could also redeem her, see Philips, "The Laws of Slavery," 51–66.

82. Erlandsson, "בגד." See also Paul, *Studies in the Book of the Covenant*, 54, for an explanation that this verb signifies a breach of contract with the woman's father, a view which, according to Chirichigno, is not at odds with Erlandsson's (*Debt-Slavery*, 250).

83. See, for example, the argument put forward in Noth, *Exodus*, 179.

84. Dozeman, *Exodus*, 530.

85. Paul, *Studies in the Book of the Covenant*, 55.

86. The translations of these three provisions are often disputed (Hebrew שְׁאֵרָהּ כְּסוּתָהּ וְעֹנָתָהּ, respectively). For an overview of this topic, see Chirichigno, *Debt-Slavery*, 252.

87. The "three things" in this verse could be referring to either the "food, clothing, and marital rights" mentioned in the previous verse (or "food, clothing, and oil" as some speculate) or the three previous conditions in vv. 8–10 (Dozeman, *Exodus*, 531; C. J. H. Wright, *Exodus*, 399).

[יצא] for free, without any payment of money" (21:11). "This is a remarkable statement of rights," states C. J. H. Wright, "since it indicates that the woman—even in her reduced status as a servant—could appeal to her family or to the elders in the community to intervene on her behalf and enforce her freedom from such an uncaring master."[88] Additionally, this closing condition repeats the principle brought up at the outset of the debt slave laws in v. 2, suggesting an intentional literary design in the arrangement of the two subsections of laws in 21:2–6 and 7–11. The entire account of the debt slave laws in the BC, then, begins and ends with the motif of freedom—a fitting emphasis with respect to the broader story in Exodus.[89]

Comparative Studies of Biblical Debt Slave Laws

In addition to those outlined in the BC, laws concerning debt slavery can also be found in Deut 15:12–18 and Lev 25:39–43. While it is true that each of these passages possess certain similarities and differences with one another (which is to be expected in parallel texts), some contend that the regulations across all of these accounts lack practical consistency or contain glaring contradictions.[90] This section will briefly touch upon some of these major claims, arguing instead for the idea that the debt slave laws of Deuteronomy and Leviticus not only operate harmoniously with those of the BC, but they also contribute additional layers of insight into the Torah's overarching humanitarian enterprise.

Exod 21 and Deut 15

Exod 21:2–11 and Deut 15:12–18 contain several similarities. For example, both passages specifically deal with the case of a native Hebrew, utilize the 6/7 motif, and make provisions for slaves who desire to stay with their masters permanently.[91] Some of the more notable differences

---

88. C. J. H. Wright, *Exodus*, 399–400.

89. See Chirichigno, *Debt-Slavery*, 352–54; Sprinkle, *'The Book of the Covenant,'* 54; and Dozeman, *Exodus*, 531.

90. See, for example, some of the ideas put forward in the reputable works of Carmichael, "The Three Laws on the Release of Slaves," 515–18; von Rad, *Deuteronomy*, 107; Levinson, "The Manumission of Hermeneutics," 301–22; Lundbom, *Deuteronomy*, 494; and Stackert, *Rewriting the Torah*, 141–64.

91. Averbeck, *The Old Testament Law for the Life of the Church*, 150–51.

include the consideration of female debt slaves as opposed to male, the usage of varying motivational elements, and the specifics of how to care for a released slave.[92] When noting such differences, it is important to remember that legal collections within the Torah may contain different "textual terrains," meaning that some passages have a tendency to highlight certain details or perspectives that others simply do not address. Such differences are important to a more complete picture of the legal and cultural phenomena.[93]

At first glance, the accounts in Exod 21 and Deut 15 seem to handle the release of female debt slaves differently. The former makes provisions for her release in the event of abuse (21:11) but otherwise enforces an indefinite servitude (21:7). The latter equates the female debt slave's term with that of the male's: "If any of your people—Hebrew *men or women*— sell themselves to you and serve you for six years, in the seventh year you must let them go free" (Deut 15:12, emphasis added; cf. Exod 21:2). Could it be that Deuteronomy made adjustments to the debt slave regulations since the giving of the laws at Sinai?[94] According to Averbeck, this is simply not the case since the account in Deuteronomy is likely referring to a completely different situation. "Exodus 21:7–11 refers specifically to a daughter of another family that is indebted to a creditor," he explains, "Deuteronomy, on the other hand, makes it clear that if a woman debt slave was not slated to be a wife when she entered into debt slavery, then she would go out free in the seventh year just like any male slave. The two passages are not contradictory."[95] Deut 15:12 is therefore not abrogating or altering the release laws in the BC; it is simply approaching the same issue of debt slavery from a different angle.[96]

The account in Deuteronomy is also much more specific regarding the welfare of the released debt slave, stating, "When you [the master] release them, do not send them away empty-handed.[97] Supply them lib-

---

92. Averbeck, *The Old Testament Law for the Life of the Church*, 151–53.

93. See Averbeck, "The Egyptian Sojourn," 163–66.

94. See the works of von Rad, Lundbom, and Levinson noted above for arguments in favor of this viewpoint. See also the helpful overview in Chirichigno, *Debt-Slavery*, 279–81.

95. Averbeck, *The Old Testament Law for the Life of the Church*, 152–53.

96. For more on this, see Tigay, *Deuteronomy*, 148–49, 466; Boecker, *Law and the Administration of Justice*, 181–82; and Philips, "The Laws of Slavery," 56.

97. The expression "empty-handed" (Hebrew ריקם) is used elsewhere in the Torah in moments of humanitarian concern. See, for example, Gen 31:42; Exod 3:21; 23:15; 34:20; and Deut 16:16.

erally from your flock, your threshing floor, and your winepress. Give to them as the LORD your God has blessed you" (15:13–14; cf. Gen 21:19–20). The incorporation of these provisions should not be viewed as unexpected or contradictory. As previously discussed in chapter 2, the laws in Deuteronomy display more explicit ethical considerations compared to those in the BC.[98] This serves to underscore the importance of upholding the dignity and autonomy of the debt slave, a concern reinforced by the reminder in the subsequent verse: "Remember that you were slaves in Egypt and the LORD your God redeemed you. That is why I give you this command today."[99] Both of the motivational elements thus far (Deut 15:14b and 15) maintain a heightened importance on imitating God's actions toward the Hebrew people in their treatment of the more vulnerable parties under them. Just as God is a חַנּוּן master to his עֲבָדִים and אָמָהֹת, so should his covenant readers aspire to be (Jer 34:8–17).

Exod 21 and Lev 25

Lev 25 represents what seems to be an even greater departure from the debt slave laws of the BC than those in Deuteronomy in that it sidesteps the 6/7 motif altogether. Rather than adhering to the law of release on the seventh year of work (Exod 21:2 and Deut 15:12), Lev 25:39–43 enforces release only on the Year of Jubilee (see Lev 25:8–38), meaning that a Hebrew debt slave could theoretically work for up to 49 years. Many take this to mean that the debt slave laws in Leviticus subvert the ones in the BC.[100] While it is true that debt slaves—or rather, "debt servants/residents" in this case, according to Lev 25:40—could indeed work for that length of time, these regulations were primarily for debt slaves who were further established than the ones detailed in Exodus and Deuteronomy. Averbeck clarifies: "Exodus 21 and Leviticus 25 are actually referring to two different categories of debt slavery: one who enters debt slavery single or married but without children (Ex 21:2–3), as opposed to one who enters debt slavery married with children (Lev 25:39–43; note esp.

---

98. See Otto, "Ethics," 276; and Morrow, *An Introduction to Biblical Law*, 98.

99. Averbeck, *The Old Testament Law for the Life of the Church*, 153.

100. See, for example, Tigay, *Deuteronomy*, 466–67; along with the survey of scholarship offered up in Chirichigno, *Debt-Slavery*, 335n1.

Lev 25:41). The latter is the head of a family who enters slavery at a point of destitution."[101]

Such destitution was often marked by the forfeiture of one's land in an attempt to settle their debts, an issue of special concern within Lev 25's debt slave regulations.[102] According to these laws, during the Year of Jubilee, all land allocations were to be returned to the original families who inherited them from their ancestors during the conquest and settlement of Israel. These regulations anticipated this event (see 25:40b–41), as it would not make much sense to release a slave and their family if they had no home or land to return to.[103] The situation of the master is also taken into account. As the one responsible for looking after family affairs and overseeing debt forgiveness, there would be little incentive to assume such a financial responsibility if the time period was limited to six years.[104] Again, the debt slave laws within the Torah are without contradiction—they simply refer to distinct situations and highlight independent humanitarian concerns.[105]

Comparative Studies of ANE Debt Slave Laws

According to Dandamayev, "The institution of slavery had a profound influence on the social structure, ideology, law, social psychology, morals and ethics of the various cultures of the ANE."[106] This much is evidenced by the sheer quantity of laws pertaining to the treatment and handling of slaves within the ancient world. For example, in addition to the slave regulations that some have identified from Nuzi,[107] "slave laws" can be identified in LU §§4–5, 17, 25–26; LL §§12–14, 25–26; LE §§16, 22–23,

---

101. Averbeck, *The Old Testament Law for the Life of the Church*, 154–55.

102. Chirichigno, *Debt-Slavery*, 355; Averbeck, *The Old Testament Law for the Life of the Church*, 154–55; Bellefontaine, "Study of Ancient Israelite Laws," 181; and Schenker, "The Biblical Legislation on the Release of Slaves," 23–41.

103. Averbeck, *The Old Testament Law for the Life of the Church*, 154–55.

104. Averbeck, *The Old Testament Law for the Life of the Church*, 155. For more on this concern elsewhere in the ANE, see Hallo, "Slave Release," 88–93.

105. Tigay notes, for example, that "Leviticus 25 represents a system for the relief of the poverty that is independent of the one in Exodus and Deuteronomy" (*Deuteronomy*, 466–67).

106. Dandamayev, "Slavery (ANE), (OT)," 58–65, quote 61.

107. For more on this topic, see Paul, *Studies in the Book of the Covenant*, 45–61; Lemche, "'The Hebrew Slave,'" 129–44; and Chirichigno, *Debt-Slavery*, 92–100, 200–218, 244–54.

31, 34–35, 40, 49–52, 55, 57; LH §§7, 15–20, 32, 116–119, 170–171, 175–176, 196–205, 209–223, 226–227, 252, 278–282; HL §§1, 3, 8, 12, 14, 16, 18, 20–24, 31–36, 52, 95, 97, 99, 194, 196; MAL A.4, 39, 41, 44, 48; MAL C+G.1–3, 7, 9; and NBL §6. The prospect of incorporating a list this lengthy into a study on the BC's debt slave regulations is nothing short of daunting. As the following pages will discuss, however, such an approach would likely complicate rather than enhance a comprehensive understanding of debt slavery in ancient times. While topical "slave laws" are abundant, parallels to "debt slave laws" are less so.

How does one go about determining which laws are appropriate for comparison? On one hand, each slave law likely provides some level of insight that could prove beneficial in exegetical endeavors. Dozeman states, for example, that all of the slave laws in the ANE "provide a broader vantage point for interpreting the role of the slave laws in the structure of the Book of the Covenant. The frequent comparison to Mesopotamian law in the exegesis of Exod 21:2–11 indicates the common culture of the legal tradition regulating slavery in the ancient Near East."[108] On the other hand, "Some connections are closer than others, and the degree of closeness that each [law] possesses must be identified and distinguished from other degrees of closeness."[109] As such, this study will aim to identify ANE laws which most closely correspond to Exod 21:2–11 for a more direct and succinct comparison while simultaneously remaining open to other laws which could provide additional understanding. "The ancient Near Eastern context and situation may not correspond precisely to biblical debt slavery," states Averbeck, "but may offer useful comparative information in spite of that fact."[110]

Wells provides several reputable metrics to discern levels of similarity between biblical and ANE laws, the most straightforward of which includes considering the "principle types of connections that biblical law appears to share with the ancient Near Eastern practice of law."[111] He goes on to explain that "three types present themselves most clearly: similar legal issues, similar legal reasoning, and similar legal remedies."[112] Upon scrutinizing the extent to which these "connections" can be discerned

---

108. Dozeman, *Exodus*, 525.
109. Wells, "The Covenant Code," 90. See also Malul, *The Comparative Method*, 68–75 for a discussion on some of the complications that arise in comparing select laws.
110. Averbeck, "Slavery in the World of the Bible," 425.
111. Wells, "What is Biblical Law?," 232.
112. Wells, "What is Biblical Law?," 232.

and the depth of their shared elements, one can categorize the relationship between a specific biblical law and its counterpart in the ANE on what Wells calls the "continuum of degrees of closeness." This continuum encompasses four levels, progressing from the lowest to the highest: resemblances, similarities, correspondences, and points of identicalness.[113] The more numerous and strong the connections between laws, the higher on the continuum their relationship climbs.

Some have posited that even if two laws are phrased in an identical manner, they may still not be directly comparable. This perspective is largely rooted in the perceived purpose and context of the legal collection to which each law belongs. For instance, the laws of the BC are situated within a canonized and religious framework, while those in the LH seemingly originate from juridical circles.[114] To be clear, it is vital to take into account the legal thoughts, expressions, values, and interests that the laws of ANE collections promoted and protected, especially with respect to their application and the way they reflect the identities of their respective authors, but these considerations should not be a deterrent to conducting fruitful legal comparisons.[115] Finkelstein offers up three principles to aid in such endeavors. Comparisons should (1) remain neutral regarding the degree of "reality" represented by the laws in question, (2) disregard the issue of enforcement, and (3) avoid deliberations with respect to the actual purpose and function of the laws in their original social and historical contexts. The overall concern should center on conceptual framework and standard of morality implied in the normative prescriptions which these law collections explicitly set out.[116]

With the above in mind, scholars have largely understood the closest cuneiform laws to those of the debt slave laws in the BC to include LU §4 and LH §117.[117] Wells, for example, considers both to at least contain

113. Wells, "The Covenant Code," 90–91.

114. For more commentary on this view, see Hallo et al., *Scripture in Context II*, 3; Westbrook, "Biblical and Cuneiform Law Codes," 247–64; and Malul, *The Comparative Method*, 70–71n80.

115. See, for example, Paul, *Studies in the Book of the Covenant*; Malul, *The Comparative Method*, 70; and esp. Tsai, *Human Rights in Deuteronomy*, 113–15, where she states that even though "the concept and situation of ANE laws in contrast to the biblical data are completely different ... the topic of slave law between the ANE and the biblical legal corpora is legitimately comparable."

116. Finkelstein, *The Ox That Gored*, 7–20. See also Tsai, *Human Rights in Deuteronomy*, 113–14.

117. For example, Greengus, *Laws in the Bible*, 86–94; Averbeck, "Slavery in the World of the Bible," 425; Wells, "The Covenant Code," 93–98; Rothenbusch,

similarities, if not correspondences, with Exod 21:2-6.[118] With respect to the institution of debt slavery in the ancient world, Tsai notes that "in the numerous ANE slave laws, debt-servitude is mentioned in only one law, LH 117. Therefore, LH 117 is the only law that can be reasonably regarded as *parallel* to the debt slave laws of Ex 21, Lev 25, and Dt 15."[119] Less similar laws, but still widely regarded as helpful, include LU §5; LH §§118-119, 148-149, 154-56, 175, 178, 280, and 282.[120] Although LU §4 and LH §117 possess similarities with the BC in terms of legal issues, reasoning, and remedies, this section will show that the humanitarian concerns presented in the biblical debt slave laws are without parallel.

Exod 21:2-6 and LU §4

The Laws of Ur-Namma (ca. 2100 BC) represent the earliest known set of laws and are widely acknowledged as establishing the format used by the later legal collections.[121] Amongst its 30-or-so discernible laws, LU §4 stands out due to its noted similarities with the BC's segment on male debt slavery (21:2-6), namely with the marriage regulation in v. 4:

Exod 21:4

אִם־אֲדֹנָיו יִתֶּן־לוֹ אִשָּׁה וְיָלְדָה־לוֹ בָנִים אוֹ בָנוֹת הָאִשָּׁה וִילָדֶיהָ תִּהְיֶה לַאדֹנֶיהָ וְהוּא יֵצֵא בְגַפּוֹ

If his master gives him a wife and she bears him sons or daughters, the wife and her children belong to her master, and the man must leave alone.

Rechtssammlung, 265-72; D. P. Wright, *Inventing God's Law*, 9 (though he now minimizes the closeness of LU 4; see 415n65); Cardellini, *Die biblischen 'Sklaven'-Gesetze*, 245-46; and the more extensive list of works included in Chirichigno, *Debt-Slavery*, 192n1.

118. See his explanation in "The Covenant Code," 93-98, esp. 94.
119. Tsai, *Human Rights in Deuteronomy*, 157.
120. D. P. Wright, *Inventing God's Law*, 9.
121. Some assert that the writings of En-metena (ca. 2500 BC) or Urukagina of Lagash (ca. 2400 BC) deserve this standing, but these accounts are more appropriately considered edicts rather than law collections. See Wilcke, "Laws of Ur-Namma," 513.

LU §4

tukum-bi arad-dè géme á-áš-a-ni in-tuk arad-bi ama-ar-gi-ni ì-gá-gá é-ta nu-ub-ta-è

If a male servant marries a female slave, his beloved, and that male slave (later) is given his freedom, she (or he?) will not leave the house.[122]

Some, such as D. P. Wright, are hesitant to label LU §4 as a parallel to Exod 21:4 since it "deals with a permanent slave [not a debt slave], does not speak of his master giving him the wife, and does not speak of children."[123] While these distinctions are no doubt worthy of consideration, they do not necessarily exclude LU §4 as a valid candidate for direct comparison.[124] For example, the circumstances of the male slave in each account are remarkably similar. Both laws deal with a single male slave who is given a wife by his master and how this marriage is handled upon his moment of release. The solution in both cases is that the wife remains behind with the master. As discussed previously, the apparent reason for a solution like this is that the slave had not yet paid the bride price for the woman to be his wife and that she still maintained value to her master as a slave.[125] In other words, they share similar legal issues, rationales, and remedies.

Observed in isolation, it can be said that LU §4 and Exod 21:4 largely address the same important matters of bride price and rightful ownership of a slave. The master's investment in his property in both cases is duly recognized.[126] It is the view of this author, however, that

---

122. Roth, *Law Collections from Mesopotamia and Asia Minor*, 17. As Averbeck notes, even though the Sumerian verb in the last clause could be rendered with "he" or "she," it probably should be rendered, "she shall not leave the house (of her owner)" (see "Slavery in the World of the Bible," 425; and Greengus, *Laws in the Bible*, 90). See also Civil, "The Law Collection of Ur-Namma," 246, 254, where he translates LU §4 as, "If a slave marries a slave girl of his choice, (and) this slave is set free, (she) will not leave the household." For an explanation of this law in the event the verb is rendered "he," see Rothenbusch, *Reschtssammlung*, 271–72, where he argues that such a translation would increase the seriousness of one's marital commitment to his wife.

123. D. P. Wright, "The Laws of Hammurabi," 16. See also Wells's response to D. Wright's reservations in Wells, "The Covenant Code," 95–96. See esp. his comments regarding D. P. Wright's stance on LH 119 and 175.

124. Regarding the absence of children in LU §4, it can be surmised that they, like in Exod 21:4, would also stay behind with the master given their treatment in LU §5 and in other ANE regulations such as LH §175 where the male slave is not granted custody. For more on this topic, see Rothenbusch, *Reschtssammlung*, 271–72.

125. Averbeck, "Slavery in the World of the Bible," 425.

126. See Exod 21:21.

Exod 21:4 encompasses only the initial part of the law, as vv. 5–6 extend the scenario by presenting a contrasting protasis and apodosis, stating, "*but if the slave declares, 'I love my master and my wife and my children and do not want to go free,'* then his master must take him before the judges," etc. The conjunction וְאִם (*but if*) at the start of v. 5 is pivotal to this understanding. It signifies a continuation of an existing scenario rather than the introduction of a new one. The "remedy" as represented in 21:4 is therefore incomplete. Only when it is read together with the following verses can the intent of the BC's account become known: it is better for the slave to remain in the care of the master rather than for him to adopt the task of redeeming his family. Such recourse is presented here as the slave's "plan B" and is needed only if the master's character has proven to be less than gracious. Propp depicts the situation well:

> What if, as is more likely, he loves his wife and children but not his master? The manservant's recourse, not spelled out here, would be to accept manumission and then try to buy his family's freedom. If he has no prospect of amassing sufficient funds, then the slave faces a difficult choice. A slave to a kindly and prosperous owner might well prefer servitude over an impoverished and lonely liberty. Deut 15:13–15 redresses this very hindrance to liberation by requiring a manumission gift. This, one imagines, was often applied toward the purchase and feeding of the former manservant's family.[127]

While both LU §4 and Exod 21:4(–6) prioritize safeguarding the master's property and assets in the event of a slave marriage, there appears to be a shift in emphasis during the slave's moment of release. The former offers a clear financial path to redemption,[128] whereas the latter offers an alternative method that does not rely on finances. This innovative approach by the BC likely stems from the Torah's overarching stance on marriage.

Exod 21:2 and LH §117

To date, Hammurabi's stela is home to the longest and most comprehensive body of laws discovered from the ancient world (ca. 1750 BC). Since its excavation, it has been a focal point of extensive scholarly attention,

---

127. See Propp, *Exodus*, 610.

128. This ironically plays into Ur-Namma's self-proclaimed title: "the king of fees, whom the god Nanna had raised for the people" (LU e3: NÍĜ.SI.A [fees] as a humorous replacement for níĝ si-sá [justice]; see Wilcke, "Laws of Ur-Namma," 516).

largely because of the numerous parallels it shares with the case laws of the BC.[129] Pertaining to the topic of debt slavery is LH 117:

Exod 21:2[130]

כִּי תִקְנֶה עֶבֶד עִבְרִי שֵׁשׁ שָׁנִים יַעֲבֹד וּבַשְּׁבִעִת יֵצֵא לַחָפְשִׁי חִנָּם

When you buy a Hebrew slave, he shall serve for six years; then, in the seventh, he shall go out as a free man without paying anything.

LH §117

šumma awīlam e'iltum iṣbassuma aššassu mārašu u mārassu ana kispim iddin ulu ana kiššātim ittandin šalaššanātim bīt šājimānišunu u kāšišišunu ippešu ina rebûtim šattim andurāršunu iššakkan

If an obligation is outstanding against a man and he sells or gives into debt service his wife, his son, or his daughter, they shall perform service in the house of their buyer or of the one who holds them in debt service for three years; their release shall be secured in the fourth year.[131]

As Wells explains, the correlation between these two laws is quite strong. Both deal with a person being acquired as a debt slave as opposed to another type of slave, place limitations on their years of servitude using similar wording within relevant clauses, and allow the debt slave to go free without having to pay off the debt. The third similarity may exist out of the assumption that the work performed during the period of debt slavery is sufficient to pay off the debt (and any interest), but that is not explicitly stated.[132]

LH §118 seems to more directly address the issue of timely repayment. It states, "If he should give a male or female slave into debt service,

---

129. Otto, "Laws of Hammurabi," 501. D. P. Wright's publication *Inventing God's Law* continues to serve as a prime resource on the comparable data between the LH and BC. For more discussion on this, see C. B. Hays, *Hidden Riches*, 142–44.

130. D. P. Wright includes Exod 21:7 into his analysis ("The Laws of Hammurabi," 14), but this is not typical since 21:2–6 and 7–11 serve distinct purposes. For more on this, see Paul, *Studies in the Book of the Covenant*, 45–61; Chirichigno, *Debt-Slavery*, 196–98; Wells, "The Covenant Code," 93–94; and Pressler, "Wives and Daughters, Bond and Free," 150–54.

131. Roth, *Law Collections from Mesopotamia and Asia Minor*, 103.

132. Wells, "The Covenant Code," 94–95. See also Greengus, *Laws in the Bible*, 89–91; and Averbeck, "Slavery in the World of the Bible," 425.

the merchant may extend the term (beyond the three years), he may sell him; there are no grounds for a claim." In this instance, the three years of labor on the part of the slave does not necessarily make full repayment for the creditor's investments.[133] However, this law does not align with Exod 21:2 because it does not involve the case of a free person temporarily going into servitude to handle a debt. Instead, it concerns itself with an already existing slave being used as a "pawn" or "human pledge." Therefore, even though both LH §§117 and 118 use the same term for "debt service" (*kiššātu*), LH §118 is not referring to debt servitude in the real sense.[134] Moreover, as Tsai points out, LH §§117 and 118 are likely part of a series of laws, namely LH §§114–119, which cover issues related to debt security, debts, debtors, and creditors in various situations. Put simply, LH §§114–119 outline different methods for resolving a loan.[135] LH §§114–116 address different contentious scenarios involving human distraint; LH 117 pertains to debt servitude; LH §§118–119 present an alternative option for repaying a loan by offering the debtor's slaves as pledge. Therefore, among ANE laws, only LH §117 deals with debt servitude in the same sense as the BC.[136]

In addition to the similarities between Exod 21:2 and LH §117 noted above, there are also noticeable differences. These include a shift in agency (in the BC, the action is initiated by the creditor; in LH §117, it is initiated by the debtor) along with specific examples as to who may be entering debt service. Although these may seem like minor details, these alterations significantly shift the legislative intent behind the law. LH §117, along with the others in its series, aims to convey to its audience that the debtor has the agency to decide how he wishes to repay his debts, whether by surrendering whatever is under debt security or

---

133. Averbeck, "Slavery in the World of the Bible," 425.

134. Tsai, *Human Rights in Deuteronomy*, 153. There is some controversy regarding the translation of *kiššātu*. For the opinion that it should be rendered as "debt service," see Roth, *Law Collections from Mesopotamia and Asia Minor*, 103; Huehnergard, *Grammar of Akkadian*, 502; and Richardson, *Hammurabi's Laws*, 79. For the understanding that it should be rendered as "ransom," see Westbrook, "Slave and Master," 169; and Neuman, "Slavery in Private Households," 21. Such a translation would likely disqualify LH 117 as being a direct parallel to Exod 21.

135. Tsai, *Human Rights in Deuteronomy*, 152.

136. Tsai, *Human Rights in Deuteronomy*, 215–19. For discussions on the difference between debt and pledge servitude, see Westbrook, "The Old Babylonian Period," 63; and Testart, "The Extent and Significance of Debt Slavery," 175–76. Examples of laws that more explicitly deal with the topic of pledge include MAL A.39, 44, 48; C+G 2–3, 7.

through another method.[137] "This should be the prime message that LH §§117–119 promote."

The most conspicuous distinction, however, lies in the duration of servitude. The BC mandates six years of service before the debt slave is released, whereas the LH stipulate only three years.[138] By way of numbers, it would seem that the latter is more readily humanitarian. While this conclusion is understandable, it fails to take into consideration the BC's emphasis on strong humanitarian concerns such as benign treatment, provision, and theological motivation.[139] "Although the lack of mentioning the spirit and method of treatment in the debt slave laws does not necessarily mean that the Babylonian masters would thus treat their debt slaves harshly," Tsai concludes, "the biblical debt slave laws noticeably speak of their humanitarian concerns and provide 'to-do' lists to reflect their concerns."[140]

Theo-Ethical Overview

The topic of slavery inherently raises questions about human dignity. How can a person simultaneously be deemed "property" and still be recognized as fully human? While there are other laws in the BC that more explicitly address such humanitarian concerns, one does not need to venture beyond the topic of debt slavery to explore this tension. First, it is valuable to once again observe the positioning of these laws within the case laws of the BC in contrast to other ANE legal codes, specifically as they relate to their respective emphases on the welfare of people and

---

137. Tsai, *Human Rights in Deuteronomy*, 153–54. Chirichigno notes that "when a debtor sells *ana kaspim* 'for money' a slave to a creditor, the creditor takes absolute possession of the slave, meaning that it is also likely that in this transaction a creditor could take permanent possession of a wife, son, or daughter," and that, even in instances when a redemption may be allowed, "debtors often lacked the means to redeem their dependents . . . LH §117, therefore, attempted to curb the power of the creditor in taking free persons as permanent possessions," a notion that, in his view, influenced Exod 21:2–6 to include the release of all debt slaves (see *Debt-Slavery*, 71–72 and 72n1).

138. For more on this, see Swiderski, "Sabbatical Patterns in the Book of the Covenant," 149–50.

139. Swiderski, "Sabbatical Patterns in the Book of the Covenant," 223. See also Bracker, *Das Gesetz Israels*, 157.

140. Tsai, *Human Rights in Deuteronomy*, 157.

the protection of property. The following table represents a simplified overview:[141]

Table 4. People vs. Property in ANE Legal Collections

LU	LL	LE	BC
Private Property	**Private Property**	**Private Property**	Debt Slaves
Marriage	Marriage & Family	Contracts	Human Offense & Injury
Injury	Injury	Marriage & Family	
Slaves	Hiring	Business & Trade	**Private Property**

Whether or not the exact ordering of ANE laws is representative of a society's primary concerns is a topic of ongoing discussion. It is telling, however, that the BC is the only law collection to begin with matters of debt slavery. This is likely the result of their shared history as slaves in the land of Egypt (see chapter 3), signifying that, at least for the Israelites, the sequence of laws held significance. This is further evidenced in the BC's more nuanced treatment of Israelite debt slaves in comparison to chattel slaves. Lemche elaborates on this point:

> In sum, the evidence about the status of slaves in Israel indicates that slavery was generally thought to be unproblematic if the slave was of foreign origin. The problem of Israelite slavery represented something abominable, which explains why Israelite slaves were to be treated differently. The Hebrew Bible repeatedly stresses that the Israelites were originally slaves to a foreign people, the Egyptians, and should therefore not let fellow Israelites become slaves of someone else—especially other Israelites.[142]

This should not be taken to mean that chattel slaves were regarded as less than human (they were granted unprecedented treatment as well).[143]

---

141. Adapted from the chart in Hess, "Structure of the Covenant Code," 126. Emphasis on "Private Property" added. The LH is not included due to its length and more sporadic categorization. See also 127 where Hess argues that the overall contents of the LH are largely similar to the LU, LL, and LE.

142. Lemche, "Ancient Near East and Hebrew Bible," 306. See also Lev 25:54–55 where the Lord explicitly designates the Israelites as belonging to him alone.

143. See, for example, Exod 21:20–21 and 26–27. According to Tsai, these laws "express the highest ethics concerning the treatment of slaves that even a chattel slave should be treated as a person, rather than as property" and attest that "the biblical slave laws overall possess a higher humanitarian respect for them as human beings than their ANE counterparts" (*Human Rights in Deuteronomy*, 141). Additionally, C. J. H. Wright

Rather, the laws concerning the acquisition of a fellow "Hebrew/Israelite" (Exod 21:2; Deut 15:12; Lev 25:39) were intended as perpetual reminders of their own history. They were meant to instill in their readers a sense of empathy and a commitment to treat both slaves and foreigners with the dignity they themselves deserved (Exod 22:20; 23:9). Indeed, the perspective emphasized was that slaves should be recognized as individuals with inherent worth, and their status as living people should take precedence over any considerations related to property management.

Second, the BC consistently addresses the needs of slaves while also upholding the rights of the masters involved.[144] For instance, it is within the master's rights to retain the wife of a released slave in order to collect her bride price (LU §4; Exod 21:4). However, the slave retains the choice to remain in servitude to be with her and avoid the potential hardships that come with her redemption. The master *must* comply (Exod 21:5–6). Similarly, the master has the prerogative to keep the slave for the agreed-upon term of servitude (LH §117; Exod 21:2a); but following that period, the slave is to be released without any payment or obligations, granting them complete freedom (Exod 21:2b; Jer 34:8–17).[145] The accounts in Deuteronomy and Leviticus reinforce and expand on these measures, whereas LH §§114–119 are not concerned with providing detailed regulations in this regard since their central concerns were mainly to protect the property and purchase rights of the owner.[146]

Finally, it is worth highlighting the fact that some of the above points, such as the possibility of the slave later paying the bride price following release, are not explicitly stated in either account and are mostly left up to (albeit reasonable) conjecture. By excluding assumptions like these and focusing solely on what is clearly stated, the BC's emphasis on humanitarian concerns stands out prominently compared to its cuneiform counterparts. While the LH stipulate only half of the service time required by the BC—a significant difference indeed—they lack

---

notes that "no other ancient Near Eastern law has been found that holds a master to account of his own slaves" (*Old Testament Ethics*, 292). See also Gane, *Old Testament Law for Christians*, 215; and Westbrook and Wells, *Everyday Law in Biblical Israel*, 55.

144. C. J. H. Wright, *Exodus*, 427–28.

145. The value of freedom is paramount in Exod 21:2–6. For an explanation on the relationship between freedom and the BC's humanitarian context, see Morrow, *An Introduction to Biblical Law*, 101–2; see also Sprinkle, 'The Book of the Covenant,' 52–54, for an illustration of how the debt slave laws form a "freedom chiasm."

146. Averbeck, "Law," in *Cracking Old Testament Codes*, 132; Tsai, *Human Rights in Deuteronomy*, 163.

the Bible's explicit clarity in safeguarding the well-being of the recently released slave. Maimonides succinctly encapsulates the position of the slave in Talmudic law: "It is permissible to work the slave hard; but while this is the law, the ways of equity and prudence are that every master should be just and merciful [and] not make the yoke heavy on his slave." He concludes that, above all, slave ownership must be guided by "mercy, compassion, and forbearance."[147]

The Case of the Goring Ox

"Few domestic animals can claim to have attracted more scholarly attention, outside the field of veterinary science, than the oxen of Exod 21:28ff., ever since the discovery of similar statutes in Mesopotamian law codes."[148] Indeed, case laws concerning the goring ox offer significant insights into fundamental ANE concepts such as legal retribution and redemption, negligence and accountability, and the sanctity of life (along with the gravity of taking it). Such laws were commonplace for a few reasons. First, oxen were often used in agriculture across the ancient world, making encounters with them a regular occurrence. Second, they are quite powerful and unpredictable animals, making them dangerous to bystanders and passersby. Lastly, due to the preceding two points, accidents resulting in harm to humans or other animals, including fatal gorings, were not unheard of.[149]

Exodus 21:28–36 is exclusively concerned with matters regarding oxen. While there is some debate on how to categorically divide up the BC's ox laws, this study finds Jackson's explanation compelling. Instead of splitting the laws into two separate sections as some propose (21:28–32 and 33–36),[150] he offers up a more unified approach with three distinct topics:[151] vv. 28–32 address laws governing injuries to humans caused by an ox (ox vs. human); vv. 33–34 cover laws regulating injury to an ox caused by a human (human vs. ox); and vv. 35–36 address laws managing injury to an ox by another ox (ox vs. ox). Unlike the debt slave laws, the

---

147. See Cohn, *Human Rights in Jewish Law*, 63. Note also the religious significance of the 6/7 motif discussed previously in chapters 2 and 3.

148. C. J. H. Wright, *God's People in God's Land*, 161.

149. C. J. H. Wright, *Exodus*, 419.

150. See, for example, Finkelstein, *The Ox That Gored*, 27–29; and Otto, *Wandel der Rechtsbegründungen*, 12–31.

151. B. S. Jackson, *Studies in the Semiotics of Biblical Law*, 189.

ox laws have no biblical parallels; they do, however, contain abundant similarities with the ox laws of other ANE legal collections. The exegetical discussion below will therefore be more integrative than the earlier segment on debt slavery. Before jumping into comparisons, it is important to briefly discuss *talion* law, as it is a significant theme in both the biblical and cuneiform ox laws and continues to be a confusing concept for modern readers.

Lex Talionis: What It Is and Is Not

The term *lex talionis* was inspired by what many consider to be the quintessential *talion* law: "eye for an eye, tooth for a tooth, foot for a foot" (Exod 21:24; cf. Deut 19:21; Lev 24:19–20). *Lex* means "law," and *talionis* means "tooth" in Latin.[152] When *talion* laws are referenced in modern discussion, they are oftentimes taken to mean something like "vengeance will be mine!" But this is actually the opposite mentality of what *lex talionis* promotes. "In fact, throughout the *mišpāṭîm* the major concern is not revenge," Morrow points out, "The goal of the legal system in the Covenant Code is the regulation of social conflict."[153] In other words, rather than emphasizing the need for retribution, *talion* laws aimed to make the punishment fit the crime. Their purpose was to restrict the extent of retribution that an individual could seek or impose for personal harm, thereby averting "unlimited retribution, personal vendetta, and excessive retaliation."[154] Cahn summarizes the spirit behind *lex talionis* well: "'An eye for an eye,' which appears to us like a barbaric maxim, was in its day merely a primitive rule of commensurability," making it a "substantial advance over . . . 'a life for an eye.'"[155] These judgments were therefore quite revolutionary and could be seen as resonating more with contemporary values than with what some might perceive as archaic.[156]

---

152. Averbeck, *The Old Testament Law for the Life of the Church*, 142.

153. Morrow, *An Introduction to Biblical Law*, 89.

154. Paul, *Studies in the Book of the Covenant*, 76. See also Otto, *Theologische Ethik des Alten Testaments*, 25–29; and C. J. H. Wright, *Exodus*, 418, esp. n16 where he states, "This understanding of the *lex talionis* has been clear among biblical scholars for over half a century, since it was first demonstrated by A.S. Diamond . . . So it is frustrating that the popular caricature still persists" (see A. S. Diamond, "An Eye for an Eye").

155. Cahn, *The Moral Decision*, 281.

156. Knight, *Law, Power, and Justice in Ancient Israel*, 143.

Beyond the purpose and intent of *talion* law is the extent to which it was put into practice. Did damaging someone's tooth, for example, always result in an identical punishment to the offender? Exod 21:27 offers a nuanced perspective: "An owner who knocks out the tooth of a male or female slave must let the slave go free to compensate for the tooth." This suggests that talion laws were often employed to determine compensation proportionate to the nature of the crime without resorting to physical harm.[157] While the deliberate taking of a life incurred the highest cost, lesser offenses like bruising carried a milder penalty.[158] It is worth noting that this concept is not unique to the Bible; *talion* laws are found in several ANE legal collections, particularly in the LH.[159] As will be illustrated below in the discussion of the goring ox, however, the biblical application of *talion* law is imbued with a uniquely humanitarian (and theological) outlook, making it difficult to isolate them from the rest of the Torah.

It is fitting to conclude this overview of *lex talionis* with Christ's words in Matt 5:38–39, as some understand his message to be revising or abrogating the *talion* laws in the Torah's legal collections.[160] At first glance, this seems to be the case: "You have heard it said, 'An eye for an eye, and a tooth for a tooth,' but I tell you ... If anyone slaps you on the right cheek, turn to them the other cheek also."[161] Rather than *amending* the law, however, Christ is instead commenting on its misapplication. *Talion* law is strictly reserved for the courts and is not to be superimposed onto personal relationships. Doing this would mean taking vengeance into one's own hands, something the law itself clearly condemns (Lev 19:18).[162]

Comparative Studies of ANE Goring Ox Laws

The goring ox laws in the BC are so similar to those in the LH and LE that, according to D. P. Wright, their resemblances "are visible even by casual

---

157. It is worth noting that within the biblical legal collections, there is only one instance where physical mutilation is mandated as a consequence of a crime; specifically in the case of a woman who defends her husband by injuring the attacker's testicles (Deut 25:11–12). See C. J. H. Wright's comments on this law in *Exodus*, 418n17.

158. C. J. H. Wright, *Exodus*, 418; Morrow, *An Introduction to Biblical Law*, 88. For more on this topic, see Huffman, "'An Eye for an Eye' and Capital Punishment," 119–31.

159. E.g., LH §§196–201.

160. E.g., Thompson, "Punishment and Restitution," 189.

161. Cf. Lam 3:30; LE §§42; LH §§202–205.

162. Averbeck, *Old Testament Law for the Life of the Church*, 240.

inspection."[163] The most conclusive comparisons include Exod 21:28–32 with LH §§250–252 and LE §§54–55, as well as Exod 21:35(–36) with LE §53, with the latter pairing having even been described as "an exact parallel" and "virtually identical."[164] Beyond these primary examples, Jackson highlights several topical similarities between the entire account in Exod 21:28–36 and LH §§244–252. His research interestingly reveals that their contents are in reverse order; the BC begins with the loss of human life to an ox while the LH begins with the loss of an ox's life to another animal.[165] While these topical and structural resemblances between Exod 21:33–36 and the accounts in LH and LE are helpful (and will receive attention as needed), the below discussion will primarily focus on Exod 21:28–32 and its aforementioned cuneiform counterparts. These verses were specifically chosen for two reasons. First, their remedies relating to the loss of human life make them especially pertinent to the goals of this project. Second, their distinctions from ANE legal collections hold significant theological import.

The ox laws begin with a primary ruling designed to answer the question, "what should be done if someone's ox kills an innocent bystander?" Following this initial law are three secondary rulings that consider alternative scenarios:

Exod 21:28–32

וְכִי־יִגַּח שׁוֹר אֶת־אִישׁ אוֹ אֶת־אִשָּׁה וָמֵת סָקוֹל יִסָּקֵל הַשּׁוֹר וְלֹא יֵאָכֵל אֶת־בְּשָׂרוֹ וּבַעַל הַשּׁוֹר נָקִי וְאִם שׁוֹר נַגָּח הוּא מִתְּמֹל שִׁלְשֹׁם וְהוּעַד בִּבְעָלָיו וְלֹא יִשְׁמְרֶנּוּ וְהֵמִית אִישׁ אוֹ אִשָּׁה הַשּׁוֹר יִסָּקֵל וְגַם־בְּעָלָיו יוּמָת אִם־כֹּפֶר יוּשַׁת עָלָיו וְנָתַן פִּדְיֹן נַפְשׁוֹ כְּכֹל אֲשֶׁר־יוּשַׁת עָלָיו אוֹ־בֵן יִגָּח אוֹ־בַת יִגָּח כַּמִּשְׁפָּט הַזֶּה יֵעָשֶׂה לּוֹ אִם־עֶבֶד יִגַּח הַשּׁוֹר אוֹ אָמָה כֶּסֶף שְׁלֹשִׁים שְׁקָלִים יִתֵּן לַאדֹנָיו וְהַשּׁוֹר יִסָּקֵל

(28) If an ox gores a man or a woman to death, the ox must be stoned and its meat may not be eaten, but the owner of the ox is free from liability. (29) But if the ox was in the habit of goring and its owner was warned yet he does not restrain it, and the ox kills a man or woman, it must be stoned and also its owner must

---

163. D. P. Wright, *Inventing God's Law*, 205. See also Wells's analysis in "The Covenant Code," 104–6; and D. P. Wright, "The Laws of Hammurabi," 24, where he states that "the goring ox laws have been recognized as the closest legal parallel between biblical and cuneiform law."

164. Paul, *Studies in the Book of the Covenant*, 84; and Westbrook, *Studies in Biblical and Cuneiform Law*, 40n4, respectively.

165. B. S. Jackson, *Studies in the Semiotics of Biblical Law*, 189.

be put to death. (30) If instead a ransom is imposed on him, he shall give for the redemption of his life according to all that is imposed on him. (31) If it gores a son or daughter, he is to be dealt with according to the same law. (32) If the ox gores a male or female slave, he must pay thirty shekels of silver to the master, and the ox must be stoned to death.

Both LH §§250–252 and LE §§54–55 operate with a similar structure in mind, though the LE begin with the case of the habitually goring ox and the negligence of its owner rather than with the instance of the ox's first offense:

LH §§250–252

šumma album sūqam ina alākišu awīlam ikkipma uštamīt dīnum šû rugummâm ul išu šumma alap awīlim nakkāpīma kīma nakkāpû bābtaašu ušēdīšumma qarnīšu la ušarrim alapšu la usanniqma alpum šû mār awīlim ikkipma uštamīt 1/2 mana kaspam inaddin šumma warad awīlum 1/3 mana kaspam inaddin

(250) If an ox gores to death a man while it is passing through the streets, that case has no basis for a claim. (251) If a man's ox is a known gorer and the authorities of his city quarter notify him that it is a known gorer, but he does not blunt its horns or control his ox and that ox gores to death a member of the *awīlu*-class, he (the owner) shall give 30 shekels of silver. (252) If it is a man's slave, he shall give 20 shekels of silver.[166]

LE §§54–55

šumma album nakkāpîma bābtum ana bēlišu ušēdīma alapšu la u<šē>širma awīlam ikkimma uštamīt bēl alpim 2/3 mana kassam išaqqal šumma wardam ikkimma ištamīt 15 šiqil kaspam išaqqal

(54) If an ox is a gorer and the ward authorities so notify its owner, but he fails to keep his ox in check and it gores a man and thus causes his death, the owner of the ox shall weigh and deliver 40 shekels of silver. (55) If it gores a slave and thus causes his death, he shall weigh and deliver 15 shekels of silver.[167]

The BC, LH, and LE share four commonalities. First, none of them prescribe a punishment for the owner of the goring ox in the case of its first

---

166. Roth, *Law Collections from Mesopotamia and Asia Minor*, 128.
167. Roth, *Law Collections from Mesopotamia and Asia Minor*, 67.

attack (this is assumed in the LE's account given the notification of the ward authorities). Second, they all concur that if the offending ox has a history of goring, a more severe repercussion is warranted. Third, each account concludes with a provision regarding slaves. If a slave is the victim of a goring ox, there is still a penalty, but it is less severe than if the victim had been someone of higher standing. Lastly, all three collections share in common the general principle that the owner who has been duly warned about his vicious ox is responsible for guarding it.[168]

Exod 21:28 and LH §250

Beyond the above legal and structural similarities, there are notable differences between the account of the BC and those of the LH and LE—some more conspicuous than others. Each of these differences will be observed in the order they appear, starting with a comparison between Exod 21:28 and LH §250. Here, there are three discrepancies to address: the BC's inclusion of (1) men and women as potential victims, (2) a death penalty for the offending ox, and (3) the prescribed means of execution which involves stoning and includes a prohibition on consuming the meat of the executed ox. Of these, the first typically receives the least attention as both accounts could be interpreted as referring to victims in a general sense, regardless of gender. While it is likely that LH §250 does not intend to exclude women through its generalization,[169] it is also likely that the BC makes it a point to include women for a deliberate purpose, namely to express consistency with the overarching theology of the Torah which asserts that all humans, both men and women, are created in the image of God (Gen 1:27).[170]

With the doctrine of the *imago Dei* acting as the motive force for justice, it is not surprising that the BC applies the death penalty for the goring ox. This is consistent with Gen 9:5-6: "And I will require a penalty for your lifeblood; I will require it from any animal and from any human. If someone murders a fellow human, I will require that person's life. Whoever sheds human blood, by humans his blood will be shed, for God

---

168. Sarna, *Exodus*, 127.

169. D. P. Wright notes, for example, that the LH show gender inclusivity elsewhere (*Inventing God's Law*, 210), though his claims that the BC's inclusivity in Exod 21:28-32 is inspired by this fact is doubtful, mainly since this very point paints the exclusion of women in LH250 as more intentional.

170. C. J. H. Wright, *Exodus*, 419.

made humans in his image."[171] Some, however, prefer to interpret this stipulation in a more utilitarian fashion, claiming that the ox was to be put down merely as a form of community protection.[172] Even though the owner is not guilty of a crime, he still suffers a major economic loss. This both encourages him to oversee his assets more responsibly in the future and serves as an example for other ox owners.

While this utilitarian interpretation is, in a practical sense, not necessarily at odds with the religious one, many understand the death sentence as being theologically motivated due to the additional requirement of stoning the offending ox and the command to refrain from eating its flesh.[173] C. Wright states, for example, "The detail that the ox is to be stoned, not merely slaughtered or eaten in a normal way, also points to [a] religious interpretation of the act."[174] Do factors like these truly necessitate a theological or ethical motivation, or can they, too, be understood in a more practical light? This topic continues to be a matter of debate with opinions ranging from complete moral failure to mere ceremonial regulation. Earlier scholars like Driver and Miles, for example, go so far as to label the offending ox as a murderer.[175] Such terminology implies that the offending ox is a moral agent, being able to, on some level, comprehend the concepts of right and wrong in its actions. Westbrook sees the pendulum as belonging to the other side. He argues that stoning in this instance should not be interpreted as assigning moral culpability equivalent to human sin. Stoning was simply a necessary precaution meant to avoid killing the ox with a knife, as using this method would mimic the sacrificial process. It was not appropriate to deal with the goring ox in such a manner following its horrendous action against the community. Regarding the ban, Westbrook concludes, its meat could not be eaten

---

171. C. J. H. Wright, *Exodus*, 419. See also Paul, *Studies in the Book of the Covenant*, 79–80; Schwienhorst-Schönberger, *Das Bundesbuch (Ex 20,22–23,33)*, 131–36; and Greenberg, "Postulates," 15–16.

172. See Jackson, *Essays in Jewish and Comparative Legal History*, 108–16; and Westbrook, *Studies in Biblical and Cuneiform Law*, 83–86. Westbrook additionally questions the notion that the LH refrains from killing the ox, labeling this take as an argument from silence (see 83–88).

173. See Sarna, *Exodus*, 128, where he states, "The killer ox is not destroyed solely because it is dangerous. This is clear from the fact that it is not destroyed when the victim is another ox [see Exod 21:35–36] and from the prescribed mode of destruction."

174. C. J. H. Wright, *Exodus*, 419.

175. Driver and Miles, *The Assyrian Laws*, 444. See also Cazelles, *Études sur le Code de l'Alliance*, 57.

simply because its blood was not properly drained, a side effect of stoning (Deut 15:23; Lev 17:13-14).[176]

Rather than labeling the ox as a morally responsible agent or mapping out a strictly practical rationale for its execution, this study sees the stoning of the ox in Exod 21:28 as somewhere in between. It points toward a greater theological reality but remains grounded in a meaningful physical application. Passages like Gen 9:5-6 are foundational for such discussions. Driver and Miles, for example, over-apply this passage to the ox laws, neglecting the differences between humans and animals delineated in other parts of the OT.[177] Westbrook leaves out Gen 9 in his explanation, leading to the general absence of theological language. The reality is that, according to Gen 9:5-6, goring oxen do, in fact, incur a divine penalty for killing a carrier of God's image (וְאַךְ אֶת־דִּמְכֶם לְנַפְשֹׁתֵיכֶם אֶדְרֹשׁ), making them "guilty" in a *legal* sense. In this case, the ox's lack of awareness of the law and its motivations for goring are not considered relevant factors in its sentencing; only the act itself is taken into account.

It is more appropriate to understand the ox's death sentence in Exod 21 as resulting from a form of supernatural cause and effect.[178] Finkelstein, for example, calls the ox's goring an "insurrection against the cosmic order itself."[179] The punishment of stoning, in his view, is fitting for the crime of goring a human for two reasons. First, a broader survey of the OT reveals that stoning is never the penalty for someone condemned to death for *intentional* homicide.[180] Second, stoning is used exclusively in the Bible to punish those who "strike at the moral and religious fibers which the community as a whole sees as defining its essence and integrity."[181] Greengus agrees, adding that there is also significance to the

---

176. Westbrook, *Studies in Biblical and Cuneiform Law*, 83-88.

177. Humans, unlike animals, are made in God's image (Gen 1:26-28; 5:1; 9:2-6), posses spirits that are held responsible for pursuing God (Job 32:8; Zech 12:1; Eccl 3:21; Isa 31:3), and are capable of moral understanding (Gen 2:16-17; Eccl 12:13-14; Ps 8:4-8; 32:9; 73:22; Job 32:8; 35:10-11; Hos 7:11).

178. See Arnold, *Genesis*, 110.

179. Finkelstein, *The Ox That Gored*, 26-29. See also Greenberg, "Postulates," 15; Paul, *Studies in the Book of the Covenant*, 79; Sarna, *Exodus*, 128; and C. J. H. Wright, *Exodus*, 419.

180. Cf. Num 35:16-19. It should also be noted that some see Lev 24:16-17 as an exception to this as the punishment of stoning in v. 16 could be implied within v. 17.

181. Finkelstein, *The Ox That Gored*, 28. Stoning, for example, was used to punish the worship of foreign gods (Deut 13; 17:2-7), the disobedient and profligate son (Deut 21:18-21), a newlywed bride found by her husband not to be a virgin (Deut 22), child sacrifice (Lev 20), sorcery and necromancy (Lev 20:27); blasphemy (Lev 24), and violation of

fact that stoning enables the offended community to act as the executioner rather than a governing body:

> Death by stoning, in the biblical tradition and elsewhere in the ancient Near East, is reserved for crimes of a special character. In those cases there is no special "executioner," for the community assembled is the mass executioner of the sentence. Offenses that entail this mode of execution must therefore in theory or in fact, "offend" the corporate community or are believed to compromise its most cherished values to the degree that the commission of the offense placed the community itself in jeopardy.[182]

This reasoning explains why the ox's meat may not be eaten. The ox is to be removed like an idolatrous town (Josh 6:15–19) or the goods of Achan (Josh 7:25) and must "therefore be destroyed, not enjoyed."[183] Since this process is seen as commonplace in ancient Israel,[184] it is not surprising that the biblical ox laws contain such particularities.

Exod 21:29–30, LH §251, and LE §54

The first alternative scenario following the principle law addresses the situation where an ox, already known to be a gorer (although no one has yet died), ends up killing someone despite the owner being aware of its tendency. All three legal accounts—the BC, LH, and LE—share the consensus that the owner's negligence is unacceptable and that he should face a penalty beyond merely losing the ox. In addition to the differences between the BC and cuneiform collections discussed earlier, two other distinctions are noteworthy. First is the increasingly apparent shift from government involvement to communal accountability. Second is the degree of punishment imposed on the owner of the ox. LH §251 and LE §54, in particular, are virtually the same. The fine's quantitative difference is largely negligible, and their respective references to a "member of the *awīlu*-class" and a "man" can be considered synonymous.[185]

---

the Sabbath (Num 15:32–36; see also the explanation of this offered in chapter 2).

182. Greengus, *Laws in the Bible*, 176.

183. Finkelstein, *The Ox That Gored*, 28. See also Westbrook's summary of Finkelstein's view in *Studies in Biblical and Cuneiform Law*, 84.

184. Loewenstamm, "Review of Goetze's 'Laws of Eshnunna,'" 192–98.

185. *Awīlu* is the Akkadian word for "free citizen."

Like in the principle law, Exod 21:29 leaves the execution of the offending ox up to the community while the cuneiform accounts hand the situation over to the city authorities. The carrying out of the owner's sentence, however, seems to imply government intervention: "and also its owner must be put to death" (וְגַם־בְּעָלָיו יוּמָת). Interestingly, rabbinic tradition understands this decree to mean "death that will be sent upon him from heaven." The rationale for this translation stems from the idea that it was not appropriate for an earthly court to mete out a death penalty to the owner of the ox for an action committed by his beast.[186] It has also been posited that the announcement of the death sentence in this instance was meant more as a moral statement in line with *talion* principles and not a direct call to literal execution.[187] Whatever the case, it remains that the BC shies away from the explicit government language found in the LH and LE, a shift that can even be seen in the warning clause: "if its owner was warned" (BC) as opposed to "if his city/ward authorities notify him" (LH/LE). This change imposes a convicting question onto the BC's readers, both ancient and modern: If it is not the responsibility of any governing body or administrative office to warn my neighbor of imminent danger or destructive habits, then whose job must it be?[188]

The differing punishments for the ox owner are more noticeable. The cuneiform accounts address the consequences of negligence by imposing a fine, a considerably lighter sentence compared to the BC's death penalty. Given Babylonia's strict application of capital punishment for intentional (and sometimes unintentional) homicide,[189] the reduction of this penalty to a fixed fine almost certainly stems from the chain of liability (the ox committed the killing, not the owner). In contrast, the death penalty for the owner in the BC, similar to the stoning mandate for the ox, was likely influenced by religious and moral considerations. Neglecting to control one's ox to the mortal detriment of others, for example, could be viewed as poor stewardship of creation (Gen 1:28; 9:1–3).

Exod 21:30 introduces an alternative consequence which initially seems to be more in line with the remedies found in the LH and LE: "If instead a ransom is imposed on him, he shall give for the redemption of his life according to all that is imposed on him." Several questions arise

---

186. Greengus, *Laws in the Bible*, 175; and Sarna, *Exodus*, 128.

187. Greengus, *Laws in the Bible*, 175.

188. See Ezek 3:20; 33:6; Matt 7:3–5; Luke 10:25–37; 17:3; Gal 6:1–2; Eph 4:25; Col 3:16; Heb 3:12–13; Jas 5:19–20; 1 John 3:17–21.

189. Greengus, *Laws in the Bible*, 161, 171.

regarding this stipulation, prompting further discussion. Why does the BC present a primary and subsequent option rather than simply imposing a fine as seen in the cuneiform accounts? Why is the amount of the fine in 21:30 left unspecified, and who is responsible for imposing this nondescript fine? According to Averbeck, the inclusion of an option to substitute the death penalty with a monetary payment emphasizes the flexibility of the Mosaic law, subject to the discretion of the court. "Not everything in the law is hard and fast."[190] In line with this interpretation, others believe Exod 21:29–30 to be arguing that, following *talion* law, the death penalty could be justified, but since the ox owner is not the direct murderer, there is room for leniency in his sentencing. Num 35:31, for example, prohibits accepting a ransom for murder, but because the ox owner did not have murderous intent, this prohibition could be mitigated.[191] In essence, the penalties in Exod 21:29–30 could be seen as establishing a spectrum, with murder on one end and involuntary manslaughter on the other. Judges could then exercise their discernment in a given case as to what end of the spectrum the crime falls, as some violations were bound to have extenuating circumstances.[192]

There are several speculations regarding the missing ransom amount in Exod 21:30. It has been argued that the amount is purposely left unstated on the assumption that the judges will provide a fair number following their examination of the case.[193] Some go further than this, asserting that the Torah refuses to place a monetary value on the life of a free person.[194] However, this view raises a critical question: If such a valuation is deemed inappropriate, how can any ransom be paid? Resolving the ox owner's redemption cost necessitates agreeing on a price for the lost life. Greengus clarifies that the ransom amount was likely never meant to represent the value of a human life; rather, it was meant to represent the "economic value" or "worth" of either the victim or the ox owner himself (Greengus sees it as the former while scholars like Finkelstein see it as

---

190. Averbeck, *The Old Testament Law for the Life of the Church*, 92.

191. Sarna, *Exodus*, 128.

192. The OT law went so far as to mandate the establishment of cities of refuge at the national level to protect accidental manslayers from being executed as premeditated murderers (Num 35; Deut 19; Josh 20–21). For more on this, see Gane, *Old Testament Law*, 116; Barmash, *Homicide in the Biblical World*; and Westbrook and Wells, *Everyday Law in Biblical Israel*, 75.

193. Finkelstein, *The Ox That Gored*, 30–31.

194. See, for example, Finkelstein, *The Ox That Gored*, 30–31; and Jackson, *Wisdom Laws*, 282.

the latter).¹⁹⁵ This understanding is supported by the almost-certain idea that the ransom was imposed by the family of the victim. They were, after all, the ones who were most impacted by the sudden and tragic loss and probably needed equitable compensation to continue making ends meet, a concept that is not too dissimilar from some modern arrangements.¹⁹⁶

Exod 21:31–32, LH §252, and LE §55

The final lines of all three texts address scenarios regarding different categories of victims. Though brief and straightforward, there are a couple differences between the BC and the cuneiform collections that further illuminate their respective value hierarchies. First, why does the BC find it necessary to include children? "If [the ox] gores a son or daughter, [the owner] is to be dealt with according to the same law" (Exod 21:31). Sprinkle sees the Hebrew terms בֵן and בַת to be referring to freeborn men and women rather than sons and daughters as this creates a more direct contrast with the following verse on slaves,¹⁹⁷ but it is more likely that these terms are used to indicate minors.¹⁹⁸ Alexander agrees, suggesting that the BC is trying to emphasize that the age of the victim has no bearing on the punishment applied.¹⁹⁹ This explanation is especially likely given the practice of "vicarious punishment" in the ancient world which enforces the concept of "a son for a son."²⁰⁰ For instance, if the BC found it fit to also enforce vicarious punishment, then Exod 21:31 would read, "If the ox gores a son or daughter, then the son or daughter of the ox's owner shall also be put to death."²⁰¹

---

195. See Greengus, *Laws in the Bible*, 174; and Finkelstein, *The Ox That Gored*, 31–32.

196. Many have pointed out that Lev 27:1–8 assigns monetary value to human life (בְּעֶרְכְּךָ נְפָשֹׁת) based on factors like gender and age. This passage, however, is most likely referring to an economic evaluation seeing that the priest was able to adjust the prices according to the economic situation of the person involved (Lev 27:8). For more on this, see Greengus, *Laws in the Bible*, 174.

197. Sprinkle, *'The Book of the Covenant,'* 108–9.

198. Fishbane, *Biblical Interpretation in Ancient Israel*, 212.

199. Alexander, *Exodus*, 490. See also Finkelstein, *The Ox That Gored*, 34–35; Jackson, *Wisdom Laws*, 218, 287; and Westbrook, *Studies in Biblical and Cuneiform Law*, 57–61.

200. Cf. LH §116, 209–210, 229, 229–230; cp. Deut 24:16.

201. For more on this, see Greenberg, "Postulates," 23; Paul, *Studies in the Book of the Covenant*, 82–83; D. P. Wright, *Inventing God's Law*, 212; and Cassuto, *A Commentary on the Book of Exodus*, 280.

Finally, the valuing of a slave at 30 shekels of silver in Exod 21:32 seems to complicate matters. If the Torah is hesitant to assign a monetary amount to the value of a human life, then why do slaves receive different treatment, especially considering this chapter's earlier conclusion that slaves are "not to be viewed as anything less than human"? Dandamayev astutely points out that this law is actually not so different from the law regarding the goring of a free person since *both* situations require ransoms. It is simply easier to calculate the value of a slave since the vocation is more explicitly stated. Again, the pricing is economic in nature; this is made abundantly clear by the BC's insistence that, even in the case of a slave, the ox must still be stoned for taking a human life, an equal carrier of the divine image.[202] The topic of human worth therefore seems to be a more complicated matter in the LH and LE where fixed prices are given even to free persons.

Theo-Ethical Overview

The goring ox laws, like those pertaining to debt slaves, offer layers of theological and ethical reflection. A common theme between the two is their determination to emphasize the value of human life over matters of property ownership. The debt slave laws did so by calling slave owners to empathize with the situation of their slaves, thus influencing their treatment of them. The ox laws more explicitly imparted the same punishment of stoning upon the goring ox regardless of the target. In the event that the owner could have prevented the goring by simply subduing his ox, even his life could be seen as forfeit.[203] Slave or free, a loss of life was to be viewed as a loss of life. C. J. H. Wright summarizes this concept well:

> This Old Testament conviction concerning the unique value of human life not only informs the hierarchy of serious offenses and the distinguishing of capital and non-capital penalties; it also extends to the offender himself and the nature and extent of the punishment meted out. When we allow ourselves to see beyond the stumbling block that the mandatory death penalty presents for some, there is a humanitarian ethos in Israelite

---

202. Dandamayev, "Slavery (ANE), (OT)," 65; Alexander, *Exodus*, 491; and Boecker, *Law and the Administration of Justice*, 164.

203. Capital punishment for a negligent owner could theoretically still apply in the case of a slave.

penal law, which is acknowledged by all who have compared it with contemporary ancient Near Eastern collections of law.[204]

Indeed, the cuneiform accounts simply do not express this same humanitarian ethos. The LH and LE command no penalties for the goring ox and require only a fine from the owner in the event that he is negligent. Such a mild consequence speaks little of the Mesopotamian worldview regarding inherent human worth. "There is good reason to suppose that [the biblical death sentence] is given not because the author expects it to be carried out," Sprinkle opines, "but to say in the strongest possible fashion, 'woe to him who in flagrant disregard of human life allows his dangerous ox to go about unrestrained.' The form may be legal, but the intent is moral."[205]

Arguments that the penalties outlined in the biblical account are too harsh (and therefore less humanitarian) are met with the stipulation in Exod 21:30 where the death penalty could be avoided through paying a ransom. This fine was most likely received by the family of the victim and not the governing authorities. This solution should not be seen as a "begrudging exception" to the death penalty, but rather the presumed normal resolution of the situation described. "A victim's family would have little to gain by having the negligent owner put to death," Sprinkle adds, "whereas if they accepted a ransom, they would both punish the culprit and compensate themselves for the economic loss of one of their members."[206] Even when extreme punishments were warranted, the BC saw it fit to provide alternative options while simultaneously keeping the well-being of the victims in mind. This much is bolstered by the fact that even if the ox owner was unable to pay the required fine, he could pursue debt slavery to satisfy the demand.

Finally, it is worth mentioning the theological language present in Exod 21:30. Even though the negligent ox owner deserved the death sentence for his crime, a כפר (ransom, form of atonement) could be payed for the פִּדְיֹן נַפְשֹׁו (redemption of his life). It is not too far fetched for modern covenant readers to, in a spiritual sense, identify with the ox owner, deserving death but instead receiving כפר. Alternatively, one may identify as the offended party, empowered to pursue a less harsh penalty for the one who caused them pain or harm. "His special concerns came

---

204. C. J. H. Wright, *Old Testament Ethics*, 309.
205. Sprinkle, 'The Book of the Covenant,' 117.
206. Sprinkle, 'The Book of the Covenant,' 217.

through loud and clear," Averbeck notes, "He was meeting them where they were in the cultural world but also taking them where they needed to go to become a nation that would show forth his character and glory in the world."[207]

SUMMARY AND CONCLUSION

By bringing in other ANE legal collections for comparative analysis, this chapter contributes to the overarching goals of the project in several ways. First, it highlights that a thorough comparison with its ANE contemporaries makes the BC's humanitarian agenda more discernible. Navigating the gap between biblical law and modern sensibilities can be challenging, and understanding that slavery in ancient Israel differed significantly from New World slavery is crucial. In ancient Israel, slavery often served as a viable option in the face of foreclosure or poverty while maintaining human dignity and providing a path back to the status quo. Even in the case of chattel slaves, humanity was not to be compromised. Further, although oxen ownership is less common in the modern world, the serious consequences of negligence leading to someone's death should be properly acknowledged rather than treated as a mere procedural liability. Retribution for such negligence is at its best when tempered by a sense of mercy, recognizing that ultimate vengeance belongs to God.

Second, using Wells's legal categorical system to analyze biblical and ANE laws reveals significant distinctions. While laws on debt slaves and goring oxen share similar topics on both sides, they differ in legal issues, legal reasoning, and legal remedies. Similarities, in his view, are best observed on a spectrum ranging from lesser to greater points of identicalness. Although various ancient laws address slavery and negligence, the number of laws considered truly "parallel" is surprisingly limited. Notable parallels include Exod 21:2–11, Lev 25:39–43, and Deut 15:12–18 with LH §117 and LU §4, as well as Exod 21:28–32 with LE §§54–55 and LH §§250–252. Even within these closer sets of laws, the humanitarian concerns emphasized in the BC stand out beyond comparison.

Third, considering that laws inherently mirror the values of their creators, this study proposed the application of C. J. H. Wright's "scale of values" as a tool to effectively discern ethical emphases within distinct legal collections. These emphases encompass (1) the safeguarding of life and

---

207. Averbeck, *The Old Testament Law for the Life of the Church*, 93.

property, (2) the treatment of peoples and the application of punishment, and (3) addressing needs and upholding rights. The analysis demonstrated that the BC consistently gave precedence to the first aspect in each category (life, people, and needs), whereas ANE laws made concessions towards prioritizing the second (property, punishment, and rights). In the context of debt slavery, each slave was ensured the right to marriage, conditions for eventual freedom, and humane treatment—prioritizing life over property. Simultaneously, the rights of the masters were acknowledged, ensuring they did not incur losses on their investments. Importantly, these masters' rights never conflicted with the essential requirements for their slaves—highlighting needs over rights. Regarding the goring ox scenario, it was emphasized that a negligent ox owner deserved the death penalty if the ox caused a fatality. However, a preferable alternative was presented, redeeming the owner's life—underscoring life over punishment and needs over rights, ultimately benefiting everyone involved.

The above findings are critical to a better understanding of the BC's unique, inherent, and innovative humanitarian outlook. However, as highlighted earlier in this chapter, the act of comparing law collections inevitably means also comparing their authors. What is it that inspires Yhwh's covenant readers to adhere to the Law of Moses compared to, for example, the followers of Shamash and the Laws of Hammurabi? The character and values of these lawgivers shape the worldviews of their adherents, molding the manner in which their written laws are then embraced. These aspects will be further explored in the next chapter using both historiographical and theological approaches. The former aids in illuminating the motivations of the legislators—what they sought to protect or promote—while the latter highlights the role that the law collections played in their readers' disposition toward life (i.e., their worldview).

5

The Book of the What?
Humanitarian Values and the "Big Picture"

I served the gods well. I even set up chapels for them! Yet no god stood by me and soothed my heart. Because of them, anything that could have been a favorable portent for me was as far away from me as the heavens. What is my reward for my desire to serve?[1]

—King Ur-Namma's Last Words, *The Death of Ur-Namma*

I am about to go the way of all of the earth, so be strong and act like a man. Keep your commitment to the Lord your God to walk in his ways and to keep his statutes, commands, ordinances, and decrees, as written in the Law of Moses. Do this so that you will prosper in all you do and wherever you turn, and so that the Lord will fulfill his promise that he made to me.

—King David's Last Words, 1 Kgs 2:2–4a

As the previous chapters demonstrated, much can be learned about a culture's values through an exploration of its laws. In this chapter, it will be seen that the reverse is equally true. By learning more about a law collection's societal background, enormous insights can be gained

---

1. Translation my own. See also Black, *The Literature of Ancient Sumer*, 60–61.

regarding the sweeping function and purpose of its decrees. "In order to properly understand and interpret the concept of law in any given society, reference must constantly be made to the total framework and overall *Weltanschauung* [worldview] which that society has evolved," Paul explains, "Law must then be seen as an integral part of the entire structural complex of the society under study."[2] What might Yhwh have had in mind for his people when he spoke his laws into existence (Exod 20:1; 21:1) as compared to human legislators?

Since it has already been shown that biblical law houses an unparalleled emphasis on humanitarian concerns, the next step is to discuss the possible motivations that inspired the authorship of the biblical and cuneiform law collections that contributed to this distinction. Both historiographical and theological/ethical methodologies play important roles in this undertaking. Though they are closely intertwined, each approaches the subject of humanitarian interest from a different vantage point. As such, this chapter will be handled in two parts. Part one will address matters of authorship. Who is the legislator? What motivated them to write their laws? To whom, exactly, were they writing? Questions like these, according to Walton, are key to discerning a society's values by way of its written decrees.[3]

Part two will then explore matters of fidelity, asserting that biblical law possesses a much greater, if not exclusive, interest in religious practice, morality shaping, and author-reader relational growth. C. B. Hays captures the inherent tensions in this arena well, posing the question:

> Does biblical law reflect a greater legal pressure to maintain the well-being of its community? Sometimes one reads that biblical law is more stringent because of its religious character. The idea is that because God is the biblical lawgiver, mere lawbreaking becomes sin, and biblical law must be harsher to maintain the holiness and purity of the divine. But since Mesopotamians saw their gods as the ultimate source of the authority behind the law as well, this assertion can be questioned: Why was Yhwh's holiness more zealously protected in some cases than Shamash's?[4]

Finally, after examining the key points discussed above, this chapter will conclude with a statement on חנן humanitarianism within the BC. Are

---

2. Paul, *Studies in the Book of the Covenant*, 1.
3. Walton, *Introducing the Conceptual World of the Hebrew Bible*, 204.
4. C. B. Hays, *Hidden Riches*, 141–42.

proper humanitarian values and practices solely a result of increased effort and intentionality, or is there a more theological basis?

PART ONE: HISTORIOGRAPHICAL CONSIDERATIONS

The authors of both biblical and cuneiform law collections fervently declared their roles as divine embodiments of compassion, espousing to notions of justice for the lawbreaker and mercy toward the needy. Their inclination to refer to themselves as "shepherds" adds another layer, indicating their perceived authority and leadership in these domains.[5] However, a proper evaluation of each author's authority, agenda, and audience (along with their chosen intermediaries/arbiters) will reveal, even near-identical laws can possess incredibly different intents, legislative spirits, and applications.

Author and Authority

While the subject of legislative authorship is generally straightforward, nuances emerge when considering the delegation of authority. Who is the *ultimate* author? This discussion revolves around two main bonds: the relationship between Yhwh and Moses within the context of biblical law and the connection between the god Shamash and Hammurabi representing cuneiform law.[6] Although other pairings exist in the ANE, such as the relationship between the god Nanna and Ur-Namma (LU) and the god Utu and Lipit-Ishtar (LL), they all conform to a similar model of authorship and authority delegation. Any of these pairings could therefore serve as a suitable representation for cuneiform law collections. However, due to the extensive scholarship available for the LH and its substantial (and generally more descriptive) source material, Shamash and Hammurabi have been selected as the key representative duo.

---

5. See, for example, Ezek 34:11–12; John 10:11–18; and Roth, *Law Collections from Mesopotamia and Asia Minor*. See also her updated translation: https://stars.library.ucf.edu/ancientneareast/134/.

6. For another reputable translation of the LH, see Frayne, RIME 4.03.06.add21: 3240'–3284' (https://cdli.mpiwg-berlin.mpg.de/artifacts/464358).

Cuneiform Law: Shamash and Hammurabi

There is little disagreement that Hammurabi is the sole author of his written decrees. He states so himself in his epilogue: "These are the just decisions which Hammurabi, the able king, has established and thereby has directed the land along the course of truth and the correct way of life . . . I have inscribed my precious pronouncements upon my stela and set it up before the statue of me, the king of justice."[7] While Hammurabi's role as author is clear, there is some ambiguity regarding the authority behind his laws. On one hand, he makes it known in his prologue that the gods chose him for the job, effectively giving him a type of divine *endorsement*: "The gods An and Enlil, for the enhancement of the people, named me by name: Hammurabi, the pious prince, who venerates the gods, to make justice prevail in the land . . . to rise like the sun-god Shamash over all humankind, to illuminate the land."[8] On the other hand, he later explains that his laws are the result of divine *empowerment*: "I am Hammurabi, king of justice (*mēšarum*), to whom the god Shamash has granted insight into the truth (*kīnātu*)."[9] Directly following this proclamation, he returns to referencing his own personal achievements as appropriate rationale for adhering to his written commands.

Paul offers insights to the above dilemma, explaining that the divine empowerment phrase possesses two different yet complementary concepts for law in the ancient world: *kittum*(sg.)/*kīnātu*(pl.) "truth" (Sumerian NÍG.GI.NA) and *mēšarum* "justice" (NÍG.SI.SÁ).[10] These terms, he goes on to explain, were likely used in place of more generic words for types of "law" since any technical terms referring to law collections did not exist yet.[11] According to Speiser, *kittum* can be understood as "the sum of cosmic and immutable truths,"[12] while *mēšarum* is the "process

---

7. Roth, *Law Collections from Mesopotamia and Asia Minor*, 133–34.

8. Roth, *Law Collections from Mesopotamia and Asia Minor*, 76–77. D. P. Wright further clarifies that the gods do not reveal the law at all; they only command the promulgation of justice. It is then Hammurabi's task to translate this ideal into reality by formulating law. For more on this, see D. P. Wright, *Inventing God's Law*, 67 and 288.

9. Roth, *Law Collections from Mesopotamia and Asia Minor*, 135.

10. Paul, *Studies in the Book of the Covenant*, 5. Paul translates *mēšarum* as "righteousness."

11. Paul, *Studies in the Book of the Covenant*, 5. See also J. Berman, *Inconsistency in the Torah*, 113; Bottéro, *Mesopotamia: Writing, Reasoning, and the Gods*, 156–84; and Malul, *Society, Law and Custom*, 12.

12. Speiser, "Authority and Law in Mesopotamia," 12.

whereby law is made to function equitably" and can be seen as "one of the ruler's principle duties."[13] The ruler who has fulfilled these obligations could therefore rightly be described as a *šar mēšarim*, a king of justice. "Kittum and mēšarum combined express eternal verities," Speiser concludes. "Jointly they spell law."[14]

The implications of this distinction is that Hammurabi's authority extended only to the institution of *mēšarim*—he was an agent of law rather than its source.[15] *Kittum/kīnātu*, on the other hand, is of divine origin, gifted to Hammurabi by Shamash. It seems conclusive, then, that Hammurabi is the author of his laws with Shamash acting as the source, a view that is widely accepted amongst scholars.[16] Reinforcing this take is the image at the top of Hammurabi's stela (see below) where Shamash appears to be granting his authority—his *kīnātu*—to Hammurabi. "Shamash is handing Hammurabi a scepter," Hays explains, "which symbolizes the authority to govern and to give laws . . . in his role as the sun-god he was seen as the one who brought all truth unto the light . . . he was the divine judge, and he has the authority to delegate that power."[17]

13. Speiser, "Early Law and Civilization," 874.
14. Speiser, "Cuneiform Law and the History of Civilization," 537.
15. Paul, *Studies in the Book of the Covenant*, 5.
16. See, for example, Levinson, "'You Must Not Add Anything to What I Command You,'" 1–51, see esp. 14; D. P. Wright, *Inventing God's Law*, 67; and C. Hays, *What's Divine about Divine Law?*, 2.
17. C. B. Hays, *Hidden Riches*, 140.

Paul, however, adds another layer by challenging Shamash's position as the ultimate source of "truth." He points to the inscription of Yaḫdun-Lim which states, "To the god Shamash, king of heaven and earth, judge of gods and mankind, whose concern is justice, *to whom truth has been given as a gift*."[18] Indeed, just as Hammurabi received *kīnātu* from Shamash, so Shamash himself received it from some even higher source.[19] "The ultimate source of law in Mesopotamia, then, was independent of the deities and belonged to a sphere of existence that surpassed both the human and divine ... In a society where *kittim* is metadivine, there can be no divine revelation of law."[20] Such a conclusion provides ground to question the authority behind cuneiform law.[21]

Biblical Law: Yhwh and Moses

In stark contrast to the cuneiform legal traditions, Yhwh himself claims to be both the author of biblical law and its ultimate source of authority, wisdom, truth, and righteousness.[22] He does not receive instruction from any other source (Isa 40:13; Job 21:22; Rom 11:34) nor, as Scripture attests, are there any others like him (Exod 8:10; 9:14; Deut 3:24; 32:31; Ps 86:8–10; Jer 10:6). Certainly, "the attribution of the ultimate authorship of a corpus of law to God and its designation as his personal will are unique in the ancient Near East to the Hebrew Bible."[23] It is no wonder, then, why the Bible prefers to avoid human supremacy (Num 23:19–21; Ps 146:3–10). Morrow adds that the Lord alone was, ideally, meant to suffice as Israel's ruler: "The social vision expressed in the mišpāṭîm is that Israel is, more or less, a community of equals whose only king is Yhwh, their God. A sign of this egalitarian tendency can be found in the covenantal framework that now surrounds the Covenant Code in Exodus

---

18. Hallo et al., *The COS*, 2:260, lines 1–6; emphasis added.

19. It is noteworthy that the verb *šarākum*, "to present a gift," is used in both texts.

20. Paul, *Studies in the Book of the Covenant*, 6–7, 99–101. For more on this, see Kaufmann, *The Religion of Israel*, 21–23.

21. For more on the topic of legal authorship in the ANE, see Charpin, *Writing, Law, and Kingship*; and LeFebvre, *Collections, Codes and Torah*.

22. Note especially the use of first-person pronouns throughout the BC as discussed in chapter 2. For more on this, see D. P. Wright, *Inventing God's Law*, 290, along with the bibliography in his footnotes. See also the explicit proclamations in Deut 4.

23. Levinson, "The Right Chorale," 32.

19 and 24."[24] Even when the Israelites later demanded a human king, he was still to be held to the same laws with no litigation power (Deut 17:18–20; 1 Sam 12).[25] (In fact, according to Deut 17:14–17, he was even to be held to a higher standard with respect to his personal gain!) Garrett summarizes this concept well: "The distinctive thing [between cuneiform law and biblical law] is this: God gave Torah to Israel, not to a king. Because Torah is the possession of the entire nation, it is their 'wisdom and sagacity' [Deut 4]. In contrast to . . . Hammurabi, no one man in Israel is categorically distinct from the populace by virtue of being the interpreter and enforcer of the laws."[26]

With the above in mind, what is to be made of Moses's role? He is not a king like Hammurabi, yet God commissioned him to hear and report the law (Deut 4:14; 5:28–31; 18:15–18; cf. Exod 19:9). Moreover, he orates with glaring authority, especially in his speeches in Deuteronomy.[27] According to Watts, the Torah paints Moses less like royalty and more like a prophet and teacher/scribe. While it is true that he possessed a form of delegated authority to give the law to Israel, Moses notes two sources for that delegated authority: Yhwh and Israel. He was a prophet in that both God *and* Israel appointed him to speak as an intermediary and intercessor: "All the people witnessed the thunder and lightning, the sound of the ram's horn, and the mountain surrounded by smoke. When the people saw it, they trembled and stood at a distance. 'You speak to us, and we will listen,' they said to Moses, 'but don't let God speak to us, or we will die'" (Exod 20:18–20). He was also a teacher/scribe in that he recorded, taught, interpreted, edited, and published the laws, but the ultimate lawgiver remains Yhwh alone.[28]

---

24. Morrow, *An Introduction to Biblical Law*, 94.

25. De Vaux, *Ancient Israel: Its Life and Institutions*, 150. For the idea that the biblical laws were purposefully written this way in order to assert absolute authority over the other nations, see Levinson, "The Right Chorale," 33; and Chavel, "A Kingdom of Priests," 169–222. See also some of the opinions discussed in Watts, *Reading Law*, 137–43; and Jackson, *Studies in the Semiotics of Biblical Law*, 138.

26. Garrett, *The Problem of the Old Testament*, 223.

27. For an interpretations suggesting that Moses was meant to represent what the ideal king of Israel should look like, see Rosenberg, *King and Kin*, x–xi.

28. Watts, *Reading Law*, 112, 117. See also Kofoed, "Encoding and Decoding Culture," 254, where he states, "It was the king, not the god(s) who issued the laws of the Sumerian and Akkadian collections, God was the law-giver in ancient Israel. Moses was merely a transmitter of the laws, a medium for God's address to the people. Neither the leader nor the people, but YHWH alone who was the all-important agent."

Author and Agenda

The previous overview allows the scope of legislative authorship to be narrowed to God, representing biblical law, and human kings, representing cuneiform law. Although figures like Moses and various deities from the ANE pantheons are involved in legal administration to some extent, they do not claim legal authorship. The next pertinent question revolves around the issue of agenda: Who or what do the laws seek to promote? What motivated the authors to establish a legal framework, and what were their ultimate goals? Similar to the examination of authority above, an introduction to this topic is best framed by the written proclamations of each author toward their respective readers. Following this will be a discussion on the nature of the prologues and epilogues in cuneiform law and if the Bible compares. Finally, leveraging the discussion up to this point, the functions of the respective law collections will be explored.

Humanitarian Proclamation

The authors of cuneiform law presented nothing short of a robust outcry for justice for the oppressed, particularly for the "orphan and the widow."[29] Samples of such proclamations are plentiful and clearly stated:

Ur-Namma:

> I did not deliver the orphan to the rich. I did not deliver the widow to the mighty. I did not deliver the man with but one shekel to the man with one mina. I did not deliver the man with but one sheep to the man with one ox. I settled my generals, my mothers, my brothers, and their families; I did not accept their instructions, I did not impose orders. I eliminated enmity, violence, and cries for justice. I established justice in the land.[30]

Lipit-Ishtar:

> ... in order to establish justice in the land, to eliminate cries for justice, to eradicate enmity and armed violence, to bring well-being to the lands of Sumer and Akkad ... I made the father

---

29. This motif existed long before the LU, the earliest known law collection. The Edicts of Urukagina, for example, state "Uru-inimgina [Urukagina] made a compact with the divine Nin-Girsu that the powerful man would not oppress the orphan or widow." See Hallo et al., *COS*, 2.408.

30. Roth, *Law Collections from Mesopotamia and Asia Minor*, 16–17.

support his children, I made the child support his father . . . I, Lipit-Ishtar, obligated those in a household of dependent workers to service ten days per month the wife of a man . . . the son of a man . . . I made weeping, lamentation, shouts for justice and suits taboo. I made right and truth shine forth and I brought well-being to the lands of Sumer and Akkad.[31]

Hammurabi:

. . . to make justice prevail in the land, to abolish the wicked and the evil, to prevent the strong from oppressing the weak . . . I established truth and justice as the declaration of the land, I enhanced the well-being of the people. I am Hammurabi, the noble king. I have not been careless or negligent toward humankind . . . I made the people of all settlements lie in safe pastures, I did not tolerate anyone intimidating them. The great gods having chosen me, I am indeed the shepherd who brings peace, whose scepter is just . . . In order that the mighty not wrong the weak, to provide just ways for the waif and the widow, I have inscribed my precious pronouncements upon my stela and set it up before the statue of me, the king of justice, in the city of Babylon.[32]

Similar outcries can also be found in the Bible, notably within the laws themselves. The BC, for example, explicitly states, "You must not mistreat any widow or fatherless child" (Exod 22:21 [22]) and immediately thereafter reveals the weighty ramifications for disobedience.[33] Neither side is lacking in explicit concern for those who are in need nor wanting in the desire for justice to be enacted on their behalf. Both are humanitarian. "There therefore seems to be no reason to suggest that the kings, lawgivers, jurists, or compilers of the ANE world were any different than those in the Bible about expressing sympathy for the socially weak in their societies."[34]

---

31. Roth, *Law Collections from Mesopotamia and Asia Minor*, 25–26, 33–35.

32. Roth, *Law Collections from Mesopotamia and Asia Minor*, 76–81, 133–34.

33. Cf. the laws in Deut 14:29; 24:19; and the proclamations in Deut 10:18; 14:29; 27:19; Isa 1:17; Jer 22:3; Job 29:12–13; Ps 82:3; Hos 14:3; Zech 7:9–10; Mal 3:5; etc. For a discussion on the widow motif in Scripture, see Kraftchick, "Widows," 421–31.

34. Tsai, *Human Rights in Deuteronomy*, 173.

Legal Prologues and Epilogues

The preceding declarations notably come from the prologues and epilogues of their respective writer's law collections. As such, it is important to examine the relationship between them and the legal corpora they claim to encapsulate. Three law collections qualify for this analysis: the LU, LL, and LH.[35] The prologues and epilogues of these law collections largely possess three major features: (1) a self-praise of the king's benevolence, achievements, and contributions for all the people and cities under his reign; (2) a declaration of his appointed kingship and power granted by divine authority; and (3) an emphasis on his role as guardian and protector of justice and the socially weak.[36]

Are these exhortations a reliable source for understanding the motivations of the ANE kings and determining the values implicit within their laws, or are they ultimately just self-contained, elaborate speeches expected of people in their position? Some see the entirety of the cuneiform legal text (prologue-corpus-epilogue) as being a literary unity—both the laws and the prologues/epilogues were written with the other in mind.[37] Others suggest that the laws existed in their own right with their own distinct purposes apart from the prologues and epilogues and were only later combined into one document.[38] Whichever the case, reading the cuneiform law collections in their final form is preferable since this approach provides further insight into their worldview/*Volksgeist* and is consistent with how this study approaches the biblical laws and their surrounding narratives.[39] "The prologues describe the political context for the composition and establish the theological, historical, and ethical legitimacy of the ruler's reforms," states Kofoed, "Since the prologues

---

35. The LH contains only a prologue and no epilogue.

36. Tsai, *Human Rights in Deuteronomy*, 243.

37. Bottéro, *Mesopotamia: Writing, Reasoning, and the Gods*; Finkelstein, "Ammisaduqa's Edict and the Babylonian 'Law Codes,'" 91–104; and Paul, *Studies in the Book of the Covenant*, 26.

38. See Westbrook, "Biblical and Cuneiform Law Codes," 247–65. See also Otto, "Laws of Hammurabi," 502–3; and Kilma, "Gesetze," 243–55.

39. Some scholars put forward that the BC, like its Mesopotamian counterparts, contains something equitable to a prologue-corpus-epilogue formula. Paul, for example, places the BC within the larger context of Exod 19–23 with 19:3–6 representing the prologue and 23:20–33 representing the epilogue (Paul, *Studies in the Book of the Covenant*, 29–35). Any resemblances between biblical and cuneiform law on this front, however, likely has nothing to do with the agenda/function of the laws themselves. For more on this, see Van Houten, *The Alien in Israelite Law*, 44–46.

provide the rationale behind and incentive for obeying these laws, they are an important and inseparable part of the compositions."[40]

Reading cuneiform law collections as a literary unity brings a new question to the table. The humanitarian outcries within the legal prologues/epilogues are clear, explicit, and zealous. Why, then, are these indignations not more readily observable within the laws themselves like in the case of the BC (see chapters 2 and 4)? "Hammurabi claims in the framework that accompanies the laws to have established social justice by preventing the strong from oppressing the weak and by providing justice for the orphan and widow," Otto explains, "[but] the collection of laws proper does not show corresponding traits of this social concern."[41] It is at this juncture that the authors' underlying motivations start to take shape. Indeed, "Officials and scribes collected, compiled, and inscribed the laws," Averbeck explains, "but the stela on which the Laws of Hammurabi appeared, for example, was a monumental royal inscription erected to laud the just rule of Hammurabi before the gods and his people—that is, royal propaganda."[42]

Legal Function and Intent

Scholars are in general agreement that the law collections of the ANE are, by and large, meant to serve as a form of propaganda used to legitimize the reign of the current king. For example, Gane states, "These collections appear to be legal treatises that provide models of judicial wisdom. As such, they could be used by kings who sponsored them to demonstrate their judicial wisdom and thereby support the legitimacy of their reigns."[43] C. B. Hays agrees: "The promulgation of laws by the king ... might have had mostly a propagandistic or votive purpose; that is to say, the king was seeking to make a statement about his authority before the people, and about his piety, before the gods."[44] C. J. H. Wright, in more certain terms, opines that ANE law collections are essentially "propaganda for the empire and its government. A country governed by *this* king, with judges whose decisions are guided by the wisdom illustrated in *these* laws, will

---

40. Kofoed, "Encoding and Decoding Culture," 243.
41. Otto, "Laws of Hammurabi," 502.
42. Averbeck, *The Old Testament Law for the Life of the Church*, 86.
43. Gane, *Old Testament Law for Christians*, 126. See also Walton, *Ancient Near Eastern Thought and the Old Testament*, 202–3.
44. C. B. Hays, *Hidden Riches*, 139.

surely be a model of justice and order. Such a society will make [the king] look good."⁴⁵

These scholars, amongst others, go on to explain that one of the core functions of ANE law collections is to express the juridical wisdom of their authors.⁴⁶ In this sense, biblical law is not too different from its cuneiform counterparts: "See, I have taught you decrees and laws as the LORD my God commanded me, so that you may follow them in the land you are entering to take possession of it. Observe them carefully, for this will show your wisdom and understanding to the nations, who will hear about them and say, 'Surely this great nation is a wise and understanding people'" (Deut 4:5–6). It can therefore be rightly said that, "In a proper sense of the word, the Book of the Covenant and related texts in the Pentateuch are propaganda for Yahweh. An Israel shaped by the wisdom of these laws would reflect the character of their God . . . Israel should make Yahweh look good" (see Jer 13:11).⁴⁷

Thus far in this segment, it has been seen that the authors of both biblical and cuneiform law lay claim to a principled and admirable humanitarian agenda and present their laws as a corpus of wisdom and guidance for their subjects, thereby legitimizing their authority. It is here, however, that their similarities in function cease to be so evident.⁴⁸ Where cuneiform law seems to double down on the legitimacy of the king, biblical collections like the BC promote religious/cultic elements; persuasive rhetoric; ethical and moral implications; and the necessity of a personal connection with the author, Yʜᴡʜ, through the establishment of a covenant, an act from which the "Book of the Covenant" gets its name

---

45. C. J. H. Wright, *Exodus*, 388. See also Kofoed, "Encoding and Decoding Culture," 247–48.

46. See esp. Walton, *Ancient Near Eastern Thought and the Old Testament*, 273, where he describes ANE law as being *exclusively* a wisdom text with no intention of serving in a proper legislative capacity; and Launderville, *Piety and Politics*, 281: "Rather than creating these laws like a legislator, Hammurabi was an executor who sustained them and made them effective . . . It is important to note that the larger fabric of the social order was shaped by the traditional and customary ways of the land, which the *Code* presupposed but made no pretense of articulating."

47. C. J. H. Wright, *Exodus*, 389.

48. C. J. H. Wright adds that both Israel and the civilizations of the ANE seek to maintain order amidst the continual possibility of chaos. This is no doubt a similarity, but it would be difficult to imagine a law collection that did not by virtue of its existence promote such a desire. Law, by its nature, brings order. Nevertheless, the cultural and cosmological rationale behind this call for order provides helpful insights for this discussion. For more on this, see C. J. H. Wright, *Exodus*, 387–88.

(Exod 24:7). This approach was innovative within the ancient world and remains unique to the laws of the Bible. Such a shift in function, as will be further explored in part two of this chapter, ultimately categorizes biblical law as a completely different type of genre or document altogether. Further illuminating the divide between biblical and cuneiform law are the expectations and benefits imparted to their intended recipients, a point to which this study now directs its attention.

Author and Audience

Cuneiform legislators had two general audiences in mind: the gods who blessed and empowered their decrees and the people who read, heard, or simply saw them. With respect to the former, it is not surprising that the authors of ANE law included so many of their personal achievements within their prologues and epilogues. While their feats would no doubt have been impressive to their human audiences (both local and foreign), the primary focus of these reports was most likely on what the king wanted the gods to know.[49] Walton elaborates, "The expectation is that through such reports the gods will be convinced that the king is doing the job well for which he was chosen ... Their role should be adequately recognized, and they should believe that their reputations and stature are growing as a result of the king's activities. Thus, as Mesopotamian historiography legitimates the king, it also serves to enhance the reputation of the deity."[50]

Regarding the latter, they had two categories of people in mind: their own subjects and those who would later come into power.[51] To the first of these groups, Hammurabi, for example, states,

> Let any wronged man who has a lawsuit come before the statue of me, the king of justice, and let him have my inscribed stela read aloud to him, thus may he hear my precious pronouncements and let my stela reveal the lawsuit for him; may he examine his case, may he calm his troubled heart, and may he praise me, saying: Hammurabi ... secured the eternal well-being of the people and provided just ways for the land.[52]

---

49. Tadmor, "Propaganda, Literature, Historiography," 331; and Albrektson, *History and the Gods*, 43.
50. Walton, *Ancient Near Eastern Thought and the Old Testament*, 211.
51. Van de Mieroop, *King Hammurabi of Babylon*, 110.
52. Roth, *Law Collections from Mesopotamia and Asia Minor*, 134–35.

As the inscription implies, not many would have been able to read his impressive stela, but its very physical presence and design continued to convey his greatness visually if not textually. "Whatever its details, the broad message the illustration communicated to even the illiterate must have been clear: King Hammurabi and the god of justice Shamash work together to protect the people of Babylonia."[53]

The "wronged man" (*awīlum ḫablum*) discussed in Hammurabi's epilogue (see the above inscription) has been the subject of ongoing conversation due to its implications on the overall function of his laws and, by extension, the laws of other cuneiform collections. Until recently, this section has generally been understood as descriptive, instructing the wronged man to bring his case to Hammurabi himself for clarification. Roth suggests, however, that Hammurabi's intention in writing the "wronged man" clause was to declare that his stela would persist as a place where those who have been wronged can find solace through prayer and by offering blessings to the king.[54] Van de Mieroop agrees, furthering the implication that the stela could have acted as some type of shrine: "Someone who felt wronged could thus find solace in the monument [itself], because it showed that justice would prevail in the end. Hammurabi guaranteed that his country was correctly ruled. He protected the weak from abuse by the powerful, he sheltered the widow and the waif, and his stela announced that to all."[55] As such, the responsibility would fall on Babylonia's future kings to ensure that Hammurabi's statutes remain enforced as originally inscribed.

ANE legislators sought to ensure that their laws would remain in effect long after their passing by extending their authority to future rulers. King Lipit-Ishtar, for example, states: "When I established justice in the lands of Sumer and Akkad, I erected this stela. He who will not do anything evil to it, who will not damage my work, who will not efface my inscription and write his own name on it—may he be granted life

---

53. Roth, "Mesopotamian Legal Traditions," 23.

54. Roth, "Hammurabi's Wronged Man," 38–45. Roth very importantly labels the nature of the "wrong" to be more practical rather than ethical. Using LH §34 for her rationale, she states, "It seems unlikely to me that the offense . . . characterized by the verb *ḫabālum* is simply some vague ethical wrong; rather, it must involve a concrete and definable—and hence prosecutable—abuse of the supervisor's position of authority" (42). She later concludes that "it is not difficult to infer that the 'wrong' that might be suffered by a *ḫablum* or *ḫabiltum* involves being denied the required and due sustenance allotments" (43).

55. Van de Mieroop, *King Hammurabi of Babylon*, 110.

and breadth of long days ... but, he who [does these things]—that man, whether he is a king [or some other great figure] ... may he be completely obliterated."[56] Hammurabi makes similar declarations: "If a future ruler heeds my pronouncements which I have inscribed upon my stela, and does not reject my judgements, change my pronouncements, or alter my engraved image, then may the god Shamash lengthen his reign, just as he has done for me, the king of justice, and so may he shepherd his people with justice."[57] Following this, Hammurabi goes on to pronounce several curses upon the future king who does not follow these instructions including afflictions like famine, loss of order, obliteration, torture, loss in battle, infertility, and disease. In this way, Hammurabi's audience included future aspiring leaders just as much as the gods and their subjects.[58] "Even the loquacious Hammurabi is high on self-claims about maintaining justice in general, and prospering the people, their cities and not least the cults of the gods."[59]

By comparison, biblical law does not seek to address or appease any other gods since the author, YHWH, is the self-declared One and Only God and is himself the source of the law's authority. In fact, he actively opposes the inclusion of any other deities (e.g., Exod 20:3; 23:32–33; Deut 4:35; 32:39). Further, biblical law does not seek to uniquely influence any king (living or yet-to-come) since there is equity amongst all peoples. Kings are held to the same standards as everyone else. "The Israelites are 'equalized,' as it were," states J. Berman, "in their status before God as members of a covenantal community but, no less, in their standing before the law."[60] The only remaining audience for biblical law to target, then, is that of the LORD's subjects—that is, those who have willingly entered into a covenant relationship with him. The Israelites were more than just hearers of the biblical decrees, however; they were their *recipients*. "Torah belongs to Israel and not to Moses," Garrett explains, "because YHWH gave Torah to all of Israel, all Israel may call upon YHWH with confidence. He is near to them and does not dwell aloof in a high ziggurat. In a nation such as Babylon, it is the king who possesses the legal text and who

---

56. Roth, *Law Collections from Mesopotamia and Asia Minor*, 34.

57. Roth, *Law Collections from Mesopotamia and Asia Minor*, 136.

58. For a discussion on how Hammurabi's intention was to endow the people with self-governing authority, see Sallaberger, "König Ḫammurapi und die Babylonier," 46–58. See also Cancik-Kirschbaum, "'Menschen ohne König...,'" 167–90.

59. Kitchen and Lawrence, *Treaty, Law and Covenant in the Ancient Near East*, 27.

60. J. Berman, *Created Equal*, 169.

has access to the god. The *people* of Babylon did not have any legal text at all; *Hammurabi* did."[61] It is not by mere personal preference that this project has consistently been referring to the adherents of biblical law as "covenant readers." Such a description applies to readers both then (in ancient times) and now (under the New Covenant),[62] meaning biblical law collections like the BC continue to have an audience.[63]

PART TWO: LAW AND RELIGION

"The authors of Exodus leave no doubt that they envisioned law as representing the essence of their religion. God promises the Israelites at the outset of the wilderness journey that the revelation of law will be the source of health for them (Exod 15:22–27)."[64] This anchoring of law within religion remains unique to the legal tradition of Israel within the ancient world.[65] "Only in biblical compilations are moral exhortations and religious injunctions combined with legal prescriptions,"[66] Paul explains, "man's civil, moral, and religious obligations all ultimately stem from God, and hence are interwoven within a single corpus of divinely given law."[67] Falk goes a step further, stating that the laws "are meant not only as norms of behavior but also as objects of contemplation to lead toward the perception and love of God."[68] It is no wonder, then, that a failure to observe biblical law is considered to be much more than just some form of civil infringement. It is sin. Put differently, to reject God's laws is to reject knowledge of his character, his sense of morality, the blessings of his covenants, and ultimately the means with which he establishes and regulates the relationship between himself and his believers.[69] Such divine-human relational concerns are simply not shared by other ANE laws.

---

61. Garrett, *The Problem of the Old Testament*, 223. See also Wells, "What is Biblical Law?," 226–27.
62. See Jer 33:33–34; 2 Tim 3:16–17.
63. For more on this, see Averbeck, *The Old Testament Law for the Life of the Church*, 225–54.
64. Dozeman, *Exodus*, 462. See also Daube, *Studies in Biblical Law*, 1.
65. See Bartor, "Biblical Law," 433; and Greengus, "Biblical and ANE Law," 243–52.
66. Paul, *Studies in the Book of the Covenant*, 43.
67. Paul, *Studies in the Book of the Covenant*, 37.
68. Falk, "Spirituality and Jewish Law," 130.
69. Bartor, "Biblical Law," 434.

The integration of law and religion within the Bible is further evidenced by its unique dealings with underlying attitudes such as love (Lev 19:18, 34; Deut 6:5) versus hatred and grudges (Lev 19:17–18), covetousness (Exod 20:17; Deut 5:21), and generous versus selfish thinking (Deut 15:9–10), which only God can detect and reward or punish (see 1 Sam 16:7; 1 Chr 28:9; Ps 139:2, 4, 23–24; Jer 11:20).[70] Biblical law also contains guidelines regarding proper sacrifice, purification rituals, modes of worship, and festival observance. None of these religious practices can be found in cuneiform law collections.[71] Finally, and perhaps most significant to the divine-human relational aspect of biblical law, is the claim of divine revelation. As Levinson explains, "It was not the legal collection as a literary genre but the voicing of publicly revealed law as the personal will of God that was unique to ancient Israel . . . There is a clear relationship between textual voice and textual authority, so that attributing a legal text to God literally gives that text ultimate authority."[72] Bartor continues on this point: "Significant as it is, this is just the first level. For the lawgiver [God] is not content only with a relationship predicated on the delivery of the laws via unmediated encounter. Rather, [he] weaves this relationship in various ways into the very nature of the laws . . . [He] maintains a relationship with the people of Israel also, and perhaps chiefly, by means of the laws."[73]

It is important at this point to repeat the fact that the biblical law collections are an inseparable part of the wider context of the Torah. They therefore ultimately seek to further the overarching goal of *instruction* present within all of its stories, dialogues, religious injunctions, histories, and ethical deliberations through their legal pronouncements. These genres are so intertwined that it can sometimes be difficult to determine where one begins and another ends, prompting scholars like Crüsemann to understand the Torah as being made up of its very own genre—that

---

70. Gane, *Old Testament Law for Christians*, 130.

71. Walton, *Ancient Israelite Literature in Its Cultural Context*, 74–78; see esp. his chart on 76–77. It should be noted that there are a few ANE laws that touch on the topic of religion, but only in a very limited sense (Walton, *Ancient Israelite Literature in Its Cultural Context*, 129n74). For example, LH §2 addresses an accusation of practicing witchcraft, LH §6 and §8 stipulate punishments for stealing things belonging to a deity. HL §44b outlines proper disposal of remnants of a ritual for purifying a person; but even in this situation, it is "a case for the king" (see Roth, *Law Collections from Mesopotamia and Asia Minor*, 223).

72. Levinson, *Legal Revision and Religious Renewal*, 27–28.

73. Bartor, "Biblical Law," 441.

is, the Hebrew tradition of melding narration, religion, ethics, and law.[74] This is, of course, not to say that the Torah completely ignored the writing styles and traditions of its time, as detailed in previous segments; rather, according to Watts, it repurposed such approaches for a new cause. "The Pentateuch adopted older legal conventions and rhetorical strategies to achieve a novel objective: the constitution of a people on the basis of religious rather than state institutions."[75] As such, the Torah became the first canon of Scripture for the Jewish and Christian faiths. "Without [it] there would be no Bible."[76]

With the above in mind, a well-rounded theological interpretation of the Bible's law collections requires intentional and meaningful consideration of their literary, canonical, and historical background—elements which this volume aimed to prioritize in the preceding and current chapters. For example, it would have been difficult to better understand the BC's stance on the value of human life, the necessity for sabbath rest, and the hierarchical order of creation without consistent reference to the foremost chapters of the book of Genesis. Indeed, the Israelites' cosmology and disclosed identity of their Creator—the foundations for their worldview—deeply informed the way in which they interpreted, cherished, and applied the laws they were gifted.[77] This same logic applies to the exodus. Evidence of this can be found in the book of Judges where the Israelites grew increasingly lawless. "The laws were violated," Kofoed opines, "because their rationale, i.e., the historical experience of what God had done for Israel in the past, was forgotten; isolated from their original setting and situated in a new context, they no longer made [any kind of compelling] sense." In other words, "Law has to be believed in, or it will not work. It involves not only a man's reason and will, but his emotions, his intuitions, and commitments, and his faith."[78]

---

74. Crüsemann, *The Torah*, 191.

75. Watts, *Reading Law*, 160.

76. Orlinsky, "The Forensic Character of the Hebrew Bible," 92.

77. Such investigations are necessary for a fuller understanding of the Bible's laws. For more on this, see Wenham, *Story as Torah*; and C. J. H. Wright, *Exodus*, 20. The same can (and should) be done for cuneiform law collections as well, though their cosmologies are separate from their laws. For very helpful insights on this topic, see Tsai, *Human Rights in Deuteronomy*, 165–74.

78. Kofoed, "Encoding and Decoding Culture," 253; and H. J. Berman, *The Interaction of Law and Religion*, 14, respectively.

Law and Morality

By this point, it can be surmised that biblical law recognizes Yhwh, who is absolute and unchanging in nature, as the sole source of ethics and morality. His written laws therefore establish absolute standards of morality by which his covenant readers are to abide. Such a concept is impossible for cuneiform law collections given their polytheistic backgrounds:

> Polytheism... implies the existence of a plurality of superhuman wills. This very condition precludes the absolute omnipotence of any one of these wills. Even if... one of these... deities... is... the head of a pantheon, he must at all times be mindful of the purposes of the other deities which are potentially vitiating to his own designs... If the first thought of the gods, as that of man, must be "to look out for himself "... moral and ethical considerations necessarily become secondary."[79]

Unterman adds that "since [God] has no real rivals, his will cannot be contested. So [God] can be viewed as motivated 'by the highest ideals.' Furthermore, he is in a position to lay down a mandate for man's behavior... in accordance with these ideals, and to guarantee man's well-being if his will is complied with, an advantage which no polytheistic god could possibly enjoy."[80] God's commandment to put no other gods before him (Exod 20:3; 21:13) is therefore a loving prescription toward his covenant readers and not, as some put forward, a competitive gesture between God and other worthy adversaries striving for ultimate authority.[81]

The use of personal pronouns within cuneiform law collections further reveals their underlying dispositions with respect to morality shaping. Tsai notes two observations worthy of thought. First, their use of the first-person voice within their prologues and epilogues neither has the intention to establish a relationship, interact with, and have dialogue with their legal subjects, nor to shape their morality or ethical values. Second, the third-person voice within their laws provides almost no inspiration for morality shaping and contains no interpersonal relationship on which their legal subjects can meditate and shape their brotherhood and peoplehood. These observations cause Tsai to conclude that "ANE laws do not hold the view that the law is a vehicle for carrying out the

---

79. Finkelstein, "The Study of Man," 438.
80. Unterman, *Justice for All*, xviii.
81. See D. P. Wright, *Inventing God's Law*, 292–300.

function of morality shaping."[82] Biblical law, on the other hand, evidences a desire for a *reciprocal* relationship with the lawgiver. This is most likely why, as chapter 4 concluded, humanitarian concerns are far less pervasive within cuneiform laws.[83]

The so-called tripartite divide within biblical law is also worthy of brief mention. That is the understanding that the law contains three distinct categories of legal application—moral, civil, and ceremonial—and that only the mutually exclusive "moral laws" persist as relevant. Such divisions become difficult to uphold given the preceding notions that proper moral living is reliant upon the imitation of God's character and the reciprocation of his personhood which the *entirety* of the law commands and reflects. Reasons for rejecting the tripartite divide abound: the Bible never alludes to it,[84] some laws fall into more than one category,[85] the Bible talks of the law as being unified,[86] etc. In his exegesis and ethical study of Lev 19, Martens opines:

> One must conclude that the distinctions between cultic, moral, and civil regulations are, if not artificial, certainly extraneous to Hebrew thought. In this single speech the stipulations about refraining from image-making (cult), insisting on truth-telling (moral), and prescribing compassionate treatment for aliens (civil) tumble about in chaotic confusion. As a grid for sorting out the way Christians deal with Old Testament law, the classification of "cultic, moral, civil," is not helpful.[87]

Instead of identifying *which* laws are moral, "we need to study and classify the laws of the Old Testament against their own social background in ancient Israel, and then discuss what significant moral features or principles emerge within *every* kind of law they had."[88] The entirety of biblical law therefore contributes to morality shaping, not just pieces of it.[89]

---

82. Tsai, *Human Rights in Deuteronomy*, 174.

83. Tsai, *Human Rights in Deuteronomy*, 247. See also Fox-Decent, "Is the Rule of Law Really Indifferent to Human Rights?," 536.

84. See Dorsey, "The Law of Moses and the Christian," 325–30.

85. For example, is keeping the Sabbath moral, civil, or ceremonial?

86. For a very helpful conversation on this point, see Averbeck, *The Old Testament Law for the Life of the Church*, 310–28.

87. Martens, "How is the Christian to Construe Old Testament Law?" 201. See also J. D. Hays, "Applying Old Testament Law Today," 21–35.

88. C. J. H. Wright, *Old Testament Ethics*, 288.

89. Cf. Ps 19:1–11.

Law and Covenant

The most glaring and fundamental difference between biblical and cuneiform law are undoubtedly the covenants associated with the former. "The laws we find in the Pentateuch were not just a list of injunctions intended to foster justice within an abstract goal of preserving cosmic order amidst the conflicting claims of different gods," states C. J. H. Wright, "Rather, they are specifically given within the story of the unique covenant relationship of Yahweh God to this one nation, Israel."[90] So important is this distinction that the initial collection of laws within the Torah (Exod 21–23) was given the title סֵפֶר הַבְּרִית "the book/scroll of the *covenant*" (Exod 24:7). Averbeck's understanding of what constitutes a covenant is helpful; a covenant contains two parties and is basically "a solemn and formal means of expressing and a method of establishing and defining a relationship." He goes on to conclude that "in one way or another, the issue at hand is always the manner in which they will practice relationship with each other."[91]

This emphasis on a formalized divine-human relationship is evidenced by a number of uniquely distinguishable features which repeatedly appear throughout the legal corpus of the BC in an unprecedented and unparalleled fashion.[92] C. J. H. Wright points out three of these features for consideration. First, the BC is based on the historical knowledge of God's election and covenant with Abraham and his redemption of the Israelites out of slavery in Egypt. Second, it constitutes a relationship that is profoundly personal in that Yhwh makes explicit promises and Israel makes reciprocal commitments. Third, it involves Yhwh's direct speech within the laws themselves, meaning that the laws are not simply impersonal formulations circulated by the government. They contain, for example, God's distinctive and hands-on comments, explanations, warnings, and exhortations, all in the first-person singular.[93]

Additional evidence is seen in the way God aligns himself with the people of Israel in anticipation of the Sinai covenant: "I will take you as my own people, and I will be your God" (Exod 6:7). Post the Sinai event,

---

90. C. J. H. Wright, *Exodus*, 390.

91. Averbeck, *The Old Testament Law for the Life of the Church*, 35. See also Knoppers, "Ancient Near Eastern Royal Grants," 696; and Davidson, "Covenant Ideology in Ancient Israel," 324.

92. C. J. H. Wright, *Exodus*, 390.

93. C. J. H. Wright, *Exodus*, 390. See also Hamilton, *Exodus*, 360; and the discussions in chapter 2.

both parties formally adopted new identities; Yhwh *became* the God of the newly formed nation of Israel and, conversely, Israel *became* a nation consecrated for God (Exod 19). "This co-identification expands the identity of Yahweh (since it is new)," Walton explains, "just as it expands the identity of Israel. As a result of this co-identification, Israel is made holy because Yahweh is holy."[94] The primary objective of biblical law, then, is "not merely (though emphatically) justice, but *holiness*. Israel is to reflect the character of Yahweh in all dimensions of life. That is what will make them 'holy'—that is, as different or distinctive from the nations as Yahweh is different from the nations' gods."[95] God's covenantal lawgiving established the framework through which Israel's moral and religious values were to function in alignment with his character, thereby intertwining law and religion.[96]

Law and Humanitarianism

Both biblical law and cuneiform law championed humanitarian ideals by promoting justice and enforcing actions that safeguard the overall well-being of their subjects. However, it is within the intersection of law and religion in the biblical account that the essential nature of its humanitarian concerns undergoes a fundamental transformation, setting it apart from its ANE contemporaries. The product of this transformation has been consistently referred to as "חָנֻן humanitarianism" throughout this project. As outlined in chapter 2, it can be further understood as promulgating "beneficent actions [which] are freely offered or received and contribute to the well-being of another or to the health of an *ongoing relationship*" and that such deeds are "not isolated actions, but constitute the *ongoing shape of life*."[97] The key term in this definition is "ongoing" and aptly works in conjunction with the priorities of relationship building and worldview commitment. Just as God sought out a meaningful

---

94. Walton and Walton, *The Lost World of the Torah*, 92.

95. C. J. H. Wright, *Exodus*, 390. See also Alexander, *Exodus*, 450–51, where he states that the BC "highlights the obligations placed upon the Israelites in order for them to be a holy nation, living under the authority of God ... to create an identity for the Israelites by distinguishing them from other nations." Biblical covenants notably contain some similarities with ANE treaties in their style. For more on this, see Greengus, "Covenant and Treaty in the Hebrew Bible," 91–126.

96. Gane, *Old Testament Law for Christians*, 42.

97. Fretheim, "חָנַן," 204. Emphasis added.

and compassionate relationship with the Israelites, so too should they build meaningful and compassionate relationships with each other. In this way, "these actions are not only pleasing to God but are considered as done unto the LORD himself and carry their own reward."[98]

What is it about the infusion of religious thought that alters the way in which adherents of the law are expected to treat each other? It might be tempting at this point to conclude that the law collections in the Bible simply placed a higher value on human life compared to the cuneiform collections. While not entirely inaccurate, this conclusion fails to acknowledge the theological underpinnings of the Bible, suggesting that all the cuneiform laws would need to do to "measure up" is elevate their standards, but the issue runs much deeper than this. Finkelstein, for instance, asserts that "it is not that the Mesopotamian thinkers held a truly low estimate of man's place in the cosmic scheme, or that they were oblivious of his uniqueness within the visible order of nature." Instead, the Bible introduces a categorical distinction, treating laws concerning people as fundamentally different from those pertaining to property.[99] While cuneiform law saw no qualitative gap between people and any other subject, biblical law strongly adheres to the principle that "nobody's life, not even that of a would-be burglar, may be taken with impunity solely in defense of property (Exod 22:1–2 [2–3]); the issue of life or death, or homicide, overrides any question of guilt related to the wrongful taking of mere 'things.'"[100] Worldview developments like these suggest that "the attitude of the [cuneiform] lawgiver or the collective sense of the society lacked the concept of equality of human life . . . [which is] the basic criterion that can defend human freedom, dignity, and rights."[101]

The BC, in particular, presents itself as a worthy focal point for such matters in the way it encapsulates them within its relatively brief corpus of legal decrees. It promotes freedom for the slave, dignity and equality for the needy or otherwise lower class, relational harmony with one's adversary, and even the well-being of animals. Such emphases are informed

98. Fretheim, "חנן," 204.

99. Finkelstein, *The Ox That Gored*, 12. See also C. J. H. Wright, *Old Testament Ethics*, 307–14.

100. Finkelstein, *The Ox That Gored*, 38–39. See also Tsai, *Human Rights in Deuteronomy*, 167–68.

101. Tsai, *Human Rights in Deuteronomy*, 169. C. J. H. Wright notes the Bible's disambiguate stance on such matters. "Equality before the law for all social groups, including aliens and immigrants, is made explicit in Exodus 12:49; Leviticus 19:34; and Numbers 15:16" (*Old Testament Ethics*, 310).

by and built upon the broader narrative backdrop of the Sinai event; the covenant established therein; and, most of all, the character and personhood of the lawgiver, Yhwh, who demonstrated proper compassion for his covenant readers to imitate. This compassion does more than simply guide readers' actions and behaviors; it grants substantial insights into the way in which God feels about and sees humans. Proper imitation, then, seeks to treat other people with his understanding of humans in mind; namely, that they have been given inherent and inalienable value and are worthy of love and affection. Theology is therefore integral to the BC's interpretation and application. On this, Spencer warns that:

> It must not be assumed that legislation related to the care of those in disadvantaged societal positions has as its singular rationale the protection of vulnerable groups within society. Instead, such legislation must be understood to have a theological basis. This theological understanding is expressed in concrete actions including, but not necessarily limited to, the maintenance of appropriate power relations, the performance of suitable theological practices and the accurate articulation of a reality in which God is sovereign.[102]

With the unique and unprecedented humanitarian concerns like the above in mind, it is not too farfetched to understand the BC to be acting as a "bridge between a present reality and an imagined future—a future in which a communal identity as Yhwh's people living in Yhwh's land in accordance with Yhwh's own mores is a goal to be realized."[103]

CONCLUSION AND SUMMARY

In the preceding chapters, specific attention was given to legal, literary, historical, and theo-ethical matters. With the underlying premise that a culture's worldview, or *Volksgeist,* plays a pivotal role in shaping the formulation and application of law, the objective of this chapter was to adopt a more comprehensive approach in comparing biblical and ANE perspectives. The first part of this exploration was historiographical in nature in the way it scrutinized the legislators' sources of authority, declared agendas, and target audiences. The second addressed what appears to be the most consequential matter: the relationship between law and religion.

---

102. Spencer, "Remembering Sabbath," 129.
103. C. Hays, *What's Divine about Divine Law?*, 52–53.

Part one revealed several helpful insights relating to the context of legal writing. First, using Hammurabi as the prime example, it was observed that cuneiform legislators explicitly asserted direct authorship while also espousing to divine endorsement for their decrees. Biblical law integrated these concepts; Yhwh, the God of the Israelites, asserts authorship *and* serves as the ultimate authority for the BC, thereby transforming any comparison between biblical and cuneiform authorship into a comparison between human and divine writers. This set the stage for the next historiographical point of interest: the respective functions of the law collections and the agendas they sought to promote.

Biblical law and cuneiform law shared some common goals, as evidenced by their mission statements advocating for justice for lawbreakers and mercy for the needy. Both served as showcases of their author's jurisprudential prowess, promoting a principled humanitarian agenda and presenting their laws as a repository of wisdom and guidance.[104] A closer examination of their intended audiences, however, revealed more divergent functions and intents. Cuneiform authors emphasized self-legitimization, aiming to establish their right to rule before their subjects, gods for continued blessings, and future kings for a lasting legacy. By contrast, the author of biblical law had no reason to appeal to other divine powers or future human rulers. Additionally, the Israelites were seen less as "subjects" and more as "recipients." The giving of the law was a way in which God continued to build a relationship with his people.

Expounding on the matter of divine-human relationship, part two identified the integration of law and religion as the primary distinction between biblical and cuneiform law. This divergence was underscored in several ways. First, unlike cuneiform law, biblical law consistently addresses "matters of the heart" (love, hate, selfishness, generosity, etc.) and includes regulations on religious practices. Second, biblical law fosters moral development through rhetoric and continual input from God within the decrees themselves, offering insight into his priorities. Third, it is embedded within a covenant framework, thereby forging a deeper connection between the Israelites and God, and promoting holy living. Finally, with respect to the BC in particular, there is a certain encouragement for covenant readers to actively demonstrate compassion toward each other, echoing the compassion exhibited and proclaimed by its author. Such compassion, at its core, possesses the desire to ensure the

---

104. It is worth noting that even secular law, to an extent, serves as a valid source of authority for covenant readers (Rom 13:1–7).

unyielding freedom, dignity, and overall well-being of others. Humanitarian concerns like these were no doubt initiated by the BC, the first of the Bible's law collections. However, the question from chapter 1 remains: Is the Bible still essential in guiding their practice today?

6

Conclusion and Final Contemplations

The law of God is a copy of the eternal mind, a transcript of the divine nature; yea, it is the brightest efflux of his essential wisdom, the visible beauty of the Most High. It is the joy of every wise believer, every well instructed child of God on earth.

—John Wesley, "The Original, Nature, Properties, and Use of the Law"

The law of the Lord is perfect, renewing one's life; the testimony of the Lord is trustworthy, making wise the simple; the precepts of the Lord are right, giving joy to the heart; the commands of the Lord are radiant, giving light to the eyes . . . Moreover, your servant is warned by them; in keeping them there is an abundant reward.

—Psalm 19:7–8, 11

Several methodological principles were outlined at the outset of this study which shaped its overall posture toward the biblical and cuneiform legal texts. First and foremost was the acknowledgment that a plurality of approaches is necessary for a more holistic comparison and interpretation. The tendency to lean too deeply into a singular method risks unwittingly silencing alternative perspectives which may further inform and build upon the objective at hand or expose critical shortcomings. As such, a robust awareness of each method's strengths, weaknesses, and limitations becomes necessary. Knowing which approach to use and when to use it was also a hurdle to overcome, leading to the next methodological principle: the commitment to working with the text "as it stands." In other words, it is preferable to allow the source material to guide one's research style rather than insisting on a certain mode of thought.[1]

The above methodological principles led to the frequent utilization of several approaches such as comparative legal study, biblical exegesis, ethics, and literary analysis. Less frequented approaches, which were needed to address certain key components, included historical criticism and historiography. Since the overarching goal of this volume was to work with the underlying value systems found within the final forms of ancient law collections, synchronous styles were naturally the most fitting while diachronous styles, such as source and redaction criticism, ultimately received little to no attention. It is important to note that this tilt toward synchrony came about organically, as it is only beneficial to remain open to both schools of thought regardless of the subject matter in question.[2] Certainly, a plurality of methods should always be consulted, but not all methods will be pertinent in every situation.

Having established the fundamental methodological guidelines, this study went on to provide clear definitions and understandings of its key frequented terms, namely "value" and "humanitarian(ism)." It was accepted that a "value" is an idea which is placed on a scale or hierarchy of relative worth or importance, as contrasted with things that are less valuable (e.g., "it is *better* to preserve life *rather than* harming or taking life").[3] The term "humanitarianism" was lacking a formal definition with respect to its practice in the ancient world. It was therefore put forward that humanitarian concerns constitute the general treatment of other people—usually the poor, marginalized, weak, oppressed, and unfortunate—that manifests itself in the form of outward service and is often coupled with the desire to enact and execute justice on their behalf. These concerns have representation in both biblical and cuneiform law collections.

1. Averbeck, "Pentateuchal Criticism and the Priestly Torah," 156. See also Averbeck, "The Egyptian Sojourn," 165.
2. Vanhoozer, *Is There a Meaning in This Text?*, 285–86.
3. Gane, *Old Testament Law for Christians*, 22–23.

From there, this study went on to critically scrutinize its primary assertion that the Book of the Covenant contains a unique, inherent, and innovative humanitarian outlook as compared to its cuneiform counterparts. Amongst the Bible's law collections, the BC was specifically chosen for this examination for a few reasons. First, it is the earliest of the biblical collections. Since it had no other biblical legal framework to reference or build upon, its changes to ANE legal traditions stand out more pointedly. Second, it set a standard that the rest of the Bible can be seen referencing thereafter. For example, the BC is largely understood as containing implicit ethical values which later biblical laws more explicitly state and expound upon.[4] Third, it is brief (only 3 chapters), making it friendly toward comprehensive examination.

Thorough comparative and textual analysis using the aforementioned methods and principles revealed the accuracy of this study's claims regarding the humanitarian concerns within biblical law. The humanitarian outlook within the BC is *unique* in that its legislator is divine, claiming to be both the author of the BC as well as its source of authority. It is *inherent* in that its values are derived not just from the laws, but also their surrounding narratives (e.g., the Mt. Sinai and exodus events), literary expressions, and the overall function and genre of Torah/instruction. It is *innovative* in the way it utilizes and incorporates the distinct compassionate character of its author, Yhwh, thereby fueling the BC's rhetoric on matters of morality, personal accountability, and religious living, amongst other such elements.

This conclusion was reached following a step-by-step expansion of focus, starting with Yhwh's statement in Exod 22:26 [Eng. 22:27], "because I am compassionate (חַנּוּן)," at its most narrow and culminating in a discussion about worldview at its most broad. chapter 2 served as the launchpad for this progressive investigation, identifying the proclamation in Exod 22:26 [27] as a structural and theological center point for the BC. The implications of this were ultimately two-fold. First, it indicates that the primary objective of the BC was to aid its covenant readers in better understanding the character of their God; this logic is only reinforced by God's earlier explicit declaration in Exod 6:7 and later expounded self-description in Exod 34:6–7. Second, it suggests that God's חַנּוּן compassion serves as the motive force behind proper obedience to the BC's decrees: "*because* I am compassionate." Humanitarian actions motivated

---

4. Otto, "Ethics," 276.

by this compassion therefore contain distinctive traits, namely, as was discussed at length in chapter 2, that they (1) seek relational growth, (2) are done with the expectation of repetition as needed, and (3) are considered acts of worship.⁵

Following this theological exploration, chapter 2 ventured into the laws themselves, focusing specifically on the laws of the collateral cloak (Exod 22:25–26), the enemy's donkey (23:4–5), and the Sabbath (23:10–12). These laws were chosen due to the fact that they have no direct parallels within cuneiform law and contain a heightened variety of literary expressions, the most notable of which being direct first-person involvement from the LORD in their contexts. By implementing Gane's suggestion to explore literary expressions in the search for implicit value structures (such as positive and negative commands, repeating formulas, manners of address, apodictic and casuistic formulations, and motivational elements),⁶ it was shown that all of the selected laws exhibit the above "חַנּוּן humanitarian" traits.

Chapter 3 further expanded the scope to include the exodus narrative with the goal of deciphering its possible influence on the BC's humanitarian outlook. This decision was not arbitrary as the BC itself references the exodus event three times (Exod 22:20 [21]; 23:9; and 23:15; cf. Exod 20:2 and 20:22). Averbeck's explanation that the biblical text contains three parallel dimensions—literary, historical, and theo-ethical—prompted a corresponding three-fold approach,⁷ the results of which were nothing short of consequential for the overall goals of this volume. For example, explorations within the BC's literary dimension revealed that the BC was not just connected with the exodus topically, but also structurally. Its entire composition was formulated using the rationale that the Israelites were delivered from bondage from the land of Egypt. The historical dimension revealed that the Israelites' collective cultural memory (or "mnemohistory") established their unique identity as an exclusive, ethnocultural group founded upon the covenant which God made with their ancestors. It also sustained their shared history as slaves in Egypt and legitimized their national existence (so long as they adhered to the law). Finally, the theo-ethical dimension identified the primary concern of the exodus as being relational, specifically that the Israelites would come to know their God more personally. Combined,

5. Fretheim, "חָנַן," 204.
6. Gane, *Old Testament Law for Christians*, 81. See also Watts, *Reading Law*, 61–88.
7. Averbeck, "Factors in Reading the Patriarchal Narratives," 116.

these three conclusions illustrate that the exodus served as a type of vertical reference point (what God did for his people) that would go on to influence Israel's horizontal lifestyle (how they proceeded to humanely and compassionately treat others in light of God's actions and person).[8] So strong is the BC's connection with the exodus that, had the Israelites never, in fact, been delivered from slavery, the BC simply would have never been written.

With the understanding that comparisons with other similar ANE texts are exceedingly helpful in bringing focus to their respective theo-ethical features,[9] chapter 4 endeavored to examine the laws of cuneiform collections alongside those of the BC. The laws regarding debt slavery (Exod 21:2–11; LH §§117–118; LU §§4–5) and goring oxen (Exod 21:28–32; LH §§250–252; LE §§53–55) were chosen for this enterprise. These laws were specifically selected due to their relatively higher amount of similarities and available history of scholarship. Moreover, they together address several of the humanitarian issues observable within the ANE, making them superior candidates for ethical deliberation.[10] Rather than opting to address any and all ethical matters, however, the debt slave and goring ox laws were read in light of C. Wright's "scale of values" which is concerned with the text's implicit value hierarchy regarding matters of life and property, persons and punishment, and needs and rights.[11]

Each set of laws was handled in three steps. The first step included prolegomenous matters (definitions, assumptions, etc.); the second involved a full-scale comparison between the biblical and cuneiform texts using the guidelines mentioned in chapter 1; finally, the third weighed and balanced each side with respect to their separate emphases on humanitarian values. The results of this analysis revealed two important distinctions. First, while the biblical and cuneiform laws certainly possess topical and structural similarities, they differ in legal issues, legal reasoning, and legal remedies.[12] Such reasoning dramatically reduces the number of laws which can truly be considered "parallel." Second, the biblical laws place a much higher significance on humanitarian concerns in that they consistently prioritize the first aspect in each category of C. J. H. Wright's scale of values (life, people, and needs), whereas ANE

8. C. J. H. Wright, *Exodus*, 400.
9. C. B. Hays, *Hidden Riches*, 4.
10. Westbrook, *Studies in Biblical and Cuneiform Law*.
11. See C. J. H. Wright, *Old Testament Ethics*, 307–14.
12. Wells, "What is Biblical Law?," 232.

law could be observed prioritizing the second (property, punishment, and rights).

Chapter 5 moved on to compare and contrast the authors themselves (Yhwh along with human kings, particularly Hammurabi). This was done with the specific effort to determine their respective motivations for writing their decrees. Several questions were utilized to guide this research: who is the legislator? What motivated them to write their laws? To whom, exactly, were they writing? Questions like these, according to Walton, are key to discerning a society's values by way of its written decrees.[13] The answers to these queries proved critical to a better understanding of the BC's humanitarian concerns. For example, both biblical and cuneiform law collections appeal to divine authority and contain explicit cries for justice and mercy, but only the former does so with the goal of forming a divine-human relationship. The latter was more concerned with maintaining order and legitimizing the current king's right to rule.[14] Put simply, the author of biblical law wants his readers to *know him* (his personhood); the author(s) of cuneiform law wanted his readers to *know about him* (his divinity and royalty).

This relational distinction ultimately led to what this study acknowledged as the most glaring difference between biblical and cuneiform law: the integration of law and religion. This intermixing on behalf of the former yielded truly unique and innovative agendas such as the ability to shape morality, establish a covenant, and persuade readers to imitate the distinct compassionate character and actions of its author. The BC's capacity to shape human morality, for example, is evidenced by the way it consistently addresses matters of the heart (love, hate, selfishness, generosity, etc.), utilizes persuasive rhetoric, and contains continual first-person input from God within the decrees themselves, thereby offering insights into how his readers can imitate him through his revealed priorities. Additionally, the BC's role within the Mosaic Covenant is left on no uncertain terms. Should the Israelites obey and keep the law, then they shall become their God's treasured possession and a "kingdom of priests" (Exod 19:5, 8; 24:7)—he will "become their God," and they will "become his people" (Exod 6:7).

Finally, chapter 5 concluded with a final statement on "חַנּוּן humanitarianism" within the BC. While it was shown through a variety of

---

13. Walton, *Introducing the Conceptual World of the Hebrew Bible*, 204.
14. Averbeck, *The Old Testament Law for the Life of the Church*, 86.

approaches that biblical law by and large contains a greater emphasis on humanitarian concerns than that of cuneiform law, it cannot be said that this distinction exists simply due to a lack of effort on behalf of the latter. The humanitarian concerns within the BC were made manifest through the historical events leading up to its ratification, the worldview promulgated by Yhwh through his acts in the early chapters of the book of Genesis, and his desire to have a relationship with his creation. His covenant readers are therefore motivated to treat each other as equals and with inherent human dignity not out of obligation, but out of worship. Should they lack practical understanding in how to go about treating their fellow Hebrews in this way, they needed only to look toward the example set for them by their God. In light of this, the BC's ultimate desire is that its readers know and imitate the compassionate character of its author, Yhwh.

There exists at least three avenues of further research worthy of pursuit following the results of this volume. First, while this study managed to cover nearly all of the laws in the BC to some capacity, there are some segments, such as Exod 22:5–13 [6–14], which were left out.[15] Given the methodological guidelines outlined in chapter 1 (chief among these being to "work the text as it stands"), all of the laws in the BC are eligible for the same treatment offered to the various segments selected in this study. Second, the field of biblical legal studies stands to benefit from the continued pursuit of "theo-ethical" measures—that is, asking the twofold questions "what does the law in question reveal about the Author's character?" and "how then should the covenant reader live in light of this information?" Such analyses sidestep some of the confusion brought about by methodologies seeking to directly apply biblical laws as written to modern society while keeping the focus on theological concerns. Finally, so long as there are ethical dilemmas in the world, there will always be a need to reaffirm and re-demonstrate the Bible's role in their handling and resolution. In the hope that this volume fruitfully participated in such an endeavor, more detailed attention will now be given to the broader talking points offered up at the outset of this work.

---

15. For more on this portion in particular, see Landman, *Legal Writing, Legal Practice*.

THE SIGNIFICANCE OF THIS STUDY FOR THE PRACTICE OF MODERN HUMANITARIAN ETHICS

Humanitarian concerns abound within biblical law.[16] Moreover, since the Book of the Covenant stands as the earliest known law collection to uniformly prioritize these concerns, it in particular serves as the foundational introduction to human rights in legislative practice.[17] The significance of this contribution can hardly be overstated. Hess points out: "This distinctive value to human persons and their basic equality, found in the earliest traditions of Israel's texts, formed the basis for the history of law and human rights in the Western world. Even though it was subject to many distortions and outright denials by various leaders and philosophers in its history, the West has again and again returned to these unique human values to define rights and freedoms."[18] Despite this, it is evident that biblical texts like the BC are gradually losing their influence on modern world events. "Much of our contemporary society . . . tends to be hostile toward unbending absolute authority or at least uncomfortable with it," states Gane, "Collective and changing human wisdom has been replacing the Bible as the ethical standard." He then goes on to ask, "What happens when members of a society set themselves adrift from the absolute anchor of morality, choosing to rely on their own subjective rationales rather than submit to divine authority, which sometimes is countercultural?"[19] This question, with respect to the aims of this study, begs another: Is the Bible still needed for contemporary humanitarian efforts?

A thorough review of the cuneiform law collections—their functions, motivations, and limitations—revealed that concepts like justice, mercy, fairness, and generosity can indeed be pursued even without reference to the biblical text. They can of their own volition properly be understood as humanitarian in their makeup. Their detachment from religious beliefs and lack of emphasis on holy living, however, disables them from fully promoting the fundamental idea that every person inherently possesses equal value and dignity. They also fall short in guiding the consistent moral and compassionate treatment of others; such was

---

16. Durham adds, "Concern for the [under]privileged and humanitarian sensitivity are reflected throughout the OT, in every major dimension of its teaching" (Durham, *Exodus*, 328).

17. Ishay, *The History of Human Rights*, 17–61.

18. Hess, "The Distinctive Value of Human Life," 228.

19. Gane, *Old Testament Law for Christians*, 21.

simply not their objective in the first place.[20] In contrast, the humanitarian values in the BC are deeply rooted in holy living and are heavily contingent upon the moral dispositions of their adherents. This much is especially evident given their implementation within a divine-human covenantal relationship. Modern humanitarian efforts therefore stand to benefit from more seriously recognizing and grappling with the rationales and motivations promoted within Scripture.[21]

While it is true that matters of justice and mercy are central within biblical law, it is also true that they do not represent the only, or even the most important, focal point for its readers. In fact, focusing too exclusively on biblical humanitarian issues can be risky since doing so would likely isolate them from the Bible's theological features.[22] Spencer, for example, explains,

> In attempting to draw out the implications of [the law] for modern life, [some have] softened the need for repentance and conversion in order to focus on more humanitarian concerns. While the desire (and demand) for justice is certainly present within the Biblical narrative, it is not separable from more theological concerns. Minimizing the theological aspects of . . . the Law more generally diminishes, if not eliminates, the uniqueness of the Biblical legal material and limits the potential functions of this material within the Old Testament toward more humanitarian concerns. Though the humanitarian value of the

---

20. For more on the complexities of this discussion, see Kolakowski, *Religion, If There is No God . . .* , 191–92; and esp. Perry, *Toward a Theory of Human Rights*, 14–29.

21. See Kofoed, "Encoding and Decoding Culture," 258, where he explains that "'paganism' is lurking at the door and is making its re-entry to the 'humane' West, because the laws and conventions created and sustained by the Judeo-Christian 'narrative' are increasingly being severed from their original setting. In 1776, when the Declaration of Independence proclaimed that 'all men are created equal, that they are endowed by their Creator with certain unalienable Rights,' this was considered self-evident truth. Although the United Nations' Declaration of Human Rights from 1948 applied the principle universally, *without* explicit reference to the Judeo-Christian Creator, the content would be unthinkable without precisely the *nomos* created and sustained by the Judeo-Christian faiths."

See also Tsai, *Human Rights in Deuteronomy*, who asks a similar question: "Does human rights need God?" Through her study of Deuteronomy, she arrives at the conclusion that respecting and defending human rights requires moral strength and convictions which can only be acquired through proper reverence of Yhwh by "obeying his words under his covenantal relationship . . . because Yhwh and his words are the universal origins and norms of righteousness and justice (e.g., Deut 4:6–8; 32:5)" (255).

22. For an example of this outcome, see Harrelson, *The Ten Commandments and Human Rights*, 10.

> Biblical legal material should not be dismissed, such concerns become nonsensical when separated from the theological elements of the text.[23]

Some scholars, such as Hiers, go so far as to praise biblical law for its continued relevance in matters of caring for the poor and disadvantaged, stating that it can "inspire contemporary efforts to achieve a society—if not a world—in which the basic welfare interests of all, even those of low degree, are protected and affirmed through appropriate public policies and legislation."[24] However, even this acknowledgment falls short of recognizing one of biblical law's primary points of concern: deliverance. There will always be a need for humanitarian discussion;[25] but such discussion, according to biblical law, is best had when it is motivated by a sincere reflection on what the law's author did on behalf of his readers. A humanitarian ethos which abandons such a motivation will inevitably divert its attention away from theological concerns like the need for deliverance by a divine Savior and the coming of a new kingdom. Instead, its focus will become increasingly centered on the rebuilding of humanity through self-interested means and the continual enhancement of the present worldly kingdom unto its own end.[26] For the Israelites, their deliverance was the exodus; just as they were foreigners delivered from bondage, so too were they called to free others and treat them with similar compassion (Exod 22:20 [21]; 22:26 [27]; 23:9; 23:15). For those under the New Covenant, the scope was broadened to include the deliverance from sin through the sacrifice of Christ on the cross. Just as God demonstrated his love through sacrifice, covenant readers today must also demonstrate their love through sacrifice on behalf of one another.[27]

---

23. Spencer, "Remembering Sabbath," 127–28.

24. Hiers, *Justice and Compassion in Biblical Law*, 218.

25. "The frequency with which the Hebrew prophets and the Christian apostles confronted their faith communities with their failures to keep the covenant obligations and challenged them to act as God has instructed them suggests that the need to speak of the requirements of justice and mercy is perennial" (Cooper and Moulder, *Social Injustice*, 15).

26. Bloesch, *Faith and Its Counterfeits*, 48.

27. Stark, *The Rise of Christianity*, 8; cf. 1 John 4:19. Stark later goes on to opine that "The embeddedness of the ethical code in a narrative on God's uncompelled and unconditional love for humankind effectively promulgated a moral vision utterly incompatible with the casual cruelty of pagan custom. Finally, what Christianity gave to its converts was nothing less than their humanity" (215). See also the reflections offered in Gane, *Old Testament Law for Christians*, 47; Averbeck, *The Old Testament Law for the Life of the Church*, 52–53; and C. J. H. Wright, *Exodus*, 440–41.

Bibliography

Aḥituv, Shmuel. *Echoes from the Past: Hebrew and Cognate Inscriptions from the Biblical Period*. Jerusalem: Carta, 2008.

Albertz, Rainer. *A History of Israelite Religion in the Old Testament Period*. Translated by John Bowden. Old Testament Library. Louisville: Westminster John Knox, 1994.

Albrektson, Bertil. *History and the Gods: An Essay on the Idea of Historical Events as Divine Manifestations in the Ancient Near East and in Israel*. Coniectanea biblica: Old Testament Series 1. Lund: Gleerup, 1967.

Albright, William Foxwell. *Yahweh and the Gods of Canaan: A Historical Analysis of Two Contrasting Faiths*. Garden City, NY: Doubleday, 1968.

Alexander, T. D. "Book of the Covenant." In *Dictionary of the Old Testament: Pentateuch*, edited by T. D. Alexander and D. W. Baker, 94–101. Downers Grove, IL: InterVarsity, 2003.

———. "The Composition of the Sinai Narrative in Exodus XIX 1–XXV 11." *Vetus Testamentum* 49 (1999) 2–20.

———. *Exodus*. Apollos Old Testament Commentary Series 2. Downers Grove, IL: InterVarsity, 2017.

———. *From Paradise to the Promised Land: An Introduction to the Pentateuch*. 3rd ed. Grand Rapids: Baker Academic, 2012.

Alt, Albrecht. *Essays on Old Testament History and Religion*. Translated by R. A. Wilson. 1966. Reprint, Biblical Seminar. Sheffield: JSOT Press, 1989.

Anderson, J. N. D. *Jesus Christ: The Witness of History*. 2nd ed. Leicester, UK: InterVarsity, 1985.

Andreasen, Niels-Erik. *The Old Testament Sabbath*. Society of Biblical Literature Dissertation Series 7. Missoula, MT: Society of Biblical Literature, 1972.

Arnold, Bill T. *Genesis*. New Cambridge Bible Commentary. Cambridge: Cambridge University Press, 2009.

Ashley, Timothy R. *The Book of Numbers*. New International Commentary on the Old Testament. Grand Rapids: Eerdmans, 1992.

Assmann, Jan. *Cultural Memory and Early Civilization: Writing, Remembrance, and Political Imagination*. Cambridge: Cambridge University Press, 2011.

Averbeck, Richard E. "The Egyptian Sojourn and Deliverance from Slavery in the Framing and Shaping of the Mosaic Law." In *"Did I Not Bring Israel Out of Egypt?" Biblical, Archaeological, and Egyptological Perspectives on the Exodus Narratives*, edited by James K. Hoffmeier et al., 143–76. Winona Lake, IN: Eisenbrauns, 2016.

———. "The Exodus, Debt Slavery, and the Composition of the Pentateuch." In *Exploring the Composition of the Pentateuch*, edited by L. S. Baker Jr. et al., 26–48. Bulletin for Biblical Research Supplement Series 27. Winona Lake, IN: Eisenbrauns, 2020.

———. "Factors in Reading the Patriarchal Narratives." In *Giving the Sense: Understanding and Using Old Testament Texts*, edited by David M. Howard Jr. and Michael A. Grisanti, 115–37. Grand Rapids: Kregel, 2003.

———. "Law." In *Cracking Old Testament Codes: A Guide to Interpreting Literary Genres of the Old Testament*, edited by D. Brent Sandi and Ronald L. Giese, 113–38. Nashville: Broadman & Holman, 1995.

———. "The Law and the Gospels, with Attention to the Relationship between the Decalogue and the Sermon on the Mount/Plain." In *The Oxford Handbook of Biblical Law*, edited by Pamela Barmash, 409–24. Oxford Handbooks. New York: Oxford University Press, 2019.

———. *The Old Testament Law for the Life of the Church: Reading the Torah in the Light of Christ*. Downers Grove, IL: IVP Academic, 2022.

———. "Pentateuchal Criticism and the Priestly Torah." In *Do Historical Matters Matter for Faith? A Critical Appraisal of Modern and Postmodern Approaches to the Bible*, edited by James K. Hoffmeier and Dennis R. Magary, 151–80. Wheaton, IL: Crossway, 2012.

———. "Slavery in the World of the Bible." In *Behind the Scenes of the Old Testament*, edited by Jonathan Greer et al., 423–30. Grand Rapids: Baker Academic, 2018.

———. "Sumer, the Bible, and Comparative Method: Historiography and Temple Building." In *Mesopotamia and the Bible: Comparative Explorations*, edited by Mark W. Chavalas and K. Lawson Younger Jr., 88–125. Journal for the Study of the Old Testament. Supplement Series 341. Sheffield: Sheffield Academic, 2002.

Baentsch, Bruno. *Exodus, Leviticus, Numeri*. Handkommentar zum Alten Testament. Göttingen: Vandenhoeck & Ruprecht, 1903.

Barmash, Pamela. "Ancient Near Eastern Law." In *The Oxford Encyclopedia of the Bible and Law*, edited by Brent Strawn, 13–24. Oxford: Oxford University Press, 2015.

———. *Homicide in the Biblical World*. Cambridge: Cambridge University Press, 2005.

———. "The Narrative Quandary: Cases of Law in Literature." *Vetus Testamentum* 54 (2004) 1–16.

Barr, James. *Biblical Faith and Natural Theology: The Gifford Lectures for 1991*. Oxford: Clarendon, 1993.

Barth, Fredrik, ed. *Ethnic Groups and Boundaries: The Social Organization of Cultural Difference*. Oslo: Universitetsforloget, 1969.

Barton, John. "Approaches to Ethics in the Old Testament." In *Beginning Old Testament Study*, edited by John Rogerson, 114–31. Philadelphia: Westminster John Knox, 1982.

———. *Understanding Old Testament Ethics*. Louisville: Westminster John Knox, 2003.

Bartor, Assnat. "Biblical Law: A Successful Relationship between Law and Religion." In *Ve-'Ed Ya'aleh (Gen 2:6): Essays in Biblical and Ancient Near Eastern Studies Presented to Edward L. Greenstein*, edited by Peter Machinist et al., vol. 1, 433–50. Writings from the Ancient World Supplement Series 5. Atlanta: SBL Press, 2021.

———. "Law and Narrative." In *The Oxford Handbook of Biblical Law*, edited by Pamela Barmash, 217–32. Oxford Handbooks. New York: Oxford University Press, 2019.

———. "Reading Biblical Law as Narrative." *Prooftexts* 32 (2012) 292–311.

Bellefontaine, Margaret. "Study of Ancient Israelite Laws and Their Function as Covenant Stipulations." PhD diss., University of Notre Dame, 1973.
Berman, Herald J. *The Interaction of Law and Religion*. Nashville: Abingdon, 1974.
Berman, Joshua. *Created Equal: How the Bible Broke with Ancient Political Thought*. New York: Oxford University Press, 2008.
———. *Inconsistency in the Torah: Ancient Literary Convention and the Limits of Source Criticism*. New York: Oxford University Press, 2017.
Birch, Bruce C. *Let Justice Roll Down: The Old Testament, Ethics, and Christian Life*. Louisville: Westminster John Knox, 1991.
———. "Moral Agency, Community, and the Character of God in the Hebrew Bible." *Semeia* 66 (1994) 23–41.
Black, Jeremy A. *The Literature of Ancient Sumer*. Oxford: Oxford University Press, 2006.
Blenkinsopp, Joseph. "Yahweh and Other Deities: Conflict and Accommodation in the Religion of Israel." *Interpretation* 40 (1986) 354–66.
Block, Daniel I. "Marriage and Family in Ancient Israel." In *Marriage and Family in the Biblical World*, edited by Ken M. Campbell, 33–102. Downers Grove, IL: IVP Academic, 2003.
Bloesch, Donald G. *Faith and Its Counterfeits*. Downers Grove, IL: InterVarsity, 1981.
Boda, Mark J. *The Heartbeat of Old Testament Theology: Three Creedal Expressions*. Grand Rapids: Baker Academic, 2017.
Boecker, Hans Jochen. *Law and the Administration of Justice in the Old Testament and Ancient East*. Translated by Jeremy Moiser. Minneapolis: Augsburg, 1980.
Bottéro, J. *Mesopotamia: Writing, Reasoning, and the Gods*. Chicago: University of Chicago Press, 1995.
Botterweck, G. Johannes, and Helmer Ringgren, eds. *Theologisches Wörterbuch zum Alten Testament*. 8 vols. Stuttgart: Kohlhammer, 1973.
Bracker, Hans-Detlef. *Das Gesetz Israels verglichen mit den altorientalischen Gesetzen der Babylonier, der Hethiter und der Assyrer*. Hamburg: Rauhen Hauses, 1962.
Brett, Mark G. "Interpreting Ethnicity." In *Ethnicity and the Bible*, edited by Mark G. Brett, 3–24. Biblical Interpretation Series 19. Leiden: Brill, 1996.
Brichto, Herbert Chanan. *The Problem of "Curse" in the Hebrew Bible*. JBL Monograph Series 13. Philadelphia: Society of Biblical Literature, 1963.
Brin, Gershon. *Studies in Biblical Law: From the Hebrew Bible to the Dead Sea Scrolls*. Journal for the Study of the Old Testament Supplement Series 176. Sheffield: JSOT Press, 1994.
Brueggemann, Walter. *The Land: Place as Gift, Promise, and Challenge in Biblical Faith*. 2nd ed. Minneapolis: Fortress, 2002.
———. "The Role of Old Testament Theology in Old Testament Interpretation." In *The Role of Old Testament Theology in Old Testament Interpretation: and Other Essays*, edited by K. C. Hanson, 1–21. Eugene, OR: Cascade Books, 2015.
Budd, Philip J. *Numbers*. Word Biblical Commentary 5. Waco: Word, 1984.
Cahn, Edmond Nathaniel. *The Moral Decision: Right and Wrong in the Light of American Law*. Bloomington: Indiana University Press, 1955.
Cancik-Kirschbaum, Eva. "'Menschen ohne König . . .' Zur Wahrnehmung des Königtums in sumerischen und akkadischen Texten." In *Das geistige Erfassen der Welt im Alten Orient: Sprache, Religion, Kultur, und Gesellschaft*, edited by Claus Wilcke, 167–90. Wiesbaden: Harrassowitz, 2007.

Cardellini, Innocenzo. *Die biblischen "Sklaven"-Gesetze im Lichte des keilschriftlichen Sklavenrechts: ein Beitrag zur Tradition, Überlieferung und Redaktion der alttestamentlichen Rechtstexte.* Bonner biblische Beiträge 55. Königstein: Hanstein, 1981.

Carmichael, Calum M., ed. *Collected Works of David Daube.* Vol. 3. Studies in Comparative Legal History. Berkeley: University of California Press, 2003.

———. *Law and Narrative in the Bible: The Evidence of the Deuteronomic Laws and the Decalogue.* Ithaca, NY: Cornell University Press, 1985.

———. *The Origins of Biblical Law: Decalogues and the Book of the Covenant.* Ithaca: Cornell University Press, 1992.

———. "A Singular Method of Codification of Law in the *Mishpaṭim*." *Zeitschrift für die altestamentliche Wissenschaft* 84 (1972) 19-25.

———. "The Three Laws on the Release of Slaves." *Zeitschrift für die altestamentliche Wissenschaft* 112 (2000) 509-25.

Carstens, Pernille. "The Torah as Canon of Masterpieces: Remembering in Archives." In *Cultural Memory in Biblical Exegesis,* edited by Pernille Castens et al., 309-26. Perspectives on Hebrew Scriptures and Its Contexts 17. Piscataway, NJ: Gorgias, 2012.

Cassuto, U. *Commentary on Exodus.* Translated by I. Abrahams. Jerusalem: Magnes, 1967.

Cazelles, Henri. *Études sur le Code de l'alliance.* Paris: Letouzey et Ané, 1946.

Charpin, Dominique. *Writing, Law, and Kingship in Old Babylonian Mesopotamia.* Translated by Jane Marie Todd. Chicago: University of Chicago Press, 2010.

Chavel, Simeon. "A Kingdom of Priests and Its Earthen Altars in Exodus 19-24." *Vetus Testamentum* 65 (2015) 169-222.

Childs, Brevard S. *Biblical Theology in a Canonical Context.* Minneapolis: Fortress, 1993.

———. *The Book of Exodus: A Critical, Theological Commentary.* Old Testament Library. Philadelphia: Westminster, 1974.

Chirichigno, Greg. *Debt-Slavery in Israel and the Ancient Near East.* Journal for the Study of the Old Testament Supplement Series 141. Sheffield: Sheffield Academic, 1993.

———. "The Narrative Structure of Exodus 19-24." *Biblica* 68 (1987) 457-79.

Christensen, Duane L. *Deuteronomy 21:10—34:12.* Word Biblical Commentary 6B. Nashville: Nelson, 2002.

Civil, Miguel. "The Law Collection of Ur-Namma." In *Cuneiform Royal Inscriptions and Related Texts in the Schoyen Collection,* edited by A. R. George, 221-88. Cornell University Studies in Assyriology and Sumerology 17. Bethesda, MD: CDL, 2011.

Clines, David J. A., and J. Cheryl Exum. "The New Literary Criticism." In *The New Literary Criticism and the Hebrew Bible,* edited by J. Cheryl Exum and David J. A. Clines, 11-25. Journal for the Study of the Old Testament Supplement Series 143. Sheffield: JSOT Press, 1993.

Cochran, Robert F., Jr., and Zachary R. Calo, eds. *Agape, Justice, and Law: How Might Christian Love Shape Law?* Law and Christianity. Cambridge: Cambridge University Press, 2017.

Cohn, Haim H. *Human Rights in Jewish Law.* New York: Ktav, 1984.

Cole, R. Dennis. *Numbers.* New American Commentary 3B. Nashville: Broadman & Holman, 2000.

Collins, John C. "Divine Action in the Hebrew Bible: Borrowing from ANE Culture and 'Inspiration.'" In *Write That They May Read: Studies in Literacy and Textualization in the ANE and in Hebrew Scriptures: Essays in Honor of Professor Alan R. Millard*, edited by Daniel Block et al, 221–39. Eugene, OR: Pickwick Publications, 2020.

Cook, Stanley. *The Laws of Moses and the Code of Ḫammurabi*. London: A. & C. Black, 1903.

Cooper, A. "The Plain Sense of Exodus 23.5." *Hebrew Union College Annual* 59 (1988) 1–22.

Cooper, Michael T., and William J. Moulder. *Social Justice: What Evangelicals Need to Know about the World*. Lake Forest, IL: Timothy Center, 2011.

Cross, F. M., Jr. "Epigraphic Notes on Hebrew Documents of the Eighth-Sixth Centuries B.C.: II The Murabbaat Papyrus and the Letter Found Near Yavneh Yam." *Bulletin of the American Schools of Oriental Research* 165 (1962) 42–46.

———. "The Structure of the Deuteronomic History." *Perspectives in Jewish Learning*, Annual of the College of Jewish Learning 3 (Chicago, 1968) 9–24.

Crüsemann, Frank. *The Torah: Theology and Social History of Old Testament Law*. Translated by Allan W. Mahnke. Minneapolis: Fortress, 1996.

Cubitt, Geoffrey. *History and Memory*. Historical Approaches. Manchester: Manchester University Press, 2008.

Dandamayev, M. A. "Slavery (ANE), (OT)." In *Anchor Bible Dictionary*, edited by David Noel Freedman, 6:58–65. New York: Doubleday, 1992

Daube, David. "The Exodus Pattern in the Bible." In *Biblical Law and Literature*, edited by Calum Carmichael. Vol. 3 of *The Collected Works of David Daube*. Berkeley: University of California Press, 2003.

———. *Studies in Biblical Law*. Cambridge: Cambridge University Press, 1947.

David, Martin. *Der Rechtshistoriker und seine Aufgabe*. Leiden: Sijthoff, 1937.

Davidson, Robert. "Covenant Ideology in Ancient Israel." In *The World of Ancient Israel: Sociological, Anthropological and Political Perspectives*, edited by R. E. Clements, 323–48. Cambridge: Cambridge University Press, 1989.

de Vaux, Roland. *Ancient Israel: Its Life and Institutions*. Translated by John McHugh. 1961. Reprint, Grand Rapids: Eerdmans, 1997.

Delitzsch, Friedrich. *Babel and Bible: A Letter on the Significance of Assyriological Research for Religion. Delivered before the German Emperor*. Translated by Thomas J. McCormack. Chicago: Open Court, 1902.

Diamond, A. S. "An Eye for an Eye." *Iraq* 19 (1957) 151–55.

Dohmen, Christoph. *Exodus 19–40*. Herders Theologischer Kommentar zum Alten Testament. Freiburg: Herder, 2004.

Donahue, John R. *Seek Justice That You May Live: Reflections and Resources on the Bible and Social Justice*. New York: Paulist, 2014.

Doorly, William J. *The Laws of Yahweh: A Handbook of Biblical Law*. New York: Paulist, 2002.

Dorsey, David A. "The Law of Moses and the Christian: A Compromise." *Journal of the Evangelical Theological Society* 34 (1991) 325–30.

Dozeman, Thomas B. *Commentary on Exodus*. Eerdmans Critical Commentary. Grand Rapids: Eerdmans, 2009.

———. *God at War: Power in the Exodus Tradition*. New York: Oxford University Press, 1996.

———. *God on the Mountain: A Study of Redaction, Theology, and Canon in Exodus 19–24*. Society of Biblical Literature Monograph Series 37. Atlanta: Scholars, 1989.

Driver, Godfrey Rolles, and John C. Miles. *The Assyrian Laws*. Vol. 1. Oxford: Clarendon, 1952.

Driver, S. R. *The Book of Exodus*. Cambridge Bible for Schools and Colleges. Cambridge: Cambridge University Press, 1911.

Durham, John I. *Exodus*. Word Biblical Commentary 3. Louisville: Westminster John Knox, 1997.

Edwards, Chilperic. *The Hammurabi Code and the Sinaitic Legislation*. London: Watts, 1904.

Eissfeldt, Otto. *The Old Testament: An Introduction, Including the Apocrypha and Pseudepigrapha, and Also the Works of Similar Type from Qumran: The History of the Formation of the Old Testament*. Translated by Peter R. Ackroyd. New York: Harper & Row, 1965.

Enns, Peter. *Exodus*. The NIV Application Commentary. Grand Rapids: Zondervan, 2000.

Erlandson, S. "*bgd*." In *Theological Dictionary of the Old Testament*, 1:470–73.

Falk, Z. W. "Exodus XXI:6." *Vetus Testamentum* 9 (1959) 86–88.

———. "Spirituality and Jewish Law." In *Religion and Law: Biblical Judaic and Islamic Perspectives*, edited by E. B. Firmage et al., 127–38. Winona Lake, IN: Eisenbrauns, 1990.

Faust, Avraham. *Israel's Ethnogenesis: Settlement, Interaction, Expansion and Resistance*. Approaches to Anthropological Archaeology. London: Equinox, 2006.

Finkelstein, J. J. "Ammisaduqa's Edict and the Babylonian 'Law Codes.'" *Journal of Cuneiform Studies* 15 (1961) 91–104.

———. "The Goring Ox: Some Historical Perspectives on Deodands, Forfeitures, Wrongful Death and the Western Notion of Sovereignty." *Temple Law Quarterly* 46 (1973) 169–290.

———. *The Ox That Gored*. Philadelphia: American Philosophical Society, 1981.

———. "The Study of Man." *Bible and Babel* 26 (1958) 431–44.

Fishbane, Michael. *Biblical Interpretation in Ancient Israel*. Oxford: Clarendon, 1985.

Fokkelman, J. P. "Exodus." In *The Literary Guide to the Bible*, edited by R. Alter and F. Kermode, 56–65. Cambridges: Harvard University Press, 1987.

Fox-Decent, Evan. "Is the Rule of Law Really Indifferent to Human Rights." *Law and Philosophy* 27 (2008) 533–81.

Frahm, Eckart. *Babylonian and Assyrian Text Commentaries: Origins of Interpretation*. Münster: Ugarit-Verlag, 2011.

Frerichs, E. S., and L. H. Lesko, eds. *Exodus: The Egyptian Evidence*. Winona Lake, IN: Eisenbrauns, 1997.

Fretheim, Terence E. *Exodus*. Interpretation. Louisville: Westminster John Knox, 1991.

———. *The Suffering of God: An Old Testament Perspective*. Overtures to Biblical Theology. Philadelphia: Fortress, 1984.

Frey, Hellmuth. "Das Ineinander von Kirche und Welt im Licht der Komposition des Bundes-buches." *Wort und Dienst* (1948) 13–35.

Freedman, Richard Elliott. *The Exodus: How It Happened and Why It Matters*. New York: HarperOne, 2017.

Gamoran, Hillel. "The Biblical Law against Loans on Interest." *Journal of Near Eastern Studies* 30 (1971) 127–34.

Gane, Roy E. *Old Testament Law for Christians: Original Context and Enduring Application*. Grand Rapids: Baker, 2017.

———. "Social Justice." In *The Oxford Handbook of Biblical Law*, edited by Pamela Barmash, 19–34. New York: Oxford University Press, 2019.
Garrett, Duane A. *A Commentary on Exodus*. Grand Rapids: Kregel Academic, 2014.
———. *The Problem of the Old Testament: Hermeneutical, Schematic & Theological Approaches*. Downers Grove, IL: IVP, 2020.
———. *Rethinking Genesis: The Sources and Authorship of the First Book of the Pentateuch*. Grand Rapids: Baker, 1991.
Gemser, B. "The Importance of the Motive Clause in Old Testament Law." In *Congress Volume: Copenhagen 1953*, edited by G. W. Anderson, 50–66. Supplements to Vetus Testamentum 1. Leiden: Brill, 1953.
Gerstenberger, Erhard S. "Covenant and Commandment." *Journal of Biblical Literature* 84 (1965) 38–51.
Gilmer, Harry W. *The If-You Form in Israelite Law*. Society of Biblical Literature Dissertation Series 15. Missoula, MT: Scholars, 1975.
Girdlestone, R. B. *Synonyms of the Old Testament*. Grand Rapids: Eerdmans, 1970.
Glatt, David A., and Jeffrey H. Tigay. "Sabbath." *HarperColins Bible Dictionary* 1:888–89.
Goetze, A. "Mesopotamian Laws and the Historian." *Journal of the American Oriental Society* 69 (1949) 115–20.
Goldenberg, Robert. "Sabbath." In *The Oxford Encyclopedia of the Bible and Law*, edited by Brent A. Strawn, vol. 2, 257–61. New York: Oxford University Press, 2015.
Goldingay, John. *Approaches to Old Testament Interpretation*. Rev. ed. Downers Grove, IL: InterVarsity, 1990.
———. *Old Testament Ethics: A Guided Tour*. Downers Grove, IL: IVP Academic, 2019.
———. "The Patriarchs in Scripture and History." In *Essays on the Patriarchal Narratives*, edited by A. R. Millard and D. J. Wiseman, 11–42. Leicester, UK: InterVarsity, 1980.
Green, Joel B., and Jacqueline E. Lapsley, eds. *The Old Testament and Ethics: A Book-by-Book Survey*. Grand Rapids: Baker Academic, 2013.
Greenberg, Moshe. "Biblical Attitudes toward Power: Ideal and Reality in Law and Prophets." In *Religion and Law: Biblical-Judaic and Islamic Perspectives*, edited by Edwin B. Firmage et al., 101–12. Winona Lake, IN: Eisenbrauns, 1990.
———. "Some Postulates of Biblical Criminal Law." In *Yehezkel Kaufmann Jubilee Volume: Studies in Bible and Jewish Religion Dedicated to Yehezkel Kaufmann on the Occasion of His Seventieth Birthday*, edited by Menahem Haran, 5–28. Jerusalem: Magnes, 1960.
Greengus, Samuel. "Biblical and ANE Law." In *Anchor Bible Dictionary*, edited by David Noel Freedman, 4:243–52. New York: Doubleday, 1992.
———. "Covenant and Treaty in the Hebrew Bible and in the Ancient Near East." In *Ancient Israel's History: An Introduction to Issues and Sources*, edited by Bill T. Arnold and Richard S. Hess, 91–126. Grand Rapids: Baker Academic, 2014.
———. *Laws in the Bible and in Early Rabbinic Collections: The Legal Legacy of the Ancient Near East*. Eugene, OR: Cascade Books, 2011.
———. "Some Issues Relating to the Comparability of Laws." In *Theory and Method in Biblical and Cuneiform Law: Revision, Interpolation and Development*, edited by Bernard M. Levinson, 60–87. Journal for the Study of the Old Testament Supplement Series 181. Sheffield: Sheffield Academic, 1994.

Halbe, Jörn. *Das Privilegrecht Jahwes Ex 34, 10–26: Gestalt und Wesen, Herkunft und Wirken in vordeuteronomistischer Zeit*. Forschungen zur Religion und Literatur des Alten und Neuen Testaments 114. Göttingen: Vandenhoeck & Ruprecht, 1975.

Hallo, W. W. "Biblical History in Its Near Eastern Setting: The Contextual Approach." In *Scripture in Context: Essays on the Comparative Method*, edited by Carl D. Evans et al., 1–26. Pittsburgh: Pickwick Publications, 1980.

———. "Compare and Contrast: The Contextual Approach to Biblical Literature." In *The Bible in the Light of Cuneiform Literature: Scripture in Context III*, edited by W. W. Hallo et al., Lewiston, NY: Mellen, 1990.

———. *Scripture in Context II: More Essays on the Comparative Method*. Winona Lake, IN: Eisenbrauns, 1983.

———. "Slave Release in the Biblical World in Light of a New Text." In *Solving Riddles and Untying Knots: Biblical, Epigraphic, and Semitic Studies in Honor of Jonas C. Greenfield*, edited by Zion Zevit et al., 79–93. Winona Lake, IN: Eisenbrauns, 1995.

Hamilton, Victor P. *Exodus: An Exegetical Commentary*. Grand Rapids: Baker Academic, 2011.

Harrelson, Walter J. *The Ten Commandments and Human Rights. 1980*. Reprint, Macon, GA: Mercer University Press, 1997.

Hartley, John E. *Leviticus*. Word Biblical Commentary 3. Dallas: Word, 1992.

Hays, Christine. *What's Divine About Divine Law? Early Perspectives*. Princeton: Princeton University Press, 2015.

Hays, Christopher B. *Hidden Riches: A Sourcebook for the Comparative Study of the Hebrew Bible and Ancient Near East*. Louisville: Westminster John Knox, 2014.

Hays, J. Daniel. "Applying Old Testament Law Today." *Bibliotheca Sacra* 158 (2001) 21–35.

Hempel, Johannes. *Das Ethos des alten Testaments*. Beihefte zur Zeitschrift für die alttestamentliche Wissenschaft 67. Berlin: Töpelmann, 1964.

Hendel, Ronald. "The Exodus in Biblical Memory." *Journal of Biblical Literature* 120 (2001) 601–22.

———. *Remembering Abraham: Culture, Memory, and History in the Hebrew Bible*. New York: Oxford University Press, 2005.

Hersey, Oliver. "The Marriage at Mount Sinai: Reading Exodus in the Context of Ancient Near Eastern Diplomatic Marriage." PhD diss., Trinity Evangelical Divinity School, 2019.

Hess, Richard S. "Alalakh Studies in the Bible: Obstacle or Contribution?" In *Scripture and Other Artifacts: Essays on the Bible and Archaeology in Honor of Philip J. King*, edited by Michael D. Coogan et al., 199–215. Louisville: Westminster John Knox, 1994.

———. "The Distinctive Value of Human Life in Israel's Earliest Legal Traditions." In *The Ancient Near East in the 12th–10th Centuries BCE: Proceedings of the International Conference Held at the University of Haifa, 2–5 May, 2010*, edited by Gershon Galil et al., 221–28. Alter Orient und Altes Testament. Münster: Ugarit-Verlag, 2012.

———. "The Structure of the Covenant Code: Exodus 20:22—23:33." Master's thesis, Trinity Evangelical Divinity School, 1980.

Hiers, Richard H. *Justice and Compassion in Biblical Law*. New York: Continuum International, 2009.

Hoffman, Yair. "A North Israelite Typological Myth and a Judaean Historical Tradition: The Exodus in Hosea and Amos." *Vetus Testamentum* 39 (1989) 169–82.

Hoffmeier, James K. *Israel in Egypt: The Evidence for the Authenticity of the Exodus Tradition*. New York: Oxford University Press, 1997.

———. "Why a Historical Exodus is Essential for Theology." In *Do Historical Matters Matter for Faith? A Critical Appraisal of Modern and Postmodern Approaches to the Bible*, edited by James K. Hoffmeier and Dennis R. Magary, 99–134. Wheaton, IL: Crossway, 2012.

Hoffmeier, James K., et al., eds. *"Did I Not Bring Israel Out of Egypt?" Biblical, Archaeological, and Egyptological Perspectives on the Exodus Narratives*. Winona Lake, IN: Eisenbrauns, 2016.

Houston, Walter J. *Contending for Justice: Ideologies and Theologies of Social Justice in the Old Testament*. Library of Hebrew Bible/Old Testament Studies 428. London: T. & T. Clark, 2006.

Houtman, Cornelis. *Exodus*. Vol. 3, *Chapters 20–40*. Historical Commentary of the Old Testament. Leuven: Peters, 2000.

Huehnergard, John A. *Grammar of Akkadian*. 3rd ed. Winona Lake, IN: Eisenbrauns, 2011.

Huffman, Herbert B. "'An Eye for an Eye' and Capital Punishment." In *The Oxford Handbook of Biblical Law*, edited by Pamela Barmash, 119–32. Oxford Handbooks. New York: Oxford University Press, 2019.

Huizinga, Johan. "A Definition of the Concept of History." In *Philosophy and History: Essays Presented to Ernst Cassirer*, edited by Raymond Klibansky and H. J. Paton, 1–10. 1936. Reprint, New York: Harper & Row, 1963.

Hyatt, J. Philip. *Exodus*. New Century Bible Commentary. Grand Rapids: Eerdmans, 1983.

Ishay, Micheline R. *The History of Human Rights: From Ancient Times to the Globalization Era*. Berkeley: University of California Press, 2004.

Jackson, Bernard S. *Essays in Jewish and Comparative Legal History*. Studies in Judaism in Late Antiquity 10. Leiden: Brill, 1975.

———. "Modeling Biblical Law: The Covenant Code." *Chicago-Kent Law Review* 70 (1995) 1745–827.

———. *Studies in the Semiotics of Biblical Law*. Journal for the Study of the Old Testament Supplement Series 314. Sheffield: Sheffield Academic, 2000.

———. *Wisdom Laws: A Study of Mishpatim of Exodus 21:1—22:16*. Oxford: Oxford University Press, 2006.

Jackson, Samuel A. *A Comparison of Ancient Near Eastern Law Collections Prior to the First Millennium BC*. Gorgias Dissertations: Near East Series 10. Piscataway, NJ: Gorgias, 2008.

Jacob, Edmund. "Les bases théologiques de l'éthique de l'Ancien Testament." In *Congress Volume: Oxford, 1959*, edited by G. W. Anderson et al., 39–51. Supplements to Vetus Testamentum 7. Leiden: Brill, 1960.

Jacob, Ernst. "Die altassyrischen Gesetze und ihr Verhältnis zu den Gesetzes des Pentateuch." *Zeitschrift für vergleichende Rechtswissenschaft* 41 (1925) 319–87.

Janzen, J. Gerald. *At the Scent of Water: The Ground of Hope in the Book of Job*. Grand Rapids: Eerdmans, 2009.

Janzen, Waldemar. *Exodus*. Believers Church Bible Commentary. Scottdale, PA: Herald, 2000.

———. *Old Testament Ethics: A Paradigmatic Approach*. Louisville: Westminster John Knox, 1994.
Johns, C. H. W. "The Code of Hammurabi." *Expository Times* 14.6 (1903) 257–58.
Josipovici, Gabrielle. *The Book of God: A Response to the Bible*. New Haven: Yale University Press, 1988.
Kaiser, Walter C., Jr. "A Principlizing Model." In *Four Views on Moving Beyond the Bible to Theology*, edited by Gary T. Meadors and Walter C. Kaiser Jr., 51–73. Grand Rapids: Zondervan, 2009.
———. *Toward Old Testament Ethics*. Grand Rapids: Zondervan, 1983.
Kaufmann, Yehezkel. *The Religion of Israel*. Chicago: University of Chicago Press, 1960.
Keil, C. F. *The Pentateuch*. Translated by J. Martin. 1864. Reprint, Grand Rapids: Eerdmans, 1978.
Kilma, J. "Gesetze." In *Reallexikon der Assyriologie*, edited by Erich Ebeling et al., 3:243–55. Berlin: de Gruyter, 1957.
Kitchen, Kenneth, and Paul Lawrence. *Treaty, Law and Covenant in the Ancient Near East*. Wiesbaden: Harrassowitz, 2012.
Knight, Douglas A. *Law, Power, and Justice in Ancient Israel*. Library of Ancient Israel. Louisville: Westminster John Knox, 2011.
Knoppers, Gary N. "Ancient Near Eastern Royal Grants and the Davidic Covenant: A Parallel?" *Journal of the American Oriental Society* 116 (1996) 670–97.
Kofoed, Jens Bruun. "Encoding and Decoding Culture." In *Write That They May Read: Studies in Literacy and Textualization in the Ancient Near East and in the Hebrew Scriptures: Essays in Honour of Professor Alan R. Millard*, edited by Daniel I. Block et al., 240–62. Eugene, OR: Pickwick Publications, 2020.
———. "The Exodus as Cultural Memory." In *"Did I Not Bring Israel Out of Egypt?" Biblical, Archaeological, and Egyptological Perspectives on the Exodus Narratives*, edited by James K. Hoffmeier et al., 177–96. Bulletin for Biblical Research Supplement Series 13. Winona Lake, IN: Eisenbrauns, 2016.
Koehler, Ludwig, and Walter Baumgartner. *The Hebrew and Aramaic Lexicon of the Old Testament*. Translated and edited by M. E. J. Richardson. 2 vols. Leiden: Brill, 2001.
Kolakowski, Leszek. *Religion, If There is No God . . . : On God, the Devil, Sin, and Other Worries of the So-Called Philosophy of Religion*. New York: Oxford University Press, 1982.
Konkel, August H. *1 & 2 Kings: From Biblical Text to Contemporary Life*. Grand Rapids: Zondervan, 2006.
Kraftchick, Stephen J. "Widows." In *The Oxford Encyclopedia of the Bible and Law*, edited by Brent A. Strawn, vol. 2, 421–31. New York: Oxford University Press, 2015.
Kristen, Julia. *Semeiotiké: Recherches pour une sémanalyse*. Paris: Seuil, 1969.
Kugel, James L. *The God of Old: Inside the Lost World of the Bible*. New York: Free, 2003.
Landman, Yael. *Legal Writing, Legal Practice: The Biblical Bailment Law and Divine Justice*. Brown Judaic Studies 370. Atlanta: SBL Press, 2022.
Laney, Carl J. "God's Self-Revelation in Exodus 34:6–8." *Bibliotheca Sacra* 158 (2001) 36–51.
Launderville, Dale. *Piety and Politics: The Dynamics of Royal Authority in Homeric Greece, Biblical Israel, and Old Babylonian Mesopotamia*. Bible in Its World. Grand Rapids: Eerdmans, 2003.

LeFebvre, Michael. *Collections, Codes and Torah: The Re-characterization of Israel's Written Law.* Library of Hebrew Bible/Old Testament Studies 451. New York: T. & T. Clark, 2006.

Lemche, Niels Peter. "Ancient Near East and Hebrew Bible," under "Slavery." In *The Oxford Encyclopedia of the Bible and Law*, edited by Brent A. Strawn, 2:302–6. New York: Oxford University Press, 2015.

———. "'The Hebrew Slave': Comments on the Slave Law Ex xxi 2–11." *Vetus Testamentum* 25 (1975) 129–44.

LeMon, Joel M., and Kent Harold Richards, eds. *Method Matters: Essays on the Interpretation of the Hebrew Bible in Honor of David L. Petersen.* Resources for Biblical Study 56. Atlanta: Society of Biblical Literature, 2009.

Levine, Baruch A. *Leviticus: The Traditional Hebrew Text with the New JPS Translation.* JPS Torah Commentary. Philadelphia: JPS, 1989.

Levinson, Bernard M. "Is the Covenant Code an Exilic Composition? A Response to John Van Seters." In *In Search of Pre-Exilic Israel: Proceedings of the Oxford Old Testament Seminar*, edited by John Day, 272–325. London: T. & T. Clark, 2004.

———. *Legal Revision and Religious Renewal in Ancient Israel.* Cambridge: Cambridge University Press, 2008.

———. "The Manumission of Hermeneutics: The Slave Laws of the Pentateuch as a Challenge to Contemporary Pentateuchal Theory." In *Congress Volume Leiden 2004*, edited by André Lemaire, 281–324. Supplements to Vetus Testamentum 109. Leiden: Brill, 2006.

———. *"The Right Chorale": Studies in Biblical Law and Interpretation.* Winona Lake, IN: Eisenbrauns, 2011.

———. "'You Must Not Add Anything to What I Command You': Paradoxes of Canon and Authorship in Ancient Israel." *Numen* 50 (2003) 1–51.

Lindenberger, James M. *Ancient Aramaic and Hebrew Letters.* 2nd ed. Writings from the Ancient World 4. Atlanta: SBL, 2003.

Loewenstam, S. E. "Din hano'ef wedin haroẓeaḥ bemishpaṭ hamiḳra uvemishpaṭ hameṣopoṭami." *Beth Miqra* 13 (1962) 55–59.

———. "Review of Goetze's 'Laws of Eshnunna.'" *Israeli Exploration Journal* 7 (1957) 192–98.

Long, V. Philips. *The Art of Biblical History.* Grand Rapids: Zondervan, 1994.

Lundbom, Jack R. *Deuteronomy: A Commentary.* Grand Rapids: Eerdmans, 2013.

Magdalene, F. Rachel. "Legal Science Then and Now: Theory and Method in the Work of Raymond Westbrook." *Maarav* 18 (2013) 25–29.

Malul, Meir. *The Comparative Method in Ancient Near Eastern and Biblical Legal Studies.* Alter Orient und Altes Testament 227. Kevelaer: Butzon & Bercker, 1990.

———. *Society, Law and Custom in the Land of Israel in Biblical Times and in the Ancient Near Eastern Cultures* [Heb.]. Ramat Gan: Bar Ilan University Press, 2006.

Marshall, Jay W. *Israel and the Book of the Covenant: An Anthropological Approach to Biblical Law.* Society of Biblical Literature Dissertation Series 140. Atlanta: Scholars, 1993.

Marsman, Hennie J. *Women in Ugarit and Israel: Their Social and Religious Position in the Context of the Ancient Near East.* Old Testament Studies 49. Leiden: Brill, 2009.

Martens, Elmer A. "How is the Christian to Construe Old Testament Law?" *Bulletin for Biblical Research* 12 (2002) 199–216.

McKay, J. W. "Exodus XXIII 1–3, 6–8: A Decalogue for the Administration of Justice in the City Gate." *Vetus Testamentum* 21 (1971) 311–25.

Mendenhall, George E. *Law and Covenant in Israel and the Ancient Near East*. Pittsburgh: Presbyterian Board of Colportage of Western Pennsylvania, 1955.

Milgrom, J. *Cult and Conscience: The Asham and the Priestly Doctrine of Repentance*. Studies in Judaism in Late Antiquity 18. Leiden: Brill, 1976.

———. *Leviticus: A Book of Ritual and Ethics*. Continental Commentaries. Minneapolis: Fortress, 2004.

Milstein, Sara J. *Making a Case: The Practical Roots of Biblical Law*. New York: Oxford University Press, 2021.

Moberly, R. W. L. *At the Mountain of God: Story and Theology in Exodus 32–34*. Journal for the Study of the Old Testament Supplement Series 22. Sheffield: JSOT Press, 1983.

Morrow, William S. *An Introduction to Biblical Law*. Grand Rapids: Eerdmans, 2017.

———. "Legal Interactions: The *Mišpāṭîm* and the Laws of Hammurabi." *Bibliotheca Orientalis* 70 (2013) 310–31.

Mott, Charles Stephen. *A Christian Perspective in Political Thought*. Oxford: Oxford University Press, 1993.

Na'aman, Nadav. "Ḫabiru and Hebrews: The Transfer of a Social Term to the Literary Sphere." *Journal of Near Eastern Studies* 45 (1986) 271–88.

Nasuti, Harry P. "Identity, Identification, and Imitation: The Narrative Hermeneutics of Biblical Law." *Journal of Law and Religion* 4 (1986) 9–23.

Naveh, J. "A Hebrew Ostracon from the Seventh Century B.C." *Israeli Exploration Journal* 10 (1960) 129–39.

Neumann, Hans. "Slavery in Private Households toward the End of the Third Millennium B.C." In *Slaves and Households in the Near East*, edited by Laura Culbertson, 21–32. Oriental Institute Seminars 7. Chicago: University of Chicago Press, 2011.

Noll, Mark. "Battle for the Bible: The Impasse over Slavery." *Christian Century* 123 (2006) 20–25.

Nora, Pierre. "Between Memory and History: *Les Lieux de Memoire*." *Representations* 26 (1989) 7–24.

Noth, Martin. *Exodus: A Commentary*. Translated by J. S. Bowden. Old Testament Library. Philadelphia: Westminster, 1962.

———. *A History of Pentateuchal Traditions*. Translated by Bernhard W. Anderson. 1972. Reprint, Chico, CA: Scholars, 1981.

Novick, P. *That Noble Dream: The "Objectivity Question" in the American Historical Profession*. Ideas in Context. Cambridge: Cambridge University Press, 1988.

Novick, Tzvi. "Social Justice in Rabbinic Judaism." In *The Oxford Handbook of Biblical Law*, edited by Pamela Barmash, 537–52. New York: Oxford University Press, 2019.

Orlinsky, H. M. "The Forensic Character of the Hebrew Bible." In *Justice and the Holy: Essays in Honor of Walter Harrelson*, edited by Douglas A. Knight and Peter J. Paris, 89–98. Scholars Press Homage Series 12. Atlanta: Scholars, 1989.

Osborne, Grant R. *The Hermeneutical Spiral: A Comprehensive Introduction to Biblical Interpretation*. 2nd ed. Downers Grove, IL: InterVarsity, 2006.

Osumi, Yuichi. *Die Kompositionsgeschichte des Bundesbuches Exodus 20,22b–23,33*. Orbis Biblicus et Orientalis 105. Göttingen: Vandenhoeck & Ruprecht, 1991.

Otto, Eckart. "Ethics." In *The Oxford Encyclopedia of the Bible and Law*, edited by Brent A. Strawn, 1:271–80. New York: Oxford University Press, 2015.

---. "Forschungsgeschichte der entwürfe einer Ethik im Alten Testament." *Verkündigung und Forschung* 36 (1991) 3-37.

---. "Human Rights: The Influence of the Hebrew Bible." *Journal of Northwest Semitic Languages* 25 (1999) 1-20.

---. "Interdependenzen zwischen Geschichte und Rechtsgeschichte des antiken Israels." *Rechtschistorisches Journal* 7 (1988) 366-67.

---. "Laws of Hammurabi." In *The Oxford Encyclopedia of the Bible and Law*, edited by Brent A. Strawn, 1:500-508. New York: Oxford University Press, 2015.

---. "Offenses Against Human Beings." In *The Oxford Handbook of Biblical Law*, edited by Pamela Barmash, 35-44. New York: Oxford University Press, 2019.

---. *Rechtsgeschichte der Redaktionen im Kodex Ešnunna und im "Bundesbuch:" Eine redaktionsgeschichtliche und rechtsvergleichende Studie zu altbabylonischen und altisraelitischen Reschtsüberlieferungen*. Orbis Biblicus et Orientalis 85. Göttingen: Vandenhoeck & Ruprecht, 1989.

---. *Theologische Ethik des Alten Testaments*. Theologische Wissenschaft 3.2. Stuttgart: Kohlhammer, 1994.

---. *Wandel der Rechtsbegründungen in der Gesellschaftsgeschichte des Antiken Israel: Eine Rechtsgeschichte des 'Bundesbuches' Ex XX 22—XXIII 13*. Studia Biblica 3. Leiden: Brill, 1988.

Parsons, Talcott. "Some Theoretical Considerations on the Nature and Trends of Change in Ethnicity." In *Ethnicity: Theory and Experience*, edited by N. Glazer and D. P. Moynihan, 53-83. Cambridge: Harvard University Press, 1975.

Patrick, Dale. "Casuistic Law Governing Primary Rights and Duties." *Journal of Biblical Literature* 92 (1973) 180-84.

---. *Old Testament Law*. 1985. Reprint, Eugene, OR: Wipf & Stock, 2011.

---. *The Rendering of God in the Old Testament*. Overtures to Biblical Theology. Philadelphia: Fortress, 1981.

---. "Studying Biblical Law as a Humanities." *Semeia* 45 (1989) 27-47.

Patterson, Orlando. *Slavery and Social Death: A Comparative Study*. Cambridge: Harvard University Press, 1982.

Paul, Shalom M. "The Book of the Covenant: Its Literary Setting and Extra-Biblical Background." PhD diss, University of Pennsylvania, 1965.

---. *Studies in the Book of the Covenant in the Light of Cuneiform and Biblical Law*. Supplements to Vetus Testamentum 18. Leiden: Brill, 1970.

Perry, Michael J. *Toward a Theory of Human Rights: Religion, Law, Courts*. Cambridge: Cambridge University Press, 2007.

Philips, Anthony C. *Ancient Israel's Criminal Law: A New Approach to the Decalogue*. Oxford: Blackwell, 1970.

---. "A Fresh Look at the Sinai Pericope, Part 1." *Vetus Testamentum* 34 (1984) 39-52.

---. "A Fresh Look at the Sinai Pericope, Part 2." *Vetus Testamentum* 34 (1984) 282-94.

---. "The Laws of Slavery: Exodus 21.2-11." *Journal for the Study of the Old Testament* 30 (1984) 51-56.

Plaut, W. Gunther, ed. *The Torah*. New York: Union of American Hebrew Congregations, 1981.

Pressler, Carolyn. "Wives and Daughters, Bond and Free." In *Gender and Law in the Hebrew Bible and the Ancient Near East*, edited by Victor H. Matthews et al., 147-

72. Journal for the Study of the Old Testament Supplement Series 262. Sheffield: Sheffield Academic, 1998.
Propp, William H. *Exodus 1–18: A New Translation with Introduction and Commentary*. Anchor Bible 2. New York: Doubleday, 1999.
———. *Exodus 19–40: A New Translation with Introduction and Commentary*. Anchor Bible 2A. New York: Doubleday, 2006.
Rad, Gerhard von. *Deuteronomy: A Commentary*. Translated by Dorothea Barton. Old Testament Library. Philadelphia: Westminster, 1966.
Rae, Scott B. *Moral Choices: An Introduction to Ethics*. 3rd ed. Grand Rapids: Zondervan, 2009.
Rendtorff, Rolf. "The Concept of Revelation in Ancient Israel." In *Revelation as History*, edited by Wolfhart Pannenberg, 23–54. New York: MacMillan, 1968.
Renz, Johannes, and Wolfgang Röllig. *Handbuch der althebräischen Epigraphik: Die althebräischen Inschriften*. Darmstadt: Wissenschaftliche Buchgesellschaft, 1995.
Reviv, Hanoch. *A Commentary on Selected Inscriptions from the Period of the Monarchy in Israel* [Heb.]. Jerusalem: Historical Society of Israel, 1975.
Richardson, M. E. J. *Hammurabi's Laws: Text, Translation and Glossary*. Biblical Seminar 73. Sheffield: Sheffield Academic, 2000.
Robinson, G. "The Idea of Rest in the Old Testament and the Search for the Basic Character of Sabbath." *Zeitschrift für die altestamentliche Wissenschaft* 92 (1980) 32–42.
Rodd, Cyril S. *Glimpses of a Strange Land: Studies in Old Testament Ethics*. Edinburgh: T. & T. Clark, 2001.
Rogerson, John. *Theory and Practice in Old Testament Ethics*. Edited by M. Daniel Carroll R. Journal for the Study of the Old Testament Supplement Series 405. New York: T. & T. Clark, 2004.
Rosenberg, Joel. *King and Kin: Political Allegory in the Hebrew Bible*. Indiana Studies in Biblical Literature. Bloomington: Indiana University Press, 1986.
Roth, Martha T. "Hammurabi's Wronged Man." *Journal of the American Oriental Society* 12 (2002) 38–45.
———. *Law Collections from Mesopotamia and Asia Minor*. 2nd ed. Writings from the Ancient World 6. Atlanta: Scholars, 1997.
———. "Mesopotamian Legal Traditions and the Laws of Hammurabi." *Chicago-Kent Law Review* 71 (1995) 13–39.
Rothenbusch, Ralf. *Die kasuistische Rechtssammlung im "Bundesbuch" (Ex 21,2–11.18–22,16)*. Alten Orients und des Alten Testaments 259. Münster: Ugarit-Verlag, 2000.
Rowley, H. H. *The Unity of the Bible*. Philadelphia: Westminster, 1953.
Ryken, Leland, and Tremper Longman III, eds. *A Complete Literary Guide to the Bible*. Grand Rapids: Zondervan, 1993.
Sallaberger, Walther. "König Ḫammurapi und die Babylonier: Wem übertrug der Kodex Ḫammurapi die Rechtspflege?" In *Who Was King? Who Was Not King? The Ruler and the Ruled in the Ancient Near East*, edited by Petr Charvát and Petra Maříková Vlčková, 46–58. Prague: Institute of Archaeology of the Academy of Sciences of the Czech Republic, 2010.
Sandmel, Samuel. "Parallelomania." *Journal of Biblical Literature* 81 (1962) 1–13.
Sarna, Nahum M. *Exodus*. JPS Torah Commentary. Philadelphia: Jewish Publication Society, 1991.

Schenker, Adrian. "The Biblical Legislation on the Release of Slaves: The Road from Exodus to Leviticus." *Journal for the Study of the Old Testament* 78 (1998) 23–41.

Schwienhorst-Schönberger, Ludger. *Das Bundesbuch (Ex 20,22—23,33): Studien zu seiner Entstehung und Theologie*. Beihefte zur Zeit-schrift für die alttestamentliche Wissenschaft 188. Berlin: de Gruyter, 1990.

Seeligmann, I. L. "Loan, Guarantorship and Interest in Biblical Law" [Heb.]. In *Mehqarim ba-Miqra uva Mizrah ha-Qadmon*, 1:183–205. Festschrift Samuel E. Loewenstamm. Jerusalem: Rubenshteyn, 1978.

Shevka, Avi. "Biblical Laws of Loans: A Comparative Perspective" [Heb.]. PhD diss., Hebrew University of Jerusalem, 2010.

Smith, Anthony D. *The Ethnic Origins of Nations*. Oxford: Blackwell, 1987.

Sonsino, Rifat. *Motive Clauses in Hebrew Law: Biblical Forms and Near Eastern Parallels*. SBL Dissertation Series 45. Chico, CA: Scholars, 1980.

Sparks, Kenton L. *Ethnicity and Identity in Ancient Israel: Prolegomena to the Study of Ethnic Sentiments and Their Expression in the Hebrew Bible*. Winona Lake, IN: Eisenbrauns, 1998.

———. *God's Word in Human Words: An Evangelical Appropriation of Critical Biblical Scholarship*. Grand Rapids: Baker Academic, 2008.

Speiser, E. A. "Authority and Law in Mesopotamia." *Journal of the American Oriental Society* 17 (1954) 8–15.

———. "Cuneiform Law and the History of Civilization." *American Philosophical Society Proceedings* 107 (1963) 536–41.

———. "Early Law and Civilization." *Canadian Bar Review* 31 (1953) 863–77.

Spencer, James. "Remembering Sabbath: An Application of Sociological Method in the Exposition of the Old Testament." PhD diss., Trinity Evangelical Divinity School, 2011.

Spina, Frank Anthony. "Israelites as *Gerim*: 'Sojourners' in Social and Historical Context." In *The Word of the Lord Shall Go Forth: Essays in Honor of David Noel Freedman in Celebration of his Sixtieth Birthday*, edited by Carol Meyers and M. O'Connor, 321–35. Winona Lake, IN: Eisenbrauns, 1983.

Sprinkle, Joe M. *Biblical Law and Its Relevance: A Christian Understanding and Ethical Application for Today of the Mosaic Regulations*. Lanham, MD: University Press of America, 2006.

———. *The Book of the Covenant: A Literary Approach*. Journal for the Study of the Old Testament Supplement Series 174. Sheffield: JSOT Press, 1994.

———. "Law and Narrative in Exodus 19–24." *Journal of the Evangelical Theological Society* 47 (2004) 235–52.

———. "Literary Approaches to the Old Testament: A Survey of Recent Scholarship." *Journal of the Evangelical Theological Society* 32 (1989) 199–210.

Stackert, Jeffrey. *Rewriting the Torah: Literary Revision in Deuteronomy and the Holiness Legislation*. Forschungen zum Alten Testament 52. Tübingen: Mohr Siebeck, 2007.

Stark, Rodney. *The Rise of Christianity: A Sociologist Reconsiders History*. Princeton: Princeton University Press, 1996.

Sternberg, Meir. *The Poetics of Biblical Narrative: Ideological Literature and the Drama of Reading*. Indiana Studies in Biblical Literature. Bloomington: Indiana University Press, 1987.

Stuart, Douglas K. *Exodus*. New American Commentary. Nashville: Broadman & Holman, 2006.

Stubbs, David L. *Numbers*. Brazos Theological Commentary on the Bible. Grand Rapids: Brazos, 2009.

Swiderski, Igor. "Sabbatical Patterns in the Book of the Covenant." Master's thesis, Trinity Evangelical Divinity School, 2013.

Tadmor, Hayim. "Propaganda, Literature, Historiography: Cracking the Code of the Assyrian Royal Inscription." In *Assyria 1995: Proceedings of the 10th Anniversary Symposium of the Neo-Assyrian Text Corpus Project, Helsinki, September 7–11, 1995*, edited by S. Parpola and R. M. Whiting, 325–28. Helsinki: Neo-Assyrian Corpus Project, 1997.

Talmon, Shemaryahu. "The 'Comparative Method' in Biblical Interpretation—Principles and Problems." In *Congress Volume: Göttingen, 1977*, edited by J. A. Emerton, 320–56. Supplements to Vetus Testamentum 29. Leiden: Brill, 1977.

Testart, A. "The Extent and Significance of Debt Slavery." *Revue française de sociologie* (Supplement: Annual English Edition) 43 (2002) 173–204.

Thompson, Trevor W. "Punishment and Restitution." In *The Oxford Encyclopedia of the Bible and Law*, edited by Brent A. Strawn, 183–93. New York: Oxford University Press, 2015.

Tigay, Jeffrey H. *Deuteronomy: The Traditional Hebrew Text with the New JPS Translation*. JPS Torah Commentary. Philadelphia: Jewish Publication Society, 1996.

———. "The Evolution of the Pentateuchal Narratives in Light of the Evolution of the Gilgamesh Epic." In *Empirical Models for Biblical Criticism*, edited by Jeffrey H. Tigay, 369–400. Philadelphia: University of Pennsylvania Press, 1985.

———. "A Talmudic Parallel to the Petition from Yavneh-Yam." In *Minḥah le-Naḥum: Biblical and Other Studies Presented to Nahum M. Sarna in Honour of His 70th Birthday*, edited by Marc Brettler and Michael Fishbane, 328–33. Journal for the Study of the Old Testament Supplements 154. Sheffield: Sheffield Academic, 1993.

Tsai, Daisy Yulin. *Human Rights in Deuteronomy: with Special Focus on Slave Laws*. Beihefte zur Zeitschrift für die alttestamentliche Wissenschaft 464. Berlin: de Gruyter, 2014.

Uitti, Roger William. "The Motive Clause in Old Testament Law." PhD diss., Lutheran School of Theology at Chicago, 1973.

Unterman, Jeremiah. *Justice for All: How the Jewish Bible Revolutionized Ethics*. JPS Essential Judaism Series. Philadelphia: JPS, 2017.

Van de Mieroop, Marc. *King Hammurabi of Babylon: A Bibliography*. Malden, MA: Blackwell, 2005.

Van Houten, Christiana. *The Alien in Israelite Law*. Journal for the Study of the Old Testament Supplement Series 107. Sheffield: JSOT Press, 1991.

Van Seters, John. "Cultural Memory and the Invention of Biblical Israel." In *Cultural Memory in Biblical Exegesis*, edited by Pernille Carstens et al., 69–96. Piscataway, NJ: Gorgias, 2012.

———. *A Law Book for the Diaspora: Revision in the Study of the Covenant Code*. Oxford: Oxford University Press, 2003.

Van Wijk-Bos, Johanna W. H. *Making Wise the Simple: The Torah in Christian Faith and Practice*. Grand Rapids: Eerdmans, 2005.

VanGemeren, Willem A., ed. *New International Dictionary of Old Testament Theology and Exegesis*. Grand Rapids: Zondervan, 1997.

Vanhoozer, Kevin J. *Is There a Meaning in This Text? The Bible, the Reader, and the Morality of Literary Knowledge*. Grand Rapids: Zondervan, 1998.

———. "The Semantics of Biblical Literature: Truth and Scripture's Diverse Literary Forms." In *Hermeneutics, Authority and Canon*, edited by D. A. Carson and John D. Woodbridge, 53–104. Leicester, UK: InterVarsity, 1986.

Viberg, A. *Symbols of Law: A Contextual Analysis of Legal Symbolic Acts in the Old Testament*. Coniectanea Biblica: Old Testament Series 34. Stockholm: Almqvist & Wiksell, 1992.

Wagner, Volker. *Rechtssätze in gebundener Sprache und Rechtssatzreihen im israelischen Recht: Ein Beitrag zur Gattungsforschung*. Beihefte zur Zeitschrift für die alttestamentliche Wissenschaft 127. Berlin: de Gruyter, 1972.

———. "Zur Existenz des sogannanten 'Heiligkeitsgesetzes.'" *Zeitschrift für die altestamentliche Wissenschaft* 86 (1974) 307–16.

———. "Zur Systematik in dev Codex Ex:21:2—22:16." *Zeitschrift für die altestamentliche Wissenschaft* 81.2 (1969) 176–82.

Walton, John H. *Ancient Israelite Literature in Its Cultural Context*. Grand Rapids: Zondervan, 1990.

———. "Biblical Texts Studied in Comparison with Other Ancient Near Eastern Documents." In *Behind the Scenes of the Old Testament: Cultural, Social, and Historical Contexts*, edited by Jonathan S. Greer et al., 573–85. Grand Rapids: Baker Academic, 2018.

———. *Introducing the Conceptual World of the Hebrew Bible: Ancient Near Eastern Thought and the Old Testament*. 2nd ed. Grand Rapids: Baker Academic, 2018.

Walton, John H., and J. Harvey Walton. *The Lost World of the Torah: Law as Covenant and Wisdom in Ancient Context*. Downers Grove, IL: IVP Academic, 2019.

Watts, James W. *Reading Law: The Rhetorical Shaping of the Pentateuch*. Biblical Seminar 59. Sheffield: Sheffield Academic, 1999.

Weeks, Noel. "Problems with the Comparative Method in Old Testament Studies." *Journal of the Evangelical Theological Society* 62 (2019) 287–306.

Weinfeld, Moshe. *Deuteronomy 1–11*. Anchor Bible 5. New York: Doubleday, 1991.

———. "Litefiṣat haḥoḵ beyisrael umeḥuẓah lo." *Beth Miqra* 17 (1964) 58–63.

———. *Social Justice in Ancient Israel and in the Ancient Near East*. Minneapolis: Fortress, 1995.

Wells, Bruce. "The Covenant Code and Near Eastern Legal Traditions: A Response to David P. Wright." *Maarav* 13 (2006) 85–118.

———. "What Is Biblical Law? A Look at Pentateuchal Rules and Near Eastern Practice." *Catholic Biblical Quarterly* 70 (2008) 223–43.

Wenham, Gordon J. *Story as Torah: Reading the Old Testament Ethically*. Edinburgh: T. & T. Clark, 2000.

Westbrook, Raymond. "Biblical and Cuneiform Law Codes." *Revue Biblique* 92 (1985) 247–64.

———. "The Female Slave." In *Law from the Tigris to the Tiber: The Writings of Raymond Westbrook*. Vol. 2, *Cuneiform and Biblical Sources*, edited by Bruce Wells and Rachel Magdalene, 149–74. Winona Lake, IN: Eisenbrauns, 2009.

———. "The Old Babylonian Period." In *Security for Debt in Ancient Near Eastern Law*, edited by Raymond Westbrook and Richard Lewis Jasnow, 63–92. Culture and History of the Ancient Near East 9. Leiden: Brill, 2001.

———. "Slave and Master in Ancient Near Eastern Law." In *Law from the Tigris to the Tiber: The Writings of Raymond Westbrook*. Vol. 1, *The Shared Tradition*, edited by Bruce Wells and Rachel Magdalene, 161–216. Winona Lake, IN: Eisenbrauns, 2009.

———. *Studies in Biblical and Cuneiform Law*. Cahiers de la Revue Biblique 26. Paris: Gabalda, 1988.

———. "What Is the Covenant Code." In *Theory and Method in Biblical and Cuneiform Law: Revision, Interpolation and Development*, edited by Bernard M. Levinson, 15–36. Journal for the Study of the Old Testament Supplement Series 181. Sheffield: Sheffield Academic, 1994.

Westbrook, Raymond, and Bruce Wells. *Everyday Law in Biblical Israel: An Introduction*. Louisville: Westminster John Knox, 2009.

Wilcke, Claus. "Laws of Ur-Namma." In *The Oxford Encyclopedia of the Bible and Law*, edited by Brent A. Strawn, 1:513–18. New York: Oxford University Press, 2015.

Williams, Peter J. "'Slaves' in Biblical Narrative and Translation." In *On Stone and Scroll: Essays in Honour of Graham Ivor Davies*, edited by James K. Aitken et al., 441–52. Beihefte zur Zeitschrift für die alttestamentliche Wissenschaft 420. Berlin: de Gruyter, 2011.

Williamson, H. G. M. "The Concept of Israel in Transition." In *The World of Ancient Israel*, edited by R. E. Clements, 141–62. Cambridge: Cambridge Press, 1989.

Witte, John, Jr., and Frank S. Alexander, eds. *Christianity and Law: An Introduction*. Cambridge University Press, 2008.

Wolterstorff, Nicholas. *Justice: Rights and Wrongs*. Princeton: Princeton University Press, 2008.

Woods, Edward J. *Deuteronomy: An Introduction and Commentary*. Tyndale Old Testament Commentary. Downers Grove, IL: InterVarsity, 2011.

Wright, Christopher J. H. *Deuteronomy*. Understanding the Bible Commentary Series. Grand Rapids: Baker Academic, 2012.

———. *Exodus*. Story of God Bible Commentary. Grand Rapids: Zondervan, 2021.

———. *An Eye for an Eye: The Place of Old Testament Ethics Today*. Downers Grove, IL: InterVarsity, 1989.

———. *God's People in God's Land: Family, Land, and Property in the Old Testament*. Grand Rapids: Eerdmans, 1990.

———. *Old Testament Ethics for the People of God*. Downers Grove, IL: InterVarsity, 2004.

Wright, David P. *Inventing God's Law: How the Covenant Code of the Bible Used and Revised the Laws of Hammurabi*. Oxford: Oxford University Press, 2009.

———. "The Laws of Hammurabi as a Source for the Covenant Collection (Exodus 20:23—23:19)." *Maarav* 10 (2003) 11–87.

———. "Methods in Studying Ancient Law." In *The Oxford Encyclopedia of the Bible and Law*, edited by Brent A. Strawn, 2:27–38. New York: Oxford University Press, 2015.

Wright, G. Ernest. *God Who Acts: Biblical Theology as Recital*. Studies in Biblical Theology 8. London: SCM, 1952.

Yamauchi, Edwin M. "חָנֻן." 302.

Younger, K. Lawson, Jr. "The 'Contextual Method': Some West Semitic Reflections." In *Context of Scripture III*, edited by W. W. Hallo and K. Lawson Younger Jr., xxxv–xlii. Leiden: Brill, 2003.

———. "Two Comparative Notes on the Book of Ruth." *Journal of Ancient Near Eastern Studies* 26 (1997) 121–32.

Zimmerli, Walter. *I am Yahweh*. Translated by Douglas W. Stott. Edited by Walter Brueggemann. 1982. Reprint, Eugene, OR: Wipf & Stock, 2018.

Subject Index

Footnotes are indicated by page numbers followed by n and then the number of the footnote, e.g., 158n177. Tables are indicated by page number followed by t.

Abrahamic covenant, 82, 102–3, 106, 106n119, 109, 187
Achan, 159
Aḥituv, Shmuel, 55
Albright, William Foxwell, 10
Alexander, T. D., 133n69, 162, 188n95
aliens. *See* foreigners/aliens
allochthony (foreign origin), 104
Alt, Albrecht, 7
altar laws, 88n38, 89, 92–93
An (god), 170
ancestry/genealogies, 103–4, 106, 109
Anderson, J. N. D., 100, 100n91
animals, 10, 63–68, 72, 75–76, 78, 78n213, 156. *See also various types*
anthropological approach, 11
apodictic laws, 7, 46t, 61, 66, 96–98, 98f, 116
apostles, 120n3, 202n25
Assman, Jan, 99, 107–8
Assyrian, Middle, Laws (MAL), 20t, 89
atonement, 164. *See also* ransom; redemption
authority
  ancient Near Eastern laws and, 21–22, 124, 168–72, 177

biblical laws and, 24, 46, 124–25, 168, 172–73, 181, 183
modern society and, 200
respect for, 71
Averbeck, Richard E.
  on ancient Near Eastern law collections, 177
  on capital crimes, 98n81, 161, 165
  on context of biblical law, 3n8, 6, 97–98, 111n140
  on covenants, 106, 187
  on creation and biblical law, 40, 93–94
  on exodus, 82–83, 98, 111n140
  on interpretation of law, 24, 79
  on Jesus Christ and law, 60n137
  on Old Testament, 120n3
  on slavery, 2, 126, 128, 128n43, 135, 135n78, 138–41, 144n122
  on source criticism, 87

Babylon/Babylonia, 160, 175, 180–82. *See also* Laws of Hammurabi (LH)
Babylonian, Neo-, Laws (NBL), 20t
Barth, Fredrik, 103
Barton, John, 41–42, 79
Bartor, Assnat, 19, 109, 113, 183
Berman, Joshua, 181

Birch, Bruce C., 38–40, 109, 111n142, 112n145
Boda, Mark J., 110n134
Boecker, Hans Jochen, 7, 92
bondage. *See* slavery
Book of the Covenant (BC). *See also* law, biblical
　overview, 1n2, 10n44, 178–79, 195
　ancient Near Eastern context of, 6–9, 15, 89
　compassion of God and, 13, 15, 15n71, 30–37, 42, 82, 190
　composition of, 84–88
　goals of, 117–18, 152, 195
　humanitarian context of, 9–14, 9n40, 14n70, 166, 195, 201
　literary context of, 4–6, 87–98, 115–18, 195–96
"The Book of the Covenant: Its Literary Setting and Extra-Biblical Background" (Paul), 4
bribes, 12, 39, 61n140
bride price, 144, 150
Brueggemann, Walter, 107, 124–25
burnt offerings, 92

Cahn, Edmond Nathaniel, 152
Canaan, land of, 91, 102, 106, 106n117, 107–8, 116. *See also* Promised Land
capital punishment. *See* death penalty
Cardellini, Innocenzo, 94
Carmichael, Calum M., 70–72
Cassuto, U., 61, 95n66
casuistic law, 7, 10–11, 45, 45t, 61, 96–98, 98f, 116
chattel slavery, 127–28, 149, 149n143, 165
chiasms, 31–32, 62, 94, 96
Childs, Brevard S., 58–59, 62, 93n59
Chirichigno, Greg, 4–5, 95, 136n82, 148n137
Christensen, Duane L., 52
Christianity, 39, 101–2, 184, 186, 202n27
circumcision, 106
cities of refuge, 161n192
Civil, Miguel, 144n122
clausal analysis, 7n31, 10

cloak as collateral, 11–12, 45–60, 46t, 67, 77, 80. *See also* pledges for loans
collateral for loans. *See* cloak as collateral; pledges for loans
collective memory. *See* cultural memory (mnemohistory)
commandments, 23, 39–40, 41, 125. *See also* Ten Commandments (Decalogue)
comparative method, 2–5, 19–21
compassion, human. *See* humanitarianism
compassion of God, 13, 15, 15n71, 30–37, 42, 82, 190
concubines, 135
contextual method. *See* comparative method
Covenant Code. *See* Book of the Covenant (BC)
covenants
　overview, 106n119, 182, 187, 188n95
　Abrahamic, 82, 102–3, 106, 106n119, 109, 187
　Sinaitic/Mosaic (*See* Sinaitic/Mosaic covenant)
　Davidic, 106n119
　new, 106n119, 182, 202
creation, 40, 48n91, 69, 74, 77–78, 80, 160, 199
Cross, F. M., Jr., 54
Crüsemann, Frank, 96, 133, 183–84
cultic laws, 69, 90–95, 91n50, 97, 116, 186
cultural memory (mnemohistory), 83, 99–104, 106, 116, 196
cuneiform law. *See* law collections, ancient Near Eastern

Dandamayev, M. A., 140, 163
Daube, David, 5n18
daughters, 130, 135–36, 138, 143, 146, 148n137, 155, 162
Davidic covenant, 106n119
de Vaux, Roland, 73
death penalty, 31, 74, 155–61, 161n192, 163–64, 163n203, 166. *See also* ransom; redemption; stoning

debt service (*kiššātu*), 147, 147n134
debt slavery. *See also* slavery
   overview, 88–89, 127–28, 163, 165–66
   ancient Near Eastern laws on, 142–48
   of males in biblical law, 129–34, 138–40
   of women in biblical law, 130, 133–38, 150
debts/loans
   in ancient Near Eastern laws, 147–48, 148n137
   avoiding, 14
   foreigners and, 50n97
   interest on, 10, 12n57, 50–51, 50n97, 71
   pledges for, 11–12, 45–60, 66–67, 71, 80, 147, 147n136
   the poor and, 50–51
Decalogue (Ten Commandments), 25, 56, 72, 90–91
Declaration of Independence, 201n21
deliverance, 111n140, 202. *See also* the exodus
deontology, 39, 41
Deuteronomic Laws (DL), 6n21, 10n44, 51–52, 65
Deuteronomy, Book of, 107–8, 107n120
diachronic method, 4, 5, 17, 17n81, 17n82, 194
Diamond, A. S., 152n154
dietary laws, 71, 93
dignity, human
   in ancient Near Eastern laws, 189, 200
   biblical humanitarianism and, 44, 79
   in Book of the Covenant, 13, 49, 149, 191, 199
   of foreigners/aliens, 150
   of the poor, 51–52
   of slaves, 94, 127–28, 132, 139, 150, 165
   in Universal Declaration of Human Rights, 27
discipline, 36–37
divorce, 135
documentary hypothesis, 86, 108. *See also* source criticism

donkey of enemy, 45–47, 46t, 60–69, 80
dowry, 133
Dozeman, Thomas B., 13, 44, 68, 91, 95–96, 141
Driver, Godfrey Rolles, 157, 158
Driver, S. R., 61
Durham, John I., 32, 71–72, 200n16

ear-piercing ritual, 130, 134
Edicts of Urukagina, 143n121, 174n29
Edwards, Chilperic, 6–8, 7n24
Egypt, 82, 90, 106n117, 109–11, 115, 127. *See also* the exodus
empathy, 82, 114, 115t, 129, 150, 163. *See also* humanitarianism
employees. *See* workers, hired
enemies, 24, 45–47, 46t, 60–69, 80
Enlil (god), 170
En-metena, 143n121
epilogues of law collections. *See* prologues/epilogues of law collections
equality, 10, 37, 37n41, 172, 181, 189, 189n101, 199–200, 201n21. *See also* dignity, human
Erlandsson, S., 136
ethics. *See also* humanitarianism; morality
   definition, 123n18
   in Book of the Covenant, 10n44, 45, 195
   in Deuteronomy, 10n44, 139
   the exodus in, 111–12
   God as ideal model of, 32, 40–42, 109, 185
ethnicity, 102–5, 131
the exodus. *See also* Book of the Covenant (BC); Sinaitic/Mosaic covenant
   Abrahamic covenant and, 82, 103, 109
   festivals and, 92–93
   God's character in, 38, 80, 83, 95, 109–10, 114, 114n155
   historicity of, 82–83, 98–102, 105n112
   humanitarianism and, 3, 76–77, 89, 95, 97–98, 113, 115, 202

SUBJECT INDEX

the exodus (*cont.*)
   Israelite identity and, 103–6, 106n117, 196
   remembering, 102
   sabbath laws and, 76–77
   Sinaitic/Mosaic covenant, 30, 33–34, 38–41, 82–84, 106–7, 106n119, 107n120, 187–88
   slavery and, 88–89, 139, 149
"eye for an eye." *See lex talionis*

Falk, Z. W., 182
fellowship offerings, 92
festivals, 14, 92–94, 92n56
Finkelstein, J. J., 124, 142, 158, 161–62, 189
first fruits, 93–94
firstborn, 71, 93
Fokkelman, J. P., 18
foreigners/aliens
   care for, 12, 39, 76–77, 97, 108, 112–13, 117, 150
   as dependents, 76
   equality of, 189n101
   God's love for, 39
   interest on loans to, 50n97
   as oppressed, 49, 57
   sabbath rest for, 48, 72, 74–76
   as slaves, 126, 128, 149
forgetfulness, 93, 99, 102
forgiveness, 35–36
form criticism, 7, 17, 32, 99
freeing of slaves/manumission, 13, 73, 88, 129–30, 132–34, 137–38, 143–46, 153, 202
Fretheim, Terence E., 43–44
Frey, Hellmuth, 61–62

Gamoran, Hillel, 12n57
Gane, Roy E.
   on ancient Near Eastern laws, 27n126, 125, 177
   on biblical law, 22–23, 24, 56, 68, 79, 196
   on humanitarianism, 3, 37–38, 60, 62–64, 69, 82, 124
   on modern society, 200
Gardiner, Alan, 105n112

Garrett, Duane A., 44, 49, 51, 85, 86, 133–35, 173, 181–82
genealogies/ancestry, 103–4, 106, 109
generosity, 32, 42, 44, 200
Gerstenberger, Erhard S., 7
Gilmer, Harry W., 11, 11n49, 45–46, 67
Girdlestone, R. B., 35
goat, young, cooked in mother's milk, 71, 93–94, 93n59
God
   as author of biblical law, 172–73, 173n28, 181, 191
   compassion of, 13, 15, 15n71, 30–37, 42, 82, 190
   as ethical model, 32, 40–42, 109, 185
   grace of, 42, 44, 59, 84, 111, 117
   image of (*imago Dei*), 41–43, 49, 79, 93, 156–58, 158n177, 163
   imitation of (*imitatio Dei*), 30, 39, 41–44, 74, 77, 79, 113, 132, 190
   justice of, 34, 36–39, 42, 79, 82, 124
   mercy of, 34–36, 42, 115t, 117
   the oppressed and, 50, 114–15
   promises of, 52, 95, 103, 106, 109, 111n140, 182, 187
   relationship with, 117, 187, 199
   revelation of, 33–34, 40, 111–12, 117, 183
   will of, 32, 39–40, 183
gods, other
   overview, 105, 174, 185
   Canaanite, 110
   Egyptian, 110
   Mesopotamian, 145n128, 168–70, 170n8, 174n29, 175, 177, 179, 181, 191
   prohibition against, 71, 91, 158n181, 181, 185
Goldingay, John, 78, 101
grace of God, 42, 44, 59, 84, 111, 117
Greenberg, Moshe, 123–24, 123n22
Greengus, Samuel, 3, 158–62

habiru/hapiru, 131–32
Hallo, W. W., 20
Hammurabi, 169–73, 170n8, 175, 177, 178n46, 179–82, 181n58, 191
Ḥaṣar Asam, 53

SUBJECT INDEX

hatred, 47, 60, 67, 68, 183, 191
Hays, Christopher B., 21, 120–21, 168, 171, 177
Hays, J. Daniel, 87
Hebrews, 131–32
Hempel, Johannes, 40
Hendel, Ronald, 106n117
Hess, Richard S., 2n7, 42n71, 149n141, 200
Hiers, Richard H., 13, 36, 202
historical-critical methods, 17, 99
historiography, 26–27, 98, 168–82
history, biblical, 19, 69, 85, 87, 102–6, 126–27. *See also* mnemohistory (cultural memory)
Hittite Laws (HL), 20t, 86n24, 89n43, 183n71
Hittite treaties, 108n125
Hoffman, Yair, 82
Hoffmeier, James K., 104–5, 105n112
holiness, 5, 41–42, 188, 191, 200–201
Holiness Collection, 6n21
homicide/murder, 156, 158, 160–61, 161n192, 189
Hoshayahu, son of Shobay, 53–54
Huizinga, Johan, 100, 105
human rights. *See also* dignity, human; equality
 ancient Near Eastern law lacking, 189
 biblical law and, 3, 9–11, 27, 52–53, 134–37, 150, 166, 200, 201n21
 Declaration of Independence and, 201n21
 Universal Declaration of Human Rights and, 27, 201n21
human trafficking, 127, 136. *See also* slavery
humanitarianism
 overview, 10, 13–14, 22, 27–28, 43–44, 113, 194
 ancient Near Eastern laws and, 164, 174–77, 188, 200–201
 in the Book of the Covenant, 9n40, 10n44, 14–15, 45–46, 57, 78–79, 188–90, 195–96
 the exodus and, 3, 76–77, 89, 95, 97–98, 113, 115, 202
 modern, 27, 201–2

 as worship, 14, 37, 43, 79–80, 112–13, 120, 199
Hyatt, J. Philip, 62, 71
hymns, 104

identity, 41, 77, 80, 83, 99, 101–9, 106n117, 188n95, 196
"if-you" laws, 11, 11n49, 14, 45–46, 46t, 57, 57n125, 67
image of God (*imago Dei*), 41–43, 49, 79, 93, 156–58, 158n177, 163
imitation of God (*imitatio Dei*), 30, 39, 41–44, 74, 77, 79, 113, 132, 190
immigrants. *See* foreigners/aliens
injustice, 38, 45, 50. *See also* justice, ancient Near Eastern; justice, biblical
institutionalism (legal positivism), 21–22, 21n102
instrumentalism (legal realism), 21–22
interest on loans, 10, 12n57, 50–51, 50n97, 71
Inventing God's Law (David P. Wright), 146n129
Ishay, Micheline R., 9–10

Jackson, Bernard S., 5n18, 123n22, 151, 154
Janzen, J. Gerald, 33–34, 43
Janzen, Waldemar, 25, 32
Jesus Christ, 23, 60, 60n137, 70, 74, 101n92, 153, 202. *See also* Christianity; new covenant
Job, 44
Johns, C. H. W., 6
Joseph, 72n191, 131
Josiah, King, 53, 102, 107
Josipovici, Gabrielle, 18–19
Jubilee, Year of, 72, 139–40
justice, ancient Near Eastern, 170–72, 170n8, 174–81, 191
justice, biblical
 biblical laws and, 16, 62, 89, 124, 156, 201–2
 of God, 34, 36–39, 42, 79, 82, 124
 impartiality of, 62
 vs. modern social justice, 37–39, 37n41

SUBJECT INDEX

Kaiser, Walter C., Jr., 10, 57–58
kindness, 3, 28, 44, 59–60, 66–68, 82
king(s)
    ancient Near Eastern, 21, 27n126, 89, 145n128, 169–72, 173n28, 175, 177–81
    God as, 172
    Israelite, 53, 102, 169, 173, 181
kiššātu (debt service), 147, 147n134
kittum/kīnātu (truth), 170–72
Kofoed, Jens Bruun, 99, 104, 108, 173n28, 176–77, 184, 201n21
Kugel, James L., 114n153

laments, 59
land, 48, 72–73, 73n192, 78, 78n213, 107–8, 140
Land, Promised, 87, 91, 93, 106–8, 106n117, 107f, 114. *See also* Canaan, land of
Laney, Carl J., 33
Launderville, Dale, 178n46
law, biblical. *See also* Book of the Covenant (BC); law collections, ancient Near Eastern
    overview, 11n140, 18–19, 84, 125, 138, 172–73, 181–92
    altar, 88n38, 89, 92–93
    authority and, 24, 46, 124–25, 168, 172–73, 181, 183
    cultic, 69, 90–95, 91n50, 97, 116, 186
    Deuteronomic Laws (DL), 6n21, 10n44, 51–52, 65
    dietary, 71, 93
    God as author of, 172–73, 173n28, 181, 191
    Holiness Collection, 6n21
    humanitarianism in, 112, 200
    modern relevance, 200–202, 201n21
law, natural, 39–40
law collections, ancient Near Eastern. *See also various law collections*
    overview, 1–2, 15, 20t, 26–27, 200–201
    audience for, 179–81, 191
    authority and, 21–22, 124, 168–72, 177
    authors of, 26n125, 170–72, 174–75, 191, 198
    prologues/epilogues of, 4, 27n129, 176–77, 176n39, 179, 185
    purpose of, 27n126, 89, 177–79, 191, 198
"Laws about Rented Oxen," 9
Laws of Eshnunna (LE), 20t, 64–65, 89, 149t, 153–55, 159–60, 163–64
Laws of Hammurabi (LH), 20t, 89, 177, 180–81. *See also* Hammurabi; Shamash (god)
Laws of Lipit-Ishtar, 20t, 149t, 169, 176
Laws of Ur-Namma (LU), 20t, 142–45, 144n122, 144n124, 145n128, 149t, 169, 174n29, 176
legal positivism (institutionalism), 21–22, 21n102
legal realism (instrumentalism), 21–22
legal theory, 21–22
Lemche, Niels Peter, 127n41, 149
Levinson, Bernard M., 8, 17n82, 18, 88, 183
lex talionis, 121, 121n10, 152–53, 152n154, 153n157, 160–62
life, human, value of, 14, 26n123, 129, 151, 160–64, 162n196, 163–64, 189, 200. *See also* image of God (*imago Dei*)
Lipit-Ishtar, 169, 174–75, 180–81
literary criticism (new criticism), 18n86
loans. *See* debts/loans
Long, V. Philips, 101–2

manna, 78
manslaughter, 159–61, 161n192, 164–66
manumission/freeing of slaves, 13, 73, 88, 129–30, 132–34, 137–38, 143–46, 153, 202
marriage, 130, 133–40, 133n69, 135n78, 143–46, 144n122, 148n137, 150, 166
Marshall, Jay W., 11, 51, 62n146, 65, 65n158, 73
Martens, Elmer A., 186
masters of slaves, 127, 130–31, 133–40, 143–45, 150–51, 150n143, 166
McKay, J. W., 61, 61n140

SUBJECT INDEX

memory, cultural (mnemohistory), 83, 99–104, 106, 116, 196
Mendenhall, George E., 7
mercy, 33–36, 42, 44, 84, 115t, 117, 169, 202n25. *See also* compassion of God
mēšarum (justice), 170–71, 170n8
messenger epilogue, 89, 91
Middle Assyrian Laws (MAL), 20t, 89
Miles, John C., 157–58
Milgrom, J., 54
Milstein, Sara J., 9
Minet Rubin, 53
mnemohistory (cultural memory), 83, 99–104, 106, 116, 196
monotheism, 110, 112
morality, 39–42, 111, 123, 123n18, 182, 185–86. *See also* ethics; humanitarianism
Morrow, William S., 9n40, 13–14, 26n122, 45, 87–88, 121n12, 129, 152, 172–73
Mosaic covenant. *See* Sinaitic/Mosaic covenant
Moses
    God's law and, 3, 27, 169, 173, 173n28, 181
    historicity of, 82
    as intermediary, 30, 90, 173
    as prophet, 173
    as servant of the Lord, 127
murder/homicide, 156, 158, 160–61, 161n192, 189

Nanna (god), 145n128, 169
Nasuti, Harry P., 41
natural law, 39–40
Naveh, J., 54
neighbor, 23, 30n3, 51–52, 56–59, 68
Neo-Babylonian Laws (NBL), 20t
new covenant, 106n119, 182, 202
new criticism (literary criticism), 18n86
Nin-Girsu (god), 174n29
Nora, Pierre, 99–100
Noth, Martin, 62
Nuzi, 140

obedience, 39–42, 68, 77, 84, 90–92, 102, 106–7, 107f, 111
offerings, 71, 92, 94
omnipotence, 185
oppression. *See also* foreigners/aliens; the poor; widows and orphans
    ancient Near Eastern laws against, 174–75, 174n29, 177
    biblical laws against, 49, 51–52, 57, 71, 97
    God fights against, 50, 114–15
    of Israelites, 59, 95, 113, 117, 131
    the prophets against, 42, 48
orphans. *See* widows and orphans
Otto, Eckart, 10, 13–14, 30n3, 31–32, 31n9, 95, 177
oxen
    sabbath rest for, 48, 74–75
    that gore, 151–65, 157n172, 157n173
    that stray, 47, 60, 63, 65, 68

paganism, 201n21, 202n27
pantheons/polytheism, 170, 174, 185, 187
parallelisms, 96
patriarchs. *See* covenants: Abrahamic
Patrick, Dale, 3–4, 11, 117
Paul, Shalom N.
    on ancient Near Eastern laws, 123–24, 170, 170n10, 172
    on prologue/epilogue of biblical law, 176n39
    on religion and law, 182
    on role of law, 4, 168
    on slavery, 132n65, 136, 136n82
Philips, Anthony C., 5n18, 123–24
Philistines, 131
pledges for loans, 11–12, 45–60, 66–67, 71, 80, 147, 147n136
polytheism/pantheons, 170, 174, 185, 187
the poor, 11–13, 37–38, 48, 50–53, 59, 71–73, 98
positivism, legal (institutionalism), 21–22, 21n102
Potiphar's wife, 131

principles in laws, 22–25, 43, 45, 122–23, 125, 178. *See also* values, scale of
prologues/epilogues of law collections, 4, 27n129, 176–77, 176n39, 179, 185
Promised Land, 87, 91, 93, 106–8, 106n117, 107f, 114. *See also* Canaan, land of
promises of God, 52, 95, 103, 106, 109, 111n140, 182, 187. *See also* Promised Land
propaganda, law collections as, 177–78
prophets, 39, 42, 102, 104, 173, 202n25
Propp, William H., 77n208, 130n52, 145
protection of others, 12, 60, 95, 112–13, 113n148, 135–36
punishment, 2, 36, 152–53, 158–59, 158n181, 162, 164. *See also* death penalty

Rae, Scott B., 123n18
ransom, 155, 160–64. *See also* redemption
realism, legal (instrumentalism), 21–22
redaction criticism, 61, 63, 66, 71, 84–85, 108, 194
redemption, 36, 89, 135–36, 145, 150, 160–64, 166, 187
refuge, cities of, 161n192
repentance, 36–37, 201
rest, Sabbath, 11, 48, 48n91, 72–78, 132
retaliation, 14, 121, 152. *See also lex talionis*
retribution, 152, 165. *See also lex talionis*
revelation, divine, 33–34, 40, 111–12, 117, 172, 183
rights, human. *See* human rights
Rodd, Cyril S., 11–12, 78n213
Roth, Martha, 9n39, 180, 180n54, 183
Rothenbusch, Ralf, 144n122

Sabbath, 48, 69–78, 80, 94–96, 132
salvation, 84
Samaritan, good, parable of, 44
šarākum (to present a gift), 172n19
Sarna, Nahum, 157n173

scribes, ancient Near Eastern, 8–9, 8n34, 22, 177
Sermon on the Mount, 60
Shamash (god), 169–72, 180, 181
shepherds, kings as, 169, 175, 181
sin, 36, 58–59, 168, 182, 202
Sinaitic/Mosaic covenant, 30, 33–34, 38–41, 82–84, 106–7, 106n119, 107n120, 187–88, 187–88. *See also* Book of the Covenant (BC); the exodus; Moses
slavery. *See also* the exodus
 overview, 126–29, 163
 in ancient Near Eastern laws, 89, 89n43, 140–48, 148n137, 150n143, 155–56
 chattel, 127–28, 149, 149n143, 165
 of children, 130, 133–34, 139–40, 143, 144n124, 145
 for debts (*See* debt slavery)
 of foreigners by Israelites, 126, 128, 149
 freedom from, 13, 73, 88, 129–30, 132–34, 137–38, 143–46, 153, 202
 injuries/death during, 152, 155–56, 163
 of Israelites by Israelites, 126–28, 149–50, 149n142
 of males, 129–34, 138–40
 masters, 127, 130–31, 133–40, 143–45, 150–51, 150n143, 166
 permanent, 130, 134
 of women, 130, 133–38, 143–46, 148n137, 150
Smith, Anthony D., 104
social justice (modern), 37–38, 37n41. *See also* justice, biblical
sojourners. *See* foreigners/aliens
Sonsino, Rifat, 57, 76n203
source criticism, 5, 17, 84–87, 108, 194
Sparks, Kenton L., 103, 103n103
Speiser, E. A., 170–71
Spencer, James, 100, 108, 190, 201–2
Spina, Frank Anthony, 76
Sprinkle, Joe M.
 on enemies, 68
 on humanitarianism, 49, 50, 63

SUBJECT INDEX 229

on literary approach, 5, 5n18, 55
on ox goring law, 162, 164
on redaction criticism, 63
on role of the law, 84
on the Sabbath, 75
on slave laws, 89
Stark, Rodney, 202n27
stoning, 154–60, 158n180, 158n181, 163. *See also* death penalty
strangers. *See* foreigners/aliens
Stuart, Douglas K., 70, 73n192
Stubbs, David L., 74
Sumerian law collections, 9, 20t, 173n28
"Sumerian Laws Exercise Tablet," 9
Swiderski, Igor, 94
sympathy, 11–12, 35, 46, 57, 68, 77, 175. *See also* compassion of God; empathy
synchronic method, 5, 17, 17n82, 194

Talmon, Shemaryahu, 20
teleology, 39, 41
Ten Commandments (Decalogue), 25, 56, 72, 90–91
thanksgiving, 92–94, 116
theology and history, 100–101, 108–9, 156, 190
Tigay, Jeffrey H., 52–53, 101, 110n137, 140n105
the Torah, 41, 45, 56, 83, 85, 156, 173, 183–84
tradition history, 99
trust in God, 78, 80
truth, 170–72
Tsai, Daisy Yulin
on ancient Near Eastern laws, 142n115, 143, 147, 185
on biblical law, 16n76, 26, 107, 107f, 122n13, 148, 149n143, 201n21

Universal Declaration of Human Rights (U.N. General Assembly), 27, 201n21
Unleavened Bread, Festival of, 92
Unterman, Jeremiah, 185
Ur, 105n114
Ur-Namma, 43n75, 145n128, 169, 174
Urukagina, Edicts of, 143n121, 174n29

Utu (god), 169

values, scale of, 26n123, 122–25, 165–66, 194, 197–98
Van de Mieroop, Marc, 180
Van Houten, Christiana, 76
Van Seters, John, 10n44
Van Wijk-Bos, Johanna W. H., 12, 30, 50, 58, 67, 112, 113, 115, 129
Vanhoozer, Kevin J., 17, 25
vengeance, 152–53, 165
violence, 12, 113n148, 174
Volksgeist (worldview), 176, 190. *See also* worldview

Wagner, Volker, 7, 8n34
Walton, John H., 19, 26–27, 168, 178n46, 179, 188, 198
Watts, James W., 45, 173, 184
Weinfeld, Moshe, 37n41, 110n137
Wells, Bruce, 8, 21n102, 25–26, 141–43, 146, 165
Weltanschauung (worldview), 168. *See also* worldview
Wenham, Gordon J., 27n128
Westbrook, Raymond, 5n18, 8, 17n81, 85–86, 86n24, 121n10, 157–58, 157n172, 158
widows and orphans, 39, 43n75, 49–50, 135, 174–75, 174n29, 177, 180
will of God, 32, 39–40, 183
wives, 130, 133–36, 138, 143–46, 148n137, 150
women
in biblical law, 2, 112, 155–56
as concubines, 135
as daughters, 130, 135–36, 138, 143, 146, 148n137, 155, 162
as slaves, 130, 133–38, 143–46, 148n137, 150
as widows, 39, 43n75, 49–50, 135, 174–75, 174n29, 177, 180
as wives, 130, 133–36, 138, 143–46, 148n137, 150
Woods, Edward J., 64
work, 11, 48, 72–73, 75, 78, 95n66, 139, 146. *See also* the Sabbath
workers, hired, 53–55, 59, 75

worldview
  ancient Near Eastern, 164, 176
  Israelite, 27n128, 39, 107, 107f, 184, 189, 199
  laws and, 166, 168, 190
worship
  the exodus and, 91–92
  the festivals and, 93–94
  humanitarianism as, 14, 37, 43, 79–80, 112–13, 120, 199
  the law and, 12–13
  the Sabbath as, 74, 80, 132
  of YHWH alone, 90–91, 95
Wright, Christopher J. H.
  on ancient Near Eastern law collections, 177–78, 178n48
  on approaches to Old Testament, 24–25
  on biblical law, 15n70, 23, 56n120, 91, 178n48, 187
  on death penalty, 163–64
  on God, 110, 111, 114n155
  on goring ox, 157
  on humanitarianism, 14n70, 37, 52–53, 95, 189n101
  on imitation of God, 41, 44, 95
  on Israelites' worldview, 107
  on *lex talionis*, 152n154
  on offerings, 92
  scale of values, 26n123, 122, 125, 126, 165, 197–98
  on slavery, 88–89, 127, 131, 132, 133, 134, 137, 149n143
  on source criticism, 86
Wright, David P.
  on ancient Near Eastern laws, 8–9, 65, 86, 96n76, 143n117, 144, 146n129, 170n8
  on biblical law, 87, 96, 146n130
  on gender inclusivity, 156n169
  on goring ox laws, 153–54, 154n163
Wright, G. Ernest, 100–101, 100n92

Yaḫdun-Lim, 172
Yamauchi, Edwin M., 35
Yavne-Yam Ostracon, 53–55
Younger, K. Lawson, Jr., 19–20

Scripture and Ancient Sources Index

Verses from the Masoretic Text are followed by (MT). All other verses are from the English Bible. Page numbers followed by n and another number indicate a footnote. For example, 6n21 indicates footnote 21 on page 6.

OLD TESTAMENT

Genesis

1–2	27n128
1:26–28	93, 158n177
1:27	156
1:28	160
1:31—2:3	77, 80
2:2–3	74, 116
2:16–17	158n177
2:24	133
3	41
5:1	158n177
9	158
9:1–3	160
9:2–6	158n177
9:5–6	156, 158
15	103
15:7–21	106
15:7	105n114
15:13	76
17:1	106
17:3–8	106
17:9–14	106
21	132
21:2–6	132
21:2	132
21:19–20	139
28:13	103
31:42	138n97
39:17	131
41:38	127
43:30	35n25

Exodus

1–18	82
1–15	82, 87
1:1	131
2:11	64
2:23–25	82, 104, 114n154
2:23b–25	103
2:24	109
2:29–30	159
3:5–6	103
3:6–8	109
3:6a	104
3:6b	104
3:7–8	114, 115, 129
3:15	103
3:16–18	104
3:21	138n97
6:2–3	104
6:6	132

Exodus (cont.)

6:7	39, 109, 117, 187, 195, 198
8:10	172
9:14	172
10:2	102
12:49	189n101
13:14	102
15:1–18	104
15:21	104
15:22–27	182
16	78
17:8–16	105
18:20	68
19–23	176n39
19–24	5, 87
19	173, 188
19:3–6	176n39
19:3	82
19:4–5a	90, 111
19:4–6	82
19:4	90, 91, 111n140, 116
19:5	68n174, 106, 198
19:5a	111n140
19:5b–6	111n140
19:6	131
19:8	198
19:9	173
20:1	168
20:2	76, 81, 90, 91, 98, 105, 196
20:3–6	91
20:3	181, 185
20:5	110, 117
20:8–11	72, 74
20:11–23:33	116
20:11	69, 74
20:12	67
20:13	22
20:16	54
20:17	38, 183
20:18–21	5
20:18–20	173
20:21–31	70
20:21–25	12
20:22–23	90, 91, 91n50
20:22–26	88n38, 89
20:22	25, 81, 90, 91, 116, 196
20:23–23:19	91
20:23	90
20:24–26	90, 92
20:24	91, 92
20:25	92n53
20:26	92n53
21–23	1n2, 187
21	129, 137, 138, 139, 143, 147n134, 158
21:1–11	12, 94, 95, 97, 98
21:1	68n174, 88n38, 168
21:2–22:28	31
21:2–22:27 (MT)	31
21:2–22:27a	31
21:2–27	95
21:2–22:26a (MT)	31
21:2–11	26, 31, 88, 90, 95, 96, 121, 126, 128, 129, 137, 141, 165, 197
21:2–6	129, 131, 137, 143, 146n130, 148n137
21:2–3	139
21:2	11, 14, 128, 133, 137, 138, 139, 145, 146, 147, 150
21:2a	150
21:2b	150
21:3	133
21:3a	133
21:3b	133
21:4–6	145
21:4	130n51, 133, 143, 144n124, 145, 150
21:5–6	128, 134, 145, 150
21:5	130n51, 133, 145
21:6b	134
21:7–11	129, 130, 134, 137, 138, 146n130
21:7	135, 138, 146n130
21:7a	135
21:8	135, 136
21:9	135, 136

SCRIPTURE AND ANCIENT SOURCES INDEX 233

21:10–11	136	22:15–26 (MT)	12
21:10	136	22:16–27	12
21:11	137, 138	22:17—23:9 (MT)	
21:12—23:9	96, 97, 98		66
21:12—22:17	96, 97, 98	22:17–19 (MT)	31, 97, 98, 98n81
21:12—22:16 (MT)		22:18—23:9	66
	96, 97, 98	22:18–20	31, 97, 98, 98n81
21:12–36	113n148	22:20—23:9 (MT)	
21:12–27	12		97, 98
21:12–17	31	22:20–30 (MT)	56n120, 96
21:12	90	22:20–26 (MT)	32, 49, 51
21:13	46, 185	22:20–26a (MT)	31
21:15	67	22:20–23 (MT)	71
21:17	67	22:20–22 (MT)	37
21:18—22:16	9	22:20 (MT)	12, 25, 49, 59, 76,
21:18–32	31		81, 89, 97, 104,
21:20–24	95		113, 117, 150, 196,
21:20–21	95, 126, 128,		202
	149n143	22:21–27a	31
21:21	127	22:21–24	71
21:24	152	22:21–23 (MT)	12, 49
21:26–27	95, 126, 128,	22:21	12, 25, 49, 59, 76,
	149n143		81, 89, 97, 104,
21:27	153		113, 117, 150, 196,
21:28–36	12, 151, 154		202
21:28–32	26, 121, 151, 154,	22:21 (MT)	46, 175
	156n169, 165, 197	22:22–24	12, 49
21:28	156, 158	22:22–23 (MT)	56, 114, 115, 117,
21:29–30	161		129
21:29	160	22:22	46, 175
21:30	160, 161, 164	22:22 (MT)	53
21:31–32	162	22:23–24	56, 114, 115, 117,
21:31	162		129
21:32	95, 126, 128, 163	22:23	53
21:33–36	151, 154	22:23 (MT)	46, 48, 50, 61
21:33–34	31, 151	22:24–26 (MT)	14, 50, 70, 71
21:35—22:15 (MT)		22:24	46, 48, 50, 61
	31	22:24 (MT)	11, 46, 48, 50, 51,
21:35—22:16	31		59, 78
21:35–36	151, 154, 157n173	22:25–27	14, 50, 70, 71
21:37—22:15	12, 113n148	22:25–27 (MT)	49
21:37—22:14 (MT)		22:25–26 (MT)	11, 12, 24, 30,
	12, 113n148		33n13, 45, 47, 48,
22	12n54, 70		51, 53, 54, 55, 56,
22:1–2 (MT)	23, 189		76, 80, 96n72, 196
22:2–3	23, 189	22:25	11, 46, 48, 50, 51,
22:5–13 (MT)	199		59, 78
22:6–14	199	22:25 (MT)	51

Exodus (cont.)

22:26–28	49
22:26–27	11, 12, 24, 30, 33n13, 45, 47, 48, 51, 53, 54, 55, 56, 76, 80, 96n72, 196
22:26	51
22:26 (MT)	13, 15, 24, 27, 31, 33n13, 39, 46, 50, 51, 52, 53, 55, 59, 61, 79, 80, 82, 114, 128, 195, 202
22:26a (MT)	42
22:26b (MT)	32, 42, 43
22:27—23:12 (MT)	31, 32
22:27–30 (MT)	12, 32, 113n148
22:27	13, 15, 24, 27, 31, 33n13, 39, 46, 50, 51, 52, 53, 55, 59, 61, 79, 80, 82, 114, 128, 195, 202
22:27 (MT)	50, 71
22:27b	32, 42, 43
22:27b (MT)	31
22:28—23:12	31, 32
22:28–31	12, 32, 113n148
22:28–29 (MT)	71
22:28	50, 71
22:28 (MT)	46, 50n96
22:28b	31
22:29–30	71
22:29	46, 50n96
22:29 (MT)	46
22:30	46
22:30 (MT)	46, 71
22:31	46, 71
23	31n9, 61, 63, 70, 72
23:1–19	70
23:1–9	12, 30n5, 61, 61n141, 66, 71, 77n208
23:1–8	62
23:1–3	32, 61, 67
23:1–2	62
23:3	45, 62
23:4–5	24, 30, 30n5, 32, 45, 46n87, 47, 60, 61, 62, 63, 64, 66, 68, 76, 80, 96n72, 196
23:4	11, 28, 62, 65, 68, 69
23:5	11, 62, 65, 65n158, 65n161, 68, 69, 80
23:6–8	32, 61
23:6–7	67
23:6	62
23:7–8	12, 62
23:7	46, 46n87, 66
23:9–19	56n120, 96
23:9	12, 25, 76, 77, 77n208, 81, 89, 90, 97, 98, 104, 113, 117, 129, 150, 196, 202
23:10–13	12, 90
23:10–12	14, 24, 30, 32, 45, 46n87, 48, 70, 71, 72, 73, 74, 75, 76, 76n203, 77, 78, 80, 94, 95, 96, 96n72, 98, 196
23:10–11	71, 72, 73
23:11	73, 78
23:12	11, 69, 72, 73, 74, 75, 76, 78, 80, 95, 113
23:13	46, 46n87, 71, 72, 77
23:14–19	13, 90, 92
23:14–19a	71
23:15–16	93
23:15	25, 81, 84, 92, 138n97, 196, 202
23:17–19	93
23:19	71, 93
23:19b	71, 93
23:20–33	89, 90, 91, 102, 106, 176n39
23:20	91
23:31–33	112
23:32–33	181
24	30, 173

24:1–8	5	24	158n181
24:3–4	68n174	24:16–17	158n180
24:5	92	24:19–20	152
24:7–8	68n174	25	73n192, 139, 140, 140n105
24:7	1n2, 102, 106, 109, 179, 187, 198	25:1–7	72, 73
31:2–6	150n145	25:2	73
31:12–17	69, 74	25:8–38	139
31:13–17	75, 77	25:23	108
31:17	48n91, 74	25:34	105
32:7	105	25:35–38	50n97
32:11	105	25:38	98
33:19	34n22, 35	25:39–43	139, 165
34	33, 34, 36	25:39	132, 150
34:6–7	30, 33, 34, 34n19, 39, 43, 79, 195	25:40	139
		25:40b–41	140
34:6	33, 34, 36, 42, 79	25:41	140
34:7	34, 36, 42, 79	25:42	104
34:10–11	33	25:44–46	128
34:14	110	25:54–55	149n142
34:20	138n97	25:55	104
34:26	93	26:13	88
35:2–3	74	26:23	105
		26:34	73
		26:40–46	106
		27:1–8	162n196
		27:8	162n196

Leviticus

3	143
5:1	38
17–26	6n21
17:13–14	158
19:2	41, 42
19:3	79n217
19:9–10	73n192
19:17–18	183
19:17	64
19:18	23, 38, 153, 183
19:19	40
19:33–34	113n150
19:34	38, 76, 104, 183, 189n101
19:36	105
20	158n181
20:27	158n181
23:4–22	92n56
23:22	37, 73n192
23:33–43	92n56
23:43	102

Numbers

5:12–13	38
5:31	55n117
14:18	33n14
15:16	189n101
15:32–36	74, 78, 159n181
15:34	74
15:35	74
15:41	105
20:14–17	104, 105
22:5	105n113
22:11	105n113
23:9	112
23:19–21	172
28:16–31	92n56
35	161n192
35:16–19	158n180
35:31	161

Deuteronomy

3:24	172
4	172n22, 173
4:5–6	178
4:6–8	201n21
4:14	173
4:24	110
4:31	35
4:32–35	109n132
4:35	110, 117, 181
4:37	82
4:39	110
5:3	111n141
5:6	98, 105
5:9	110
5:12–15	72
5:14	69, 75
5:15	69, 76, 77, 102
5:21	183
5:28–31	173
6:4–5	23
6:4	110, 117
6:5	183
6:12	102
6:15	110
6:21	102
7:6–8	83
7:8	82
8:14	102
8:18	75n199
10:12–13	2
10:17–19a	39
10:17	45
10:18	175n33
10:19	76
12–26	6n21
13	158n181
14:21–23	93
14:21	71, 93
14:29	175n33, 175n33
15	137, 138, 143
15:1–18	73
15:1–15	71
15:7–11	37, 38
15:7–8	51
15:9–10	183
15:12–18	126, 137, 165
15:12	64, 132, 138, 139, 150
15:13–15	145
15:13–14	139
15:14b	139
15:15	76, 89, 104, 111n141, 115, 139
15:16	134
15:23	158
16:1–17	92n56
16:11	93
16:14	93
16:16	138n97
17:2–7	158n181
17:14–17	173
17:15	64
17:18–20	173
18:15–18	173
19	161n192
19:15	54
19:21	152
21:18–21	67, 158n181
22	158n181
22:1–4	63, 64, 65
22:2	64
22:2b	64
22:3	63
22:6–7	40
22:10	40
23:20–21	50n97
24:10–13	51
24:12	52
24:13	52, 53
24:14–15	59
24:16	162n200
24:17–18	104
24:17	56n122
24:18	76
24:19	175n33
25:4	40
25:11–12	153n157
25:17–19	105
26:8	83
26:11	108
27:19	175n33
28:50	44
31:10–11	73
31:12	58
32:5	201n21

32:31	172
32:39	181

Joshua
6:15–19	159
7:25	159
20–21	161n192
24:19	110

Judges
5:4–5	104
6:8–10	104

Ruth
2:13	135n74

1 Samuel
2:27–28	104
12	173
15:2	105
15:6	105
16:7	183
25:41	135n74

2 Samuel
7:23–24	83

1 Kings
8:53	83

2 Kings
22:11	102n100
22:13b	102

1 Chronicles
17:20–21	83
28:9	183

2 Chronicles
30:9	33

Nehemiah
9:17	33

Job
19:21	44
21:22	172
22:6	59
24:3	59
25:10–11	158n177
29:12–13	175n33
32:8	158n177

Psalms
1	23–24
4:1	59
8:4–8	158n177
10:17	52
19:14	41, 55n117
22:26	52
25	84
25:9	52
32:9	158n177
34:2	52
40:8	41
66:5–6	104
73:22	158n177
74:12–13	104
77:19–20	104
78	104
78:34–35	37
78:38	35
81:10	105
82:3	175n33
86:8–10	172
86:15	33
103	84
103:8	33
103:13	35
105	104
106	104
111:4	33
112:1	44
112:4	44, 79n217
116:5	33
119:1–8	117
139:2	183
139:4	183
139:23–24	183
145:8	33
146:3–10	172

Proverbs

3:12	37
12:10	75n199
14:21	59
19:17	59, 80
21:13	37
22:2	45
28:8	44

Ecclesiastes

3:21	158n177
12:13–14	158n177

Isaiah

1:17	175n33
10:26	104
11:16	105
30:18	117
31:3	158n177
40:13	172
41:8–9	127
43:1–3	83
55:8–9	68
58:13–14	78

Jeremiah

2:6	105
7:22	105
7:25	105
10:6	172
11:20	183
13:11	178
14:9	55n118
16:14	105
17:19–27	78
22:3	175n33
22:15–16	37
22:16	42, 45
30:11	37
31:31–32	105
33:33–34	182n62
34:8–17	139, 150

Lamentations

3:22–23	36
3:30	153n161

Ezekiel

3:20	160n188
20:5–10	105
20:22–31	105
23:19	105
23:27	105
33:6	160n188
34:11–12	169n5

Daniel

4:27	44
9:15	105

Hosea

2:15	102
7:11	158n177
11:1	102
12:9	104, 105
13:4	105
13:14	102
14:3	175n33

Joel

2:13	33

Amos

2:7a	48
2:8	48
2:10	102
3:1	102

Jonah

4:2	33

Micah

6:4	102
6:8	2, 3n7, 42, 42n71, 79n217
7:15	102

Nahum
1:2   110

Haggai
2:5   105

Zechariah
7:9–10   39, 175n33
12:1   158n177

Malachi
3:5   175n33

NEW TESTAMENT

Matthew
2:27   70
5:17   60n137
5:21–27   74
5:38–39   153
5:43–48   80
5:43–45   60, 68
5:48   60
6:26a   67
7:3–5   160n188
22   23
23:23   44, 122
25:31   69
25:40   59, 80

Mark
6:34   35n25
8:2   35n25

Luke
6:36   42, 79n217
7:13   35n25
10:25–37   44, 160n188
10:37   44
17:3   160n188

John
6:27   28
10:11–18   169n5
13:35   80
20:31   110n135

Acts
4:32—5:11   94
10:34   45

Romans
11:34   172
13:1–7   191n104

Galatians
6:1–2   160n188

Ephesians
4:25   160n188
5:1–2   68

Colossians
3:10   42n69
3:16   160n188
3:25   45

2 Timothy
3:15–17   120
3:16–17   182n62
3:16   25

Hebrews
3:12–13   160n188
12:5–6   37

James
1:27   28, 37
2:13   36
2:19   110
5:11   36
5:19–20   160n188

1 John
2:6   68
3:17   37
3:17–21   160n188
4:19   42, 202

LAWS OF UR-NAMMA (LU)

4–5	121, 140, 197
4	142, 143, 144, 144n122, 144n124, 145, 150, 165
5	143, 144n124
25–26	140

LAWS OF LIPIT-ISHTAR (LL)

12–14	140
25–26	140

LAWS OF ESHNUNNA (LE)

16	140
22–23	140
31	140
34–35	141
40	141
42	153
49–52	89, 141
50	64, 65
52–55	197
53–55	121
53	154
54–55	154, 155, 165
54	159
55	141, 162
57	141

LAWS OF HAMMURABI (LH)

2	183n71
6	183n71
7	141
8	183n71
15–20	141
32	141
34	180n54
114–119	147, 150
114–116	147
116–119	141
116	162n200
117–119	148
117–118	121, 197
117	142, 143, 145, 146, 147, 147n134, 148n137, 150, 165
118–119	143, 147
118	146, 147
148–149	143
154–156	143
170–171	141
175–176	141
175	143, 144n124
178	143
196–205	141
196–201	153
202–205	153
209–223	141
209–110	162n200
226–227	141
229–230	162n200
229	162n200
244–252	154
250–252	121, 154, 155, 165, 197
250	156, 156n169
251	159
252	141, 162
278–282	89, 141
280	143
282	143

HITTITE LAWS (HL)

1	141
3	141
8	141
12	141
14	141
16	141
18	141
20–24	141
31–36	141

44b	141
52	141
95	141
97	141
99	141
194	141
196	141

MIDDLE ASSYRIAN LAWS (MAL)

A.

4	141
39	141, 147n136
41	141
44	141, 147n136
48	141, 147n136

C+G.

1–3	141
2–3	147n136
7	141, 147n136
9	141

NEO-BABYLONIAN LAWS (NBL)

6	141

YAVNE-YAM OSTRACON

lines 1–14	53–54

www.ingramcontent.com/pod-product-compliance
Lightning Source LLC
Chambersburg PA
CBHW072023240426
43667CB00044B/2256